T0328358

TAPESTRY

THE HISTORY AND CONSEQUENCES OF AMERICA'S COMPLEX CULTURE

TAPESTRY

THE HISTORY AND CONSEQUENCES OF AMERICA'S COMPLEX CULTURE

BY JERRY CARRIER

Algora Publishing
New York

Library of Congress Cataloging-in-Publication Data —

Carrier, Jerry, 1948-
   Tapestry: the history and consequences of America's complex culture / Jerry Carrier.
      pages cm
   Summary: "Ethnic minorities are about to become 'the majority.' We need to become
more conscious of the complex minority cultural influences that have long been working in
the background. The many threads create a richly interwoven social fabric that allows for
varied views on economic relations as well as on religious belief"—Provided by publisher.
   Includes bibliographical references and index.
   ISBN 978-1-62894-048-0 (soft cover: alkaline paper)—ISBN 978-1-62894-049-7
(hard cover: alkaline paper)—ISBN 978-1-62894-050-3 (ebook) 1. United States—Ethnic
relations. 2. United States—Civilization. 3. Cultural pluralism—History. 4. United
States—Social conditions. I. Title.
   E184.A1C336 2014
   973—dc23
                              2014025541

Printed in the United States

To the future of America and most specifically: Brandon, Madeline, Lucy, Ethan, Henry, and Kathleen.

Table of Contents

Introduction to American Culture

> I want to show that gospel, country, blues, rhythm and blues, jazz, and rock 'n' roll are all just really one thing. Those are American music and that is the American culture.
>
> —Etta James

> No culture can live, if it attempts to be exclusive
>
> —Mahatma Gandhi

> Just as the soil, however rich it may be, cannot be productive without cultivation, so the mind without culture can never produce fruit.
>
> —Seneca Indian proverb

American culture has been both magnificent and disastrous. It has been both inclusive and intolerant, and it stands at a crossroad requiring a decision as to which direction it will turn. Is it entering a renaissance or a dark age?

> *Culture: The characteristic features of everyday existence, as diversions or a way of life, shared by people in a place or time.*

American culture is a rich and complex tapestry of colorful threads from at least five continents, North and South America, Europe, Africa and Asia. It also includes influences from Polynesia. While the mainstay of American culture is Christian, capitalist, and ethnically of European (particularly British) heritage, to think that this is all there is to American culture, or that they are the most important parts of American culture, is to not understand the depth and the constantly changing dynamics of this rich, vast, and rapidly expanding culture.

All cultures must change as the world around them changes — and with the dynamics of a rapidly changing world, if American culture does not change quickly, too, that failure will be at the great expense of American prosperity. In fact the increasing diversity of these cultural threads and the changes they will bring, if they are allowed to unfold in a timely fashion, will mean an even richer culture and continued American prosperity. The United States has arrived at a moment when the mainstay majority is slowly, sometimes unwillingly, accepting complex minority cultural influences. These important and long existing minority threads will become more significant as America becomes a minority-majority rather than mostly a White European Christian capitalistic dominated country. These minority threads, including the many minority European-American threads, have always been important contributing factors in American culture, but they have been lingering in the shadows of the collective subconscious of mainstream America. This book explores these shadows and their consequences.

Much of this book is specifically about the United States, but many of the same trends examined here are part of the history of Canada and, to some extent, Mexico too, and the phenomena discussed in this book began while the continent was first being explored by Europeans, before there was such an entity as the United States. Thus, for simplicity, I often use the term "America." That being said, I do highlight many specific details about Canada and Mexico, which certainly have distinct and complex cultures and histories of their own. I also use the term "American" for the people of the US, although I realize that everyone else living in the Americas may legitimately call themselves Americans. This book uses the term "America" to mean the US and "Americans" to refer to the people of the US, without intending to slight anyone else.

I will also put this disclaimer up front: The social science of identifying the sources and implications of various aspects of American culture and subcultures is complicated and has become dominated by empiricists using replicable sets of mathematical and statistical algorithms. And sometimes in the length of time it takes to research and develop these complex models, the culture or subculture has already changed. I believe that in order to understand the whole of the society, a work like this needs to provide descriptions more in social-cultural terms and less in terms of mathematical justification and empirical data (although some statistical analysis is necessary). The Empiricists have their place, but they complicate culture perhaps even more than they do the other social sciences. Relying on empirical data in culture is akin to describing a Mondrian painting by precisely measuring and describing each rectangle, square and line of color. This method, while highly accurate, certainly does no justice to the art, nor does it add to the enjoyment or even the understanding of those who see and appreciate the art of either a Mondrian painting or a culture.

I use the word race in this book as it is commonly used, especially in America and even by the US census. However, in pure biological terms, there is no such thing. Humans are too close and intermixed to have significant genetic differences; we all come from a common ancestor less than 200,000 years ago and have been inter-marrying since. Race is much more about culture and ethnicity.

I should note that culture is complex, and customs and words and ideas frequently have more than one source. They may come into use precisely because they come from more than one source. One example of this that is discussed early in this book is that the "Soul food" known as "chitlins" comes from both African-American and Southern Native American roots, as both cultures fried and ate the intestines and organs of slaughtered animals. In this way White Southerners were also exposed to both cultures and adopted this practice.

Construction of log buildings is present in many northern European cultures, but early Americans were only exposed to log cabins built by the original Swedish colony in Pennsylvania and the eastern Native American long huts, which are considered to be the inspiration for the American log cabin.

In another example it can be argued that the word "savvy" in American usage comes from the French word "savoir-faire," meaning "knowing your way around and how to get things done." However, Americans first began to use the word "savvy" in the West as part of cowboy culture. Cowboys were not exposed to French, but they were exposed to Spanish language. I conclude, as do many linguists, that the word comes from the Spanish word "sabe" where the "b" is pronounced like a soft "v" and means "he knows." A person who knows is "savvy." However, just as the food "chitlins" comes from exposure to two cultures, perhaps the word came from exposure to both languages, and that one reinforced the other.

I have also attributed American Sign Language to both Native American Sign Language and French Sign Language, as the first use of sign language in America by the deaf was a "Creole" version inspired by Native Americans. This was in use and occurred before an American educator looking to improve on the system went to France to study their more complex version, bringing it back to adapt it to American English.

It is also important to note that this book is not a cheerleader piece for American culture. The good is presented along with the bad. It is meant to be an honest portrayal. Some readers may find my examples and criticisms harsh; however, it should be noted that criticisms of American culture and American exceptionalism are rare and needed — and this is the purpose of the book. I have tried to be balanced, and I believe that on the whole I present a positive and accurate picture of American culture.

Some German and Irish Catholic readers may find certain sections, such as those on Charles Lindbergh and Father Coughlin, uncomfortable. These are not made to demean the many contributions of the Germans or Irish to America, but are important, albeit negative, elements. At the same time, many other prominent individuals who were not German or Irish Catholics in pre-

World War II America, like Henry Ford, also endorsed Hitler. The same is true of parts of this book concerning the elements of organized crime that came from Italian and Russian Jewish immigrants. There have been many positive contributions from both of these groups, but the negative impacts are also important in understanding our composite culture. Similarly, this book is neither anti-Black nor anti-Muslim, but I believe it was necessary to fairly portray the negative impacts of the Black Supremacy religious movements in American culture.

I have also used "race" in some sections of this book. However, I also explain that genetically speaking, there are really no major physical or genetic differences among people. Race is really about cultural differences. I have used the word race in this book because in the United States people are categorized by "race," even in the US census, so it is difficult to write about American culture without the use of this word. It is very complicated as American Latinos of all colors and ethnicities sometimes refer to themselves as "la raza," the race, and even some Jewish-Americans consider their Jewish ethnicity to be a race and identify themselves as "non-white" in the U.S. Census. I have tried in this book to do my best to describe culture in the United States without giving any sustenance to the concept that people differ because of differences due to "race."

CHAPTER 1. AMERICAN ETHNOCENTRISM & THE MYTH OF AMERICAN EXCEPTIONALISM

> The American culture promotes personal responsibility, the dignity of work, the value of education, the merit of service, devotion to a purpose greater than self, and at the foundation, the pre-eminence of family.
>
> —Mitt Romney

> You can call it mysticism if you want to, but I have always believed that there was some divine plan that placed this great continent between two oceans to be sought out by those who were possessed of an abiding love of freedom and a special kind of courage
>
> —Ronald Reagan

Perhaps there is no better start to a discussion about American culture than a quote from Mitt Romney, a millionaire born into the leisure class, about the merits of work, service, and devotion to things greater than self: a quote easily said by a man with too much money and too many houses to count. America has some interesting cultural universals but none as powerful or potentially detrimental as the myth of American Exceptionalism, which is based upon America's dominant religion, which has two faces: Christianity and capitalism. These two concepts are virtually inseparable in a majority of American minds and form the primary belief system for about eighty percent of US citizens.

Capitalism and Christianity have merged to become one religion and are fixed in our national psyche. American pundits from both the Right and Left, from George W. Bush to Barack Obama, will shout with conviction about "American

Exceptionalism" as if the world and all agree to its validity. In 2006, Howard Zinn wrote an article in the *Boston Review*, "The Power and Glory, the Myths of American Exceptionalism," where he stated:

> The notion of American exceptionalism—that the United States alone has the right, whether by divine sanction or moral obligation, to bring civilization, or democracy, or liberty to the rest of the world, by violence if necessary—is not new. It started as early as 1630 in the Massachusetts Bay Colony when Governor John Winthrop uttered the words that centuries later would be quoted by Ronald Reagan. Winthrop called the Massachusetts Bay Colony a "city upon a hill." Reagan embellished a little, calling it a "shining city on a hill." . . . In reality, we have never been just a city on a hill. A few years after Governor Winthrop uttered his famous words, the people in the city on a hill moved out to massacre the Pequot Indians.

In his 2012 article *American Exceptionalism — Our Tedious Boast*, Eric Zorn wrote in an editorial for the *Chicago Tribune*: "Now it is flung about as the ubiquitous, defensive measure of America's global standing. And it's often used, Joe McCarthy style, as a cudgel to bash those who are judged to have hastened our decline by being insufficiently jingoistic."

American Exceptionalism is the myth that America has been blessed by the Christian god, that by this "divine sanction" it has the best economic system, capitalism. This myth also implies that Americans are better people, and are smarter, more devout and harder working than others, and that the nation and its beliefs are a model for political and economic freedom everywhere. It is used to justify the lies of President George W. Bush and Vice President Cheney who told the public about "weapons of mass destruction" so that they could "nation build" in Iraq. They suggested we have a duty to try to make Iraq (not coincidently an oil-rich country) into a quasi American state. It is what enabled Lyndon Johnson and Richard Nixon to conduct a war in Vietnam and attempt to create an artificial Catholic-capitalist southern Vietnamese state. It is the rationale used by the China Lobby to support the Christian convert and capitalist Chiang Kai-shek so that China might also become a Christian-capitalist nation. The China Lobby included many noted Americans like Henry Luce, Congresswoman Clare Booth Luce, Congressman Walter Judd, and Senators William Knowland and Joe McCarthy, along with other powerful American businessmen many of whom who were, or whose parents were, Christian missionaries in China. The fact that all these foreign missionary attempts failed miserably in spreading Americanism has not deterred their devotion to their belief in the myth of American Exceptionalism. Nor has their failure caused a very serious reconsideration by most other Americans. President George W. Bush dedicated his new presidential library to spreading his version of democracy through "nation building" around the globe.

American exceptionalism begs the question, is it factual? The quick answer is no. Even if you are a Christian, why would you believe that the United States is more blessed than all other Christian nations? America is not a nation more blessed than others by a Christian god. Americans are not wiser. They do not have a superior culture, nor are Americans better than other people. And capitalism, America's chosen path to prosperity, has not shown itself to be the perfect economic system—even in America, especially in the light of the recent economic meltdown by the banks and Wall Street which was caused by capitalist greed and the systemic failure of the unregulated free market.

The fact that both Christianity and capitalism are held in such high, unquestioned reverence is a severe a limitation to growth and freedom. American exceptionalism is pure ethnocentrism. It is a jingoistic intolerant generality married to the American version of militant missionary Christianity, and it is cause for many concerns around the world. The song *Onward Christian Soldiers* is not just a hymn, here, it is a military anthem. The propensity to try and force these beliefs on others is a prominent reason why many people around the world harbor animosity toward the United States. Americans' belief in their own exceptionalism is a foreign policy nightmare; it reduces American intellectual dialogue; and it gives way to dogmatic responses to complex problems. At the same time, it seems to be preventing the United States from making the changes necessary for growth and prosperity in the twenty-first century.

American exceptionalism distorts and in many ways demeans an otherwise great culture and also frequently serves to belittle and exclude non-European, non-Christian cultural influences. It is a leftover of European Christian imperialism and it is unfortunately one of the strongest and most dominate cultural traits in America. Will this trait continue or will it die, or change, over time? We will explore this.

Chapter 2. Native Roots

The American Indian is of the soil, whether it be the region of forests, plains, pueblos, or mesas. He fits into the landscape, for the hand that fashioned the continent also fashioned the man for his surroundings. He once grew as naturally as the wild sunflowers. He belongs just as the buffalo belonged.

—Luther Standing Bear

Where today are the Pequot? Where are the Narragansett, the Mohican, the Pokanoket, and many other once powerful tribes of our Indian peoples? They have vanished before the avarice and the oppression of the White Man, as snow before a summer sun.

—Chief Tecumseh

As a man walked across the land, the land owner came to him and said, Get off my land. So the man asked, Why is it your land? The owner replied, Because I got it from my father. Where did he get it? asked the man. From his father, the owner said. And where did he get it? the man asked again. He fought the Indians for it, the owner said. The man replied, Okay, then I will fight you for it.

—Fletcher Knebel, *Trespass*

There are just over 5.2 million Native Americans in the United States, or 1.7% of the total population, according to the US Census. There are 562 recognized tribes and the largest are the Cherokee with a population of 819,105, the Navajo 332,129, the Choctaw 195,764, the Chippewa 170,742, the Sioux 170,110, the Apache 111,810, and the Blackfeet with 105,304. No other tribe has more than a hundred thousand. The Census does list a mixed category of "Mexican American Indians" with a population of 175,494, which helps show the difficulty and complexity of defining ethnicity and culture in America.

At the time of European arrival in North America, there were about five hundred tribes and about 22 million Native people. However there are only 5 million Native Americans in the US today. Most Native people died due to the new diseases brought in by the Europeans, for which the Native Americans had no immunities. Small pox, tuberculosis, measles, and influenza took millions of lives. According to Jared Diamond, in his book *Guns, Germs and Steel* over 95% of the pre-Columbian Native population died of disease shortly after European arrival. That made conquering a continent much easier.

The death toll from disease wasn't enough to satisfy the European invaders, so the US government also developed a deliberate policy to kill or assimilate Native Americans and eradicate their Native culture. Indian reservations were created for this purpose, as were Indian boarding schools with compulsory attendance for Native children. In these schools their Native Culture and languages were forbidden so as to "civilize these children into the ways of Whites." Many of the reservations and Indian schools were managed by Catholic priests and Protestant clergy to take away Native beliefs and Christianize them.

Even today the federal government still controls who can be recognized as a Native so as to control their populations and reduce their numbers through inter-marriage with Whites. The actual policy was "to breed them out of existence." And while the government doesn't use this phrase anymore the policy of who is Native still remains in the hands of the federal government. The federal government through the Bureau of Indian Affairs firmly also controls the Native Americans on the reservations. Much of Native culture languishes on the reservations due to a gross lack of resources and generations of poverty and their forced dependency on the government handouts. This forced dependency and the forced enculturation in Indian boarding schools was, and in many cases still is, truly genocide.

Before Europeans came to what has now become the United States, a complex network of Native American tribes and cultures populated the vast continent. There were over 250 Native languages in the US and Canada. Much of Native society was matrilineal, unlike the male-dominated European society. Women played a central role in tribal decision-making and Native Americans traced their ancestors through their female lines. In the Seneca tribe, one of the more powerful and feared of the five Iroquois nations, women were the decision makers and leaders. This was a difference well noted by the English colonists. Paula Gunn Allen in her essay, *Who Is Your Mother? Red Roots of White Feminism* claims this was the spark that later helped to start the American feminist movement.

American democratic representative government also came in part from the Native Americans. It was a government the Iroquois had used successfully for over a thousand years. According to some Native historians, like David Grinde Jr., when Ben Franklin and the founding fathers began to shape the American government, they modeled theirs on the Iroquois Nation's democratic representative government. Franklin would later credit the Native Iroquois leader Canassatego for recommending this style of government. Franklin was an admirer of Canassatego and printed many of his political speeches. In October 1988, the US Congress formally recognized these contributions and passed Resolution 331 to recognize the strong influence the Iroquois had upon the American government, the Constitution and the Bill of Rights.

Some still claim that American democracy was fashioned after the Greeks and Romans, but where the founding fathers had some academic knowledge of these ancient societies, their experience with governments was limited to European monarchies. It is also no coincidence that the Iroquois tribal symbol, the bald eagle, was taken by the new government as its symbol. Ben Franklin had originally proposed the wild turkey. Even the political word and process "caucus" comes from the Native Algonquian language and was their custom.

The habit of bathing in water can also be attributed in part to the Native Americans. Oddly enough Europeans, at the time of colonization, particularly the Puritans, held religious objections to bathing in water, believing that it was an act of temptation causing sexual arousal and promiscuity. Although bathing was practiced in ancient Rome, in Arab cultures—including Moorish Spain before 1492, and in Japan, there were few bath houses in Europe at this time, mostly for the gentry, and strictly divided by gender. But the prudish Puritans frowned even on this practice. Initially the Native Americans were called "heathens and hedonists", as Puritan hygiene took second place to this religious taboo. Eventually the European colonists, including the Puritans, began emulating their much cleaner and less odorous Native neighbors.

The vast number of Native languages and their complexity was such that the Native population had for many years used a form of sign language to communicate with neighboring tribes and their many trading partners. This sign language is still part of American culture, in the form of American Sign Language for the hearing impaired. According to Ceil Lucas in, *The Sociolinguistics of the Deaf*, while ASL has its roots nineteenth century French Sign language (LSF), it was greatly influenced by Native Sign language.

There are also about 2200 Native words in use in current American English. These borrow words, as linguists call them, describe weather phenomena such as hurricanes, chinooks, blizzards, and climatic and land types such as savannah and bayou. The borrow words also include animal names like moose, caribou, skunk, raccoon, opossum, puma and jaguar, plant names like mahogany, hickory, yucca, mesquite, very many food plants—and some native plants called tobacco, coca, and marijuana, which when taken out of their traditional context came to have very unfortunate cultural side effects and consequences.

Place names that derive from Native language include about half the states, like Massachusetts, Minnesota, and Mississippi, as well as the names of many counties, cities, rivers, lakes, and mountains. According to Edward Vajda, a professor of Linguistics at Western Washington University, because of Native influence, Americans, unlike Europeans, also name places after animals, such as Turtle Mountain or Beaver Lake. Naming places after animals was a practice given up in Europe after their conversion to Christianity and their disdain for older religions based upon the natural environment.

The colonists took many Algonquian words directly into the English language. Words such as wampum, toboggan, tomahawk, papoose, squaw, and powwow are used and understood today by most Americans. "Podunk," which Americans use to describe a small out-of-the-way place, is a Native word meaning place of isolation. "Honk" is the Native word for the sound wild geese make, and it is now applied in American English to car horns as well as to geese. American English also began to copy Native languages in the compounding of nouns, not generally found in English before this exposure, to create new words such as bullfrogs, warpath, catfish, chokecherry, peanut and rattlesnake. Many American phrases also come from Native languages such as "walk a mile in my moccasins (or shoes)" "burying the hatchet," "the Great Spirit," and "smoking the peace pipe."

Food is the most commonly noted Native contribution to both American and world culture. Today most of the food eaten in the world, an estimated sixty percent of world foodstuffs, came to us through Native Americans. These foods and their names (such as tomato, potato, and cocoa) are also of Native language origin. The big three foods, called the "Three Sisters" by many Native Americans, are corn, beans and squash. These foods were cultivated by most North American Native tribes.

Blueberries, hominy, cranberries, wild rice, chokecherries, currents, persimmons, sassafras, raspberries, sage, sunflowers, pumpkins, many kinds of melons, and maple syrup (produced by a Native American technique known as "sugar bushing"), and turkey are foods from Native America that became part of the early American diets and eventually world cuisines. Dishes like buffalo, moose, bear, elk, prairie chicken, squirrel, wild geese, turtles, wild duck and antelope were early parts of the American diet and are still enjoyed by hunters and outdoor enthusiasts. American fish like salmon, smelt, bass, catfish, walleye and pickerel are also enjoyed. Native dishes like cornbread mush (cornmeal cereal) became common foods of the European Americans. Foods like jerky, pemmican, succotash, and more recently, fry bread, came from Native America.

According to historian Charles Hudson, in his book, "*A Conquered People,*" *The Southeastern Indians* even the Southern and Soul food dish "chitlins" owes its roots in part to a Native dish called "chitterlings." Southeastern Indians, like African-Americans ate the entire slaughtered animal, including and eating the intestines and organ meats fried in animal fat. The popular

Southern Soul food likely came from exposure to both cultures.

Many important Native foods came from the Caribbean, Mexico, and the US Southwest, such as tomatoes, potatoes, sweet potatoes, pineapples, avocado, tapioca, papaya, passion fruit, coconuts, peanuts, peppers both hot and sweet, chocolate, and vanilla which spread quickly around the globe shortly after their European discovery. Stevia, the non-sugar sweetener, is another American plant cultivated by Native Americans that is just now coming into fashion. Even the word barbeque is an Anglicized version of barbacoa, a Native Taino word and method of slow roasting meat over a fire pit. Jamaican Jerk also comes from the Taino Indians of Jamaica who applied a dry rub of allspice and pepper to meat before the slow roasting.

What Americans call Mexican food is actually Native American cuisine from the Southwestern US and the northern parts of Mexico. These foods were already staples in Texas, New Mexico, Arizona, California and parts of Colorado, Nevada and Utah long before they became part of the United States. In an interesting mix of cultures the fry bread taco is now a common favorite food on many American Indian reservations.

The tortilla, guacamole, mole sauce, salsa, tacos, gorditas and tamales are Native foods from this region and are as much American as they are Mexican. In fact in overseas international groceries, these food items can be found in the American as well as Mexican food sections. Far more tacos are eaten in the US than in Mexico, and guacamole was listed as the most popular American Superbowl snack in a poll by *American Demographics*, a US marketing magazine.

Another cultural trait of the Native Americans which has been very slowly adopted by European Americans was the tolerance for gays and lesbians, according to Sue-Ellen Jacobs, Wesley Thomas, and Sabine Lang in their book *Two Spirit People*. This tolerance was another reason the Europeans considered Native Americans to be "heathens and hedonists." To the shock of Europeans, gays and lesbians lived openly in Native society and were accepted without much thought. In Ojibwe, for example, gays and lesbians were called the "egwakwe" and were considered as an equal third sex. In Lakota they were called "wiŋkte" and in Navajo "nádleehé." In many tribal cultures like the Iroquois, particularly the Seneca, there was little difference in sexual roles and since women were considered decision makers, it made the acceptance of the gays and lesbians very easy. In some tribal cultures, gays and lesbians were considered spiritually enhanced with the powers of both males and females. The traditional Christian and biblical concept of two complete and separate sexes of males and females was not prevalent in Native cultures. In the few tribes that gave it much thought, like the Ojibwe, the Lakota and the Navajo, believed there were three genders with gays and lesbians being a third equal gender.

The American log cabin is likely a combination of Swedish and Native influences, These dwellings strongly resemble both the long huts of the Iroquois and Ojibwe and the original housing of the American Swedish colony in what is now Pennsylvania, whose cabins were fashioned after Swedish cabins in the old country. Other things like toboggans, canoes and snowshoes come from Native culture. The Native game of lacrosse is still played and it, along with English rugby, inspired the game of American football. Relay races and tug of war are also of Native in origin. Hockey is thought to have origins in a very similar Native game called shinny. Stickball, another Native game, along with English cricket, is thought to be the inspiration of for baseball.

There are other obvious Native contributions such as moccasins and kayaks. And there are some not so well known like hammocks from the Caribbean, chewing gum from sap from the spruce tree in North America and from the Mayan chicle where rubber was used. Quinine, for both pleasure and medicinal purposes, and rubber are both Native contributions. While cotton was domesticated independently in both the old world and the Americas, the American variety *Gossypium hirsutum*, cultivated by Native Americans, is thought superior. Today over 90% of the world's cotton production are from these Native varieties. Some cotton weaving techniques also came from Native America. And although most know that tobacco was a Native product, few know that pipe smoking and cigars also came from Native culture. The use of coca, marijuana, peyote, and dantura also came from Native culture, but their use in pre-European Native culture was purely ceremonial or as an anesthetic for surgery and other medical uses.

Drug addiction was not a significant problem prior to European settlement. The Europeans introduction of alcohol began Native problems with addiction. Native Americans also used willow bark for fevers and swelling; it wasn't until the 19th century that modern medicine discovered that salicylic acid from the willow bark could be made into the drug we now call aspirin.

Native Americans art forms, in both North and South America, were abstract and thought to be primitive by European colonists; however, appreciation of their concepts, design and color by American artists began in the late 19th century. They were a major inspiration for the American Abstract Expressionists. Many other American painters like Georgia O'Keefe were deeply influenced by Navajo and other Native art. American pottery and jewelry, especially turquoise and silver, woodcarving and weaving and textiles like Navajo blankets, are Native influences found in mainstream America. Native leather craft, beadwork and color patterns and dyes are significant influences in American art. And unique Native art pieces like sand painting, dream catchers and totem poles are still part of American art and culture. Much of American crafts are of Native origin and lore. Most of the outdoors skills and woodcrafts that are taught in the Boy Scouts and Girl Scouts owe their foundations to Native culture.

Native music and dance have made contributions to American culture. Call and response patterns in songs, where a lead singer will sing a verse which is then repeated by many in chorus, derive from both Native American and African traditions, and contemporary American music is influenced by both. Native drums are an important part of American music tradition. Music with a heavy beat and drum solos in particular have both Native and African origins.

But perhaps the major contribution by Native America to American culture is the ecology movement. Beginning with the first contact of Europeans with the North American, Europeans slowly came to appreciate the Native reverence for the land, water, sky and the mineral, plant and animal kingdoms. Native life was an expression of harmony with the natural world, as Native Americans saw themselves as a small part of this world. They called animals and plants brothers and sisters, and said they were all of one mother. This philosophy stood in stark contrast to that of the Europeans, who saw nature as god's gifts for man to exploit and the natural environment as something to be dominated and overcome by man. The wilderness was for conquering. Land was to be put under the plow. Trees were to be felled and cut for building or burned for heat and fuel. Animals were to be killed or tamed, worked, eaten or skinned. And water was to be harnessed and used in mills, wells and irrigation.

Europeans related to the natural world as separate and outside of themselves, and had little appreciation of the beauty and bounty of nature in and of itself. It took a few hundred years to shift that attitude and to start what today has become the environmental or green movement. Teddy Roosevelt summed it up at the beginning of the 20th century: "It is also vandalism wantonly to destroy or to permit the destruction of what is beautiful in nature, whether it be a cliff, a forest, or a species of mammal or bird. Here in the United States we turn our rivers and streams into sewers and dumping-grounds, we pollute the air, we destroy forests, and exterminate fishes, birds and mammals, not to speak of vulgarizing charming landscapes with hideous advertisements. But at last it looks as if our people are awakening."

Roosevelt was one of the first significant voices in the ecology movement, but Rachel Carlson in her book *Silent Spring*, published in 1962, was an important and a significant step forward. Because of her work on the hazards of chemicals and pesticides, for the first time Americans began questioning the safety of fertilizers, pesticides, other chemicals and technology and their detrimental environmental impacts on the natural world. Her book sold 500,000 copies in twenty-four countries and was at the time one of the most successful books ever published.

However, many consider that the birth of the modern environmental movement to be April 22, 1970, when Senator Gaylord Nelson of Wisconsin declared a "national teach-in on the natural environment." As a result an estimated 20 million Americans held rallies, events, and demonstrations protesting the deteriorating natural environment. The movement became international in a very short time. At the time Nelson said: "The ultimate test of man's conscience may be his willingness to sacrifice something today for future generations whose words of thanks will not be heard." Nelson was also fond of quoting a Native American proverb giving credit to the people who started the movement: "We do not inherit the earth from our ancestors; we borrow it from our children."

The Second Wounded Knee 1973

> It is hard for me to believe that the FBI that I have re-
> vered so long has stooped so low.
>
> —Judge Fred J. Nichols of the Federal District Court of
> South Dakota

In February of 1973, Native Americans from the Pine Ridge Indian Reservation and a small group from the American Indian Movement (AIM) met at Wounded Knee, on the Pine Ridge Indian Reservation in South Dakota. It was the site of a government massacre of the Sioux Indians, mostly women and children, in 1890. The Native Americans of the Pine Ridge Reservation met with AIM members at Wounded Knee to have open discussions and to present to the government their grievances and to make people aware of the unimaginable poverty at the Pine Ridge Indian Reservation, which was then and continues to be one of the poorest places in the United States. They also wanted the federal government to investigate the oppressive and corrupt local tribal government that they believed was protected by the US Bureau of Indian Affairs.

As the talks began, the streets leading into and out of the small rural reservation town of Wounded Knee were quickly barricaded by US marshals. They had been ordered to do so by President Nixon's Justice Department. Nixon said, "We already have Negroes protesting civil rights and Hippies protesting the war, and we aren't going to put up with an Indian protest."

The US marshals quickly surrounded the Native gathering, which was being held on Native sovereign land. They surrounded the group with overwhelming government forces, refusing to let them disperse even if they had chosen to do so. The Native Americans then claimed, and they were later proven to be correct in Court, that they had little choice and were forced to make a stand similar to that of their ancestors at Wounded Knee in 1890.

The Native Americans stated that the government blockaded them in at Wounded Knee in order to starve them out, break up their protest and stifle their complaints about injustice and government inflicted poverty. The Nixon Justice Department claimed to the press that it had only responded to stop "Indian violence."

Former US Senator James Abourezk of South Dakota later verified that the Native version was the truth. He said that US Marshals, knowing of the meeting at Wounded Knee through FBI undercover agents they had planted as members in AIM, had arrived in force on the scene a day before the Native Americans gathered. And when the Native Americans met, the government forces almost immediately surrounded and trapped them. Then, at the direction of the Nixon Justice Department, more US Marshals and the FBI arrived with an even larger military force the next day. The government forces included fifteen armored personnel carriers, military helicopters, machine guns and M-16 combat rifles, military and FBI trained snipers, grenade launchers, and over 130,000 rounds of ammunition—all in response to a small Native meeting about poverty and injustice.

The Native Americans hoped that media attention would protect them from government violence and make the world aware of their poverty and injustice, and that this attention would help resolve these problems peacefully. It wasn't to be. The Nixon White House wanted to make an example so that other Indians across the nation would continue unquestioningly to accept their role as second class citizens.

A reporter later chronicled that a group of racist local Whites were actually the first to open fire, shooting at the Native Americans. The government forces claimed they were fired upon, but it is still unclear if it was the Native Americans or these local vigilantes hoping to have the government kill the Native Americans. The government forces then fired upon the Native Americans, using deadly snipers from helicopters. The first casualty at Wounded Knee was a Native man. He was shot in the head and killed through a window by a government sniper as he slept in bed. The second casualty was another Native man who was shot through the heart, while peacefully walking across a street, by another professional government sniper.

The Native Americans were afraid they would all be killed by the overwhelming force now firing indiscriminately at them. They rounded up a few small weapons and they began smuggling in a few more for their protection. After being fired upon and killed, they began to fire back to keep the government men with their guns away. In one of these exchanges a US Marshal was struck by a bullet which left him paralyzed from the waist down. Media coverage was controlled by the government. They restricted press access to the tragedy, and they fed them false propaganda during the incident making the Native group appear more menacing. The national media pushed the story of the wounded US Marshal without mentioning the Native fatalities, particularly that the first man killed by a government sniper was asleep at the time. The one-sided media coverage worked and the nation, including many Native Americans, sided with the government against AIM and the Indian protestors.

The crisis ended when a deputy attorney general, horrified by what was happening, insisted on entering Wounded Knee unarmed to talk to the Indians, despite the government's and the FBI's strong objections and claims that the Native Americans would kill him or take him hostage. The Native Americans told him that they had never intended, nor did they ever want, any violence, and insisted that they had not fired upon the government until they had been fired upon and two of their people killed. They said they responded because they thought the government forces intended to massacre them and were afraid for their lives.

His talks eventually led to the peaceful ending of the second Wounded Knee. The government, in ending the crisis, promised the Native Americans to have hearings about the oppressive poverty conditions and government treaty violations, and also promised to investigate the corrupt and oppressive tribal government. These hearings were never held. The government had lied again. And in the years since, poverty has become even more horrific on the Pine Ridge Reservation, especially after the second incident at Wounded Knee.

In the aftermath, both sides claimed it was the other who started the gunfire. However some news correspondents who managed to get access to the site later reported that the government forces had indeed allowed some local White racists and trouble makers, with weapons, direct access to the site they controlled. They said the government actions and granting of access to the site seemed to further encourage and sanction the White racists and their violence. The news crews claimed it was this group who fired the first shots, firing at both the Native Americans and also on the government forces to provoke and justify a government attack.

The White racists were never charged. The FBI brought 542 separate charges against the Native Americans at Wounded Knee. All but fifteen charges were eventually dismissed by the courts and these fifteen were very minor offenses—mostly nebulous charges of interfering with government law officers in the performance of their duties.

The longest trial in US history resulted from the FBI charges brought against two AIM leaders at Wounded Knee, Dennis Banks and Russell Means.

During the trial, the Judge found out that AIM had been infiltrated by the FBI, who had tried to incite Native violence. Even more appalling, the judge also discovered that the Natives' defense counsel had also been infiltrated by an FBI informant who was illegally spying for the prosecution in preparation for their defense and during the trial. The judge also discovered that the government had coached and encouraged perjured testimony given by the government witnesses. He also discovered that it was FBI infiltrators at Wounded Knee that were the only Native Americans advocating violence. The Court also discovered that the FBI and the government prosecution team had deliberately lied and also withheld some vital evidence that would disprove the government's case during the trial. Presiding Judge Fred J. Nichols of the Federal District Court of South Dakota criticized the FBI and the prosecutors for being "more interested in convictions than in justice." He also said, "It is hard for me to believe that the FBI that I have revered so long has stooped so low."

After dismissing all charges against the two men Judge Nichols concluded: "The fact that incidents of misconduct formed a pattern throughout the course of the trial leads me to the belief that this case was not prosecuted in good faith or in the spirit of justice. The waters of justice have been polluted, and dismissal, I believe, is the appropriate cure for pollution in this case."

The poverty on Pine Ridge continues. Native Americans have the highest rates of poverty of any people in the United States. Reservations are places of extreme poverty, as in Pine Ridge much of this is caused by federal government policies. Suicide, chemical dependency, and teen pregnancies many from unprosecuted rapes and statutory rapes are an epidemic on reservations. In 2010 on the White Earth Indian Reservation, the largest reservation in Minnesota, a PBS Radio team looked into the issue of epidemic teen rape on the reservation. They interviewed the local White county sheriff and White county attorney whose sworn job it was to investigate and prosecute these crimes. When they asked why the cases were not investigated or prosecuted, both justified their inaction by stating that because the Indians were on the Reservation, they didn't pay any property taxes, and then implied that they were therefore undeserving of their attentions.

With all the contributions that Native Peoples have made to America, including serving as a model of representative democracy, Natives have the fewest rights of any Americans to enjoy these once given benefits.

Discrimination is still very much a part of everyday life for Native Americans. Government policies governing reservations, and about who may be considered Native Americans, and how Native Americans may live on their own lands, are meant to control and eventually completely assimilate and obliterate Native peoples and culture. Derogatory colloquialisms such as "redskins," "blanket ass," and "chief" for males and "squaw" for females are frequently used by Americans to denigrate Native Americans; this remains an ugly and regrettable part of the American culture.

CHAPTER 3. LATINOS, HISPANICS, CHICANOS, TEJANOS, AND NUYORICANS

> As a child of West Texas, I identify with Hispanic culture every bit as much as North American culture.

> —Tommy Lee Jones

> Mexico's African presence has been relegated to an obscured slave past, pushed aside in the interest of a national identity based on a mixture of indigenous and European cultural mestizaje. In practice, this ideology of racial democracy favors the European presence; too often the nation's glorious indigenous past is reduced to folklore and ceremonial showcasing.

> —Dr. Maria Jimenez Roman

There are over 50 million people with Spanish ancestry in the United States, with about 37 million Spanish speakers. For lack of a better generic term, we will simply refer to them here as Latinos. Estimates are that over 10 million non-Latino Americans are fluent in Spanish with many more speaking limited Spanish. The influence of Latinos on American culture is both deep and very complicated. To begin with, the term Latino isn't universally accepted, nor does it adequately describe the ethnic diversity in this group of Spanish speakers. Some prefer the term Hispanic, particularly people from Cuba or Puerto Rico, where social and class status is sometimes determined by the amount of Spanish ancestry a person has. And there are some American-born Spanish-surnamed people who prefer the use of the term "Chicano," especially those who have lived for many generations in New Mexico and California. Some of these families have been living on land that is now part of the United States much longer than any English-speaking Whites. In Texas, American-born Latinos are frequently called and prefer the term "Tejanos." Many Americans from Mexico and Central Americans prefer the term "Latino." In New York, some second and third generation Puerto Ricans identify themselves as "Nuyorican." And there are many other less-informed Americans who refer to all Latinos regardless of where they come from as "Mexicans."

Contrary to the generalized ideas of many White, Black and Asian Americans, "the Latinos" do not constitute one culture or one people. To understand Americans with Spanish ancestry, more thought is necessary. First, Latino is less a racial designation and more cultural. Some Mexican-Americans call themselves "La Raza," meaning they are descendants from Aztecs, Mayans or other Indian peoples. Latinos are not all brown or coffee-colored as is sometimes generalized. They are varied in their ethnic composition including White Europeans (mostly Spanish, but also some French and Portuguese, among others). Latinos also include Native-Americans from North America, Mesoamerica, South America and the Caribbean. There are many Latinos of African descent that have come to America from the Caribbean and Mesoamerica. And there are Asian components, both East and West Asian, including South and Central Americans from India and also some Chinese and Japanese. In the former British colonies of Jamaica, the Bahamas, Guyana and Belize, East Indians are very common and many of these have immigrated to the United States. Many of them are English- as well as Spanish-speakers. Each of these varied ethnic groups has brought their version of Latino culture to the United States.

Just like there is no single "European Culture," Latino culture varies by country and region as well as by race and ethnicity. Cuban culture and Puerto Rican culture are not the same as Mexican culture, which in itself varies widely. And not everything is from Spanish culture. For an example, the Jamaican use of curry (which was brought to the United States) did not originate in Spain, England, Africa or Native America, but came from East India.

But perhaps the biggest myth about Latino or Mexican culture is that it was brought to the United States recently, rather than being part of American culture from the very beginning. The Spanish, just like the French, Dutch and English, played an important role in the development of what is uniquely American. In fact Spanish settlement in the territories that now comprise the United States pre-dates the arrival of both the British and the French.

Puerto Rico, which of course has been part of the United States since the Spanish–American War in 1898 (and which has been debating whether to become a state or retain their current commonwealth status as an unincorporated US territory), was the site of the first European settlement in the new world. Caparra was settled in 1508 by some six hundred Spanish people. The next colony in what is now the United States was named San Miguel Gualdape. It was established in Georgia in 1526, but the colony was abandoned because the Spanish clashed with the local Native Americans, who then made their lives so miserable that they left. In 1589, the Spanish established two colonies, Ochuse and Santa Elena, in Florida, near what is now Pensacola. However, after a great storm (most likely a hurricane), their supply ships were destroyed. The colonies were greatly damaged by the storm and they too were abandoned.

During this time the Spanish territory of Florida, which was comprised of what is now the State of Florida and the southern halves of Georgia, Alabama, Mississippi and Louisiana, was uncontested and under complete Spanish power. Many Spanish expeditions explored the area. However, the Spanish soldiers were very hostile to the Native Americans and conflicts were so frequent and so fierce that they prevented colonization. This was also before the Native population was dramatically decimated by European diseases.

On one such expedition, corn was discovered by the Spanish, and shortly thereafter they introduced it to the rest of the world. In 1566, the Spanish built a new colony named for Santa Elena in what is now Parris Island, South Carolina. From there, the Spanish settled six forts, moving as far inland as Tennessee. However, the Spanish were gold-seekers, and after about twenty years of failure to find gold, they abandoned both the forts and the colony. In 1565, the Spanish established St. Augustin (now St. Augustine) in Florida, which is the oldest continually inhabited European settlement in the continental United States. The Spanish developed many missions and small communities in the Southern US from St. Augustin, but all these missions were later destroyed by the French and English during St. Anne's War. In 1696, the Spanish settled the colony of Pensacola on the site of their former colony of Ochuse.

The Spanish developed many ranches in Florida and used captured Native Americans as slave labor. A series of Native revolts along with French raids took its toll on Spanish Florida. Pensacola was also captured by the French. The Spanish responded and captured Fort Carolina, the French settlement in what is now North Carolina; they renamed it Fort San Mateo. It was eventually re-taken by the French. These back and forth conflicts greatly damaged both the Spanish and French hopes of colonizing what is now the American South.

In 1763 the British defeated the French in the Seven Years War and seized the French possessions in America. The French, in their conflicts with Spain, had taken Havana, Cuba. This now fell into British hands; the Spanish then traded what we know as Florida to the British for the return of Havana and Cuba. However, western Florida, including what are now southern Alabama, Mississippi, and Louisiana, were still in the possession of the Spanish. During the American Revolution, Spain re-claimed territories and occupied forts at what are now Vicksburg, Mississippi, and Memphis, Tennessee. This competition for land eventually resulted in the Seminole Wars of the early nineteenth century, where the Spanish along with Native Americans, particularly the Seminoles, fought the United States. During this time the Spanish had also encouraged US Black slaves to escape and come to Florida as free men. These former slaves lived alongside the Seminole Indians of Florida and inter-married, eventually becoming known as the "Black Seminoles."

The US Army, financed by Southern slave holders, invaded Florida in many attempts to reclaim the former slaves. After much conflict, the US and Spain agreed to a treaty whereby Florida was turned over to the US in 1821 in exchange for Americans giving up their claims on the Spanish territory of Texas. That year hundreds of Black Seminoles left Florida and escaped to the Bahamas to prevent their re-enslavement. Many of the Black Seminoles of mixed heritage also continued to live with the tribe.

In 1527, a Spanish ship sailing to Florida was hit by a hurricane which stranded them in a shipwreck near the present-day Galveston, Texas. Four of the survivors spent the next eight years wandering through what is now Texas and New Mexico. They eventually were able to share the tales of these explorations with the Spanish viceroy in Mexico. They embellished what they had found in their telling. Their tales of Indian cities and minerals, gold, silver and turquoise enchanted the viceroy and he organized a formal exploration of the area in 1539. The Spanish were consumed by visions of the mythical Seven Cities of Cibola made of gold, which they believed were hidden somewhere in Native America. The explorers actually found the Zuni pueblo of Hawikah and they enthusiastically exaggerated their findings to curry favor with the viceroy, who allowed himself to believe he had possibly found one of the seven cities. He organized another expedition, led by Francisco Vasquez de Coronado.

When the explorers reached Hawikah, it did not appear to be any golden city, but the Spanish thought the Indians were hiding their gold. A fight soon ensued and the Zuni were defeated by the horse-mounted Spanish and their superior weapons. The Spanish took their provisions from the conquered pueblo and continued their quest to find the seven cities. Although the two-year exploration found no cities of gold, they did find the Grand Canyon and explored much of what is now the Southwestern US, journeying as far north as Kansas before returning to Mexico in 1542.

The Spanish explored the newly-claimed area for another fifty years and in 1595 a colonization effort was privately financed to settle the area. Juan de Onate, a wealthy resident of Mexico, was given the rights to settle what would be called New Mexico. On July 11, 1598, the Village of San Juan de los Caballeros near the junction of two rivers, the Rio Grande and Rio Chama, was founded in what is now the United States twenty-two years before the Puritans landed in the new world and founded Plymouth Colony in 1620. Spanish influence in today's America is older than the English.

Other settlements quickly followed. A few months later the village of San Gabriel was founded and served as the capital of New Mexico, until Santa Fe was founded and the capital was moved there in 1610, ten years before Plymouth Colony.

In addition to creating new wealth, the Spanish were zealously spreading

Catholicism. Having only recently thrown the Muslims out of Spain and reclaimed it for Catholicism, the Spanish colonists, like the English, had little tolerance for other religions, particularly Native religions and customs, all of which they considered pagan. Their intolerance and missionary zeal led to frequent violence between the Spanish colonists and the Native population. It was so frequent and brutal that it hampered the growth of the New Mexico Spanish colonies, but the culture of the area was slowly changed by the Spanish, and Catholicism and Spanish culture began to slowly dominate the region. The Spanish also brought horses to Texas and New Mexico, some of which were taken by Native Americans and some got away or were left when colonies or explorations ended, and within a surprisingly short time wild horses dotted the plains. The plains Indians quickly became expert horsemen.

However, these Spanish colonists were also changed. There was a lot of inter-marriage with the Native Americans and gradually much of Native culture was adopted by the Spanish particularly their cuisine. Corn, tomatoes, and peppers became favored foods, and tortillas, tacos, enchiladas, burritos, and all the cuisine Americans have come to call Mexican food became standard fare in New Mexico and Texas. All of this is woven into American culture, particularly American Western culture. Cowboys, cowboy hats, guitars, cowboy boots, Western saddles, ranches, patios, corrals, lassos, chaparral, burros, mustangs, wranglers, rodeos and the Texas long horns are "American" things from this "Spanish" culture. English saddles, riding gear, and farming are very different from these. There are more than 10,000 words in American English that come from Spanish. Words like amigo, adios, bonanza, bronco, buckaroo, bandoleer, butte, canyon, cargo, chaps, coyote, desperado, guerilla, hammock, hacienda, hoosegow (meaning jail), macho, the phrase "mano a mano," margarita, marijuana, mesa, mosquito, muchacho and muchacha, mulatto, negro (meaning a black person), ocelot, peccadillo, poncho, pronto, renegade, sarsaparilla, sassafras, savvy, siesta, serape, shack, spaniel, stampede, tango, tornado, tequila, turquoise, vigilante, vinegraroon, and vamos (frequently pronounced "vamoose" in English and meaning "let's go" in Spanish), came into usage in American Western culture.

Mexico gained its independence from Spain in 1821. The Southwestern US then became part of the New Republic of Mexico, although the new Republic's rule over her territory was fairly weak and Texas, California and New Mexico were fairly independent. Mexico also had a different trade policy than Spain. The Spanish had seen the Americans as rivals to their new world colonies, but Mexico wanted to develop trade with the United States and welcomed Americans as traders and settlers, and soon Americans began appearing in their territories in greater numbers.

Although the Spanish had granted Florida to the US in exchange for guaranteeing the right of Spain to rule Texas, Texas still remained in dispute. In the years from 1519 to 1848 Texas was claimed by France, Spain, the Republic of Mexico, the Independent Republic of Texas and the United States.

Texas

The first European colony in Texas was the short-lived French colony of Fort St. Louis in 1682. In response the Spanish constructed several mission colonies in East Texas, which were also abandoned by 1691. But during the following hundred years, the Spanish built many small settlements in Texas. In 1821, when Mexico became free from Spain, Texas was a part of the new Republic of Mexico. To encourage more settlement in the vast under-populated land, Mexico encouraged immigrants from the US to settle in Texas and to become Mexicans. By the 1830s this open door immigration resulted in about 30,000 Anglos living in Texas compared to about 7,800 original Mexican citizens.

In 1824, Mexican President Santa Anna revoked the Mexican constitution and began a dictatorial government. While he could control most of Mexico, he had trouble forcing his will on Texas and New Mexico, where both the US and Mexican populations revolted in 1825. Santa Anna sent his army to put down the revolt and the Texans, both Anglo and Latino, fought against Santa Anna and his forces. One of the more memorable battles was a loss for the Texans, at the Alamo Mission, but contrary to American belief the majority of those who died at the Alamo were Latinos, not Anglos. But the Alamo only served to rally the Texans and to persuade even more Americans and Latinos to come to Texas to defeat Santa Anna which they accomplished in 1826 and a new Texas Republic was created.

California

Although Texas likes to brag it is the only State that was a Republic before it joined the United States, the claim is false. Vermont, in 1791, and Hawaii from 1894 to 1898, were independent republics, and California was also an independent republic before becoming part of the Union. Californians revolted from Mexico in 1846, and California was declared an independent Republic. It was called both The Bear Republic and The Republic of California. The Californians never formed a complete government. They did not know at the time that war had been declared between the US and Mexico. The California revolt only took 26 days, and when the Californians learned that the Americans were also at war with Mexico and had sent troops to California to assure its independence from Mexico, the leaders of the revolt and the new Republic of California abandoned their new government and asked for immediate annexation to the United States as a territory. The only modern remnant of the Republic is its flag which is now the State Flag of California, with its Bear and the proud proclamation, "The Republic of California."

California was variously claimed by the Spanish, the English and the Russians. In 1840 a French visitor wrote: "It is evident that California will belong to whatever nation that chooses to send there a warship and two hundred men." The name California came from a Spanish novel about a mythical island called California which was home to the beautiful Amazon women warriors of Greek mythology. The first European explorer to California was Cabrillo, a Portuguese captain who was commissioned by the Spanish to explore the land for Spain and to find a northwest passage to Europe from the Pacific in 1542. Cabrillo spent a winter on Santa Catalina Island, where he injured himself while exploring. He died of his wounds and the exploration ended.

In 1579, Sir Francis Drake sailed up the California coast and claimed it for England. In 1812, the Russians came to California as traders and established Fort Ross on the California coast about sixty miles north of present day San Francisco. It remained a Russian colony until 1841.

California remained lightly settled by Europeans until late. It was reachable primarily by ships sailing the Pacific; two physical boundaries kept explorers and colonists from accessing California by land. In the south were two difficult deserts to cross, the Sonora and the Mojave, and the central and northern part of the state were bordered by the rather formidable Sierra Nevada Mountain range. The disastrous attempt of 1846 Donner Party to cross these mountains illustrates their effectiveness as a barrier.

The Spanish Church began the first colonization of California by Europeans. They established missions to bring Christianity to the Native population. These missions started small, with usually two Franciscan priests and six to eight Spanish soldiers. A trail called the El Camino Real (The Royal Highway), which later became known as the Mission Trail, linked these missions which were placed about sixty miles apart, from San Diego to San Francisco. Many of these missions eventually became the sites of California's first cities.

After Mexican independence from Spain, the Mexicans took the missions from the Spanish Church and the Franciscans, but they lacked funds to support them, and they were closed. When California achieved US statehood, the US Supreme Court restored the mission ownership to the Franciscans and they were resurrected by the Catholic Church. The Mission style of architecture, furniture, wrought iron fences and accents became prominent in California and the Southwestern United States. In addition to the missions the Spanish introduced the Ranchos system to California. A rancho was a large land grant given to Spanish colonists who were then expected to raise cattle and sheep. The colonists modeled their ranchos on the estates of the Dons of Spain. It was also the Spanish who introduced many fruits, including dates, citrus, and grapes for wine making to California on the ranchos. The workers on these ranchos were called cowboys and were mostly Native Americans. These Spanish customs are at the roots of the American Western culture.

California remained a sleepy place until the Gold Rush of 1848, but even then it remained remote and isolated until the transcontinental railway was completed in 1876. The gold rush, while not long lasting, brought the benefits of California's climate and amenities to the attention of those in the American East and internationally. The new railroad eliminated the need to travel by ship or wagon train, and only a hundred years later California became the most populous state. California's large Central Valley is one of the most important agricultural regions of the United States as well as the world.

Puerto Rico

Puerto Rico was inhabited by Native Peoples sometime between 3000 and 2000 in the Pre Christian Era (B.C.). Christopher Columbus during his second voyage of discovery landed on the island in 1493. He named it San Juan Bautista. A colony called Caparra was settled by Ponce de Leon in 1508. A year later the settlement was moved to a nearby islet off the coast called Puerto Rico (Rich Port), and the name stuck. It was from Puerto Rico that the Spanish began their colonization of Florida and what is now the United States. The Spanish enslaved the Native population, the Taino. Because of the harsh and inhuman treatment by the Spanish of the Taino, and European diseases, they were eventually wiped out on the island. In 1513 the Spanish began bringing the first African slaves to Puerto Rico to replace their Native slave labor.

The first school in the Americas, "Escuela de Gramatica," was founded on Puerto Rico in 1513. By 1860 Puerto Rico had a population of about 583,000. About 300,000 of these were White Europeans and the others were people of color, including a few Native Americans and many Blacks and many of mixed race.

The Puerto Ricans attempted to gain independence from Spain in the late nineteenth century but were unsuccessful. At the conclusion of the Spanish American War in 1898, the Treaty of Paris gave Puerto Rico along with Cuba and the Philippines to the victorious United States. An American government was created on the island in 1900. In the 1940s, due largely to the economic hardships on the island during and after the Great Depression, a large migration of Puerto Ricans began, mainly to New York City. Puerto Ricans today are a large ethnic group in New York, and New York born people of Puerto Rican ancestry and ethnicity sometimes refer to themselves as "Nuyoricans."

After 1900, Puerto Rican schools taught in both English and Spanish, but in the 1960s the English language education was mostly dropped, and some Puerto Ricans now speak less English than their parents and grandparents. However, the island is bi-lingual.

Puerto Ricans are US citizens and Puerto Rico is sometimes called the fifty-first state, but Puerto Ricans have still not voted for statehood. Many Puerto Ricans want statehood, while some find it advantageous to remain a US territory. As of this is writing, the Statehood faction seems to have the upper hand.

Cuba

In the nineteenth century Cuba fought three wars for liberation from Spain, the last of which escalated into the Spanish–American War when the US battleship the *Maine* was mysteriously sunk and the United States declared war on Spain. After the US victory, the Treaty of Paris made Cuba a US protectorate, but her independence was also assured by the treaty—although with no timeframe. Many in the US preferred that Cuba remain an American territory.

Columbus had discovered Cuba on his first voyage in 1492. In 1511, the Spanish decided to conquer Cuba from the Taino Indians. It took three bloody years, but the Spanish Conquistadors were eventually successful. Spanish cruelty was horrific and when the Taino were captured in battle they were tied to wood piles and burned alive. The Spanish justified these horrific acts by claiming that since the Taino were not Christians, they lacked a soul and were therefore not humans. After the conquering the Island the Spanish continued to roundup and massacre the Taino population. After decimating the Native population the Spanish had no workforce to grow the newly discovered and popular tobacco crops, so they began to import African slaves, However the Spanish government greatly restricted the slave trade in Cuba fearing it would eventually become a Black colony. The British captured the capital city, Havana, in 1762 during the Seven Years War and during their brief reign, before the Spanish took back Cuba, they brought in many thousands of African slaves during a ten month period.

During the Haitian Slave Rebellion from 1791 to 1804, thousands of French colonists escaped Haiti with their slaves and were allowed to colonize in Cuba after swearing allegiance to Spain. These new immigrants brought the sugar and coffee industry to Cuba. In the nineteenth century slavery was abolished in Cuba. In the early nineteenth century Cubans began to entertain a break with Spain and many wanted annexation to the United States. As early as 1805 the Americans held secret discussions with Cuban rebels about possible annexation. Much of the impetus for this discussion was due to Spain's abolition of slavery and the Cuban plantation owners desire to continue as an American slave state. In 1898 the Americans backed Cuba's move for independence which escalated into the Spanish American War and after the Treaty of Paris Cuba became a protectorate of the United States.

In 1902 Cuba was granted independence, in name only, and the US continued to govern Cuba as a puppet state. American corporations, business and the US Mafia controlled Cuba and her government from so-called independence until Castro's revolution in 1959. In 1940 the US puppet, Fulgencio Batista, won election as president in a corrupt election that was contrived by the Americans. Batista was ineligible to run again in 1944 because of the Cuban Constitution. The US Mafia began operating in Cuba in the 1930s and soon controlled most of Havana. Eduardo Chibas, a progressive, was expected to easily win in the 1952 elections with his campaign to rid Cuba of corruption, the Mafia and US corporate influence. He very mysteriously committed suicide just before the election and Batista with the support of the Americans, the CIA, and the Mafia, took over the Cuban government in a bloodless coup three months before the elections. Batista remained in power as the Cuban dictator with US support until the Castro led Cuban revolution of 1959.

As a consequence of the Cuban Revolution, thousands of mostly upper class Cubans fled to the United States, particularly to the Miami area (which would become known as "Little Havana"). Many of these upper class Cubans were part of the corrupt Batista Government, or had worked as managers for American business enterprises. And while there were some Cuban refugees that genuinely did not want to live under Castro's rule they too were also very conservative, and unlike most other Latinos in America, the Cubans supported and continue to support rightwing American political philosophy.

The CIA engineered an attack on Cuba now known as the Bay of Pigs fiasco. When the CIA's Bay of Pigs invasion went horribly wrong they asked President Kennedy to commit US troops to invade Cuba and he refused. This further cemented many of the Cuban-Americans to the rightwing conservatives and Republicans in American politics. It also cemented the American right to the Cubans and to "free Cuba." Politicians like President George Herbert Walker Bush lost family fortunes when Castro took Cuba and nationalized American businesses and possessions there. Although he has denied any involvement in the CIA and the Bay of Pigs fiasco, it is curious to note that three of the ships used by the American-trained Cuban forces in the CIA-supported Bay of Pigs Invasion were named Barbara J. after Bush's wife and the World War II ship that he served upon, another named Houston, after his home, and Zapata after his oil company. It is also noteworthy that Bush was later named CIA Director under Nixon, who, as the Vice President in the Eisenhower Administration, had been the point person for the Bay of Pigs Invasion. John Foster Dulles, the Secretary of State who was involved in the planning of the invasion along with his brother, CIA Director Allen Dulles, also had business ties to the Bush family and also lost fortunes when Castro nationalized their businesses. Nixon and his partner Bebe Rebozo also lost a hotel and casino in the revolution. These losses explain much of American foreign policy toward Cuba since 1959.

The 2010 census counts just over 50 million Hispanics in the United States and 37 million Spanish speakers. The ethnic breakdown is as follows: Mexicans 63%, Puerto Ricans 9.2%, Central Americans 8%, South Americans 5.5%, and Cubans 3.5%, and the census also includes another category of "all others" of 10.8%.

The distribution of Latinos in the US is fairly predictable. In the 2010 Census the state with the highest Latino population is New Mexico with 46.3%, followed by California 37.6%, Texas 37.6 %, Arizona 29.6%, Nevada 26.5%, Colorado 20.7%, as you would expect all in the previously Spanish

Southwest. Florida with its large Cuban population is next at 22.5%, followed by New York with 17.5% with its large Puerto Rican population. New Jersey would be a surprise to many people with 17%, also mostly Puerto Rican. If Puerto Rico becomes a state, it would of course lead the list of states with a Hispanic population of 99%. In 2000, no other states had a population of more than more than a ten percent Hispanic population. However, by 2010, another eight more states recorded Hispanic populations of over 10%. The major metropolitan areas that list Latino as their largest single ethnic group are Los Angeles, San Diego, Dallas-Ft. Worth, San Antonio, Houston, and Miami.

One of the more confused arguments has been American Anglos arguing for laws demanding English as the official American language, and keeping an English-only policy with all official records. These protests ignore the fact that Spanish has always been spoken in the United States, even longer than English, and that the descendants of the original Spanish colonists still live here. The languages do borrow from each other, including words accepted into English like adobe, aficionado, albino, alcove, alfalfa, alligator, armadillo, armada, and arroyo. It also works both ways: many English words are now used in Spanish, such as television, and radio.

There are also a few Spanish dialects that are unique to the United States; these have been labeled New Mexican Spanish, Cali-Mexi, Tex-Mex or Tejano. These versions of Spanish include Native-American words, and English words and phrases mixed with Spanish, along with newly created words. For example the phrase "Hay que watcho" means very little in either English or Spanish but its Cali-Mexi/New Mexican Spanish meaning is "I'll be seeing you," with the word "watcho" coming from English. The Cali-Mexi/New Mexican word for fire is "fiero," while the word "fire" in formal Spanish is fuego (original Latin meaning, "hearth"). The meaning of fiero in Spanish is fierce or cruel.

Latino religion is more complex than a first glance would indicate. While about 70% of Latinos are Catholic, 23% are Protestant or other Christians such as Mormons and Jehovah Witnesses, and about 7% are others, mostly atheists and agnostics. The number of Protestant Latinos is growing and about 85% of Latino Protestants define themselves as evangelicals. The Catholic Church has begun to worry about this recent rapid change. Latinos made important early contributions to American Catholicism.

Latinos mostly attend American public schools, but a significant number attend parochial schools, mostly Catholic, and some schools are Spanish-speaking. And while Latinos mostly attend English-speaking public and private higher education, there is a Hispanic Association of Colleges and Universities (HACU) with 238 member institutions in the United States that teach courses in Spanish. The places with the most Hispanic colleges and universities, as may be expected, are in California, Texas and Puerto Rico.

Many Mexican-American things are misunderstood as being Mexican.

The holiday Cinco de Mayo is primarily an American celebration. Contrary to what many Americans think, May 5th is not Mexican Independence Day: that is celebrated in Mexico on the 16th of September. Cinco de Mayo is a minor celebration in the Mexican state of Pueblo, where it commemorates a Mexican army victory in a battle with the French. However Cinco de Mayo is a widely recognized Mexican-American holiday in the United States celebrating Mexican-American heritage and culture. As an Anglo child growing up in Barstow, California, in the 1950s and 1960s, I celebrated Cinco de Mayo each year by marching with my Boy Scout troop in our city's parade. As an Anglo child in Barstow, California, I also grew up speaking my share of Spanish and Spanglish and eating more than my fair share of Mexican-American cuisine; I also listened to Mariachi music, and Herb Alpert and the Tijuana Brass, along with our generation's favorite Mexican-American performers Richie Valens, Santana and Los Lobos. In fact I could speak Spanish as well as or better than many of my Chicano friends. Cheech Marin, the Mexican-American actor and comedian, once joked that a Chicano is someone who goes to community college and takes a Spanish class in the hope of getting a B, which was true of many of my Chicano friends. I can identify strongly with the quote by Tommy Lee Jones at the beginning of this chapter. Growing up in California, I am as at ease with Mexican-American culture as I am with Anglo culture.

An American Hero, Cesar Chavez

Cesar Chavez was a Chicano born in Yuma, Arizona, in 1927. He grew up in an adobe home with his six siblings. His father at one time owned a small ranch and grocery store, but both were lost during the Great Depression. After losing everything the family moved to California and became migrant farm workers.

In 1942 Chavez, who was in the seventh grade, had to quit school to become a fulltime farm worker to help his family survive. He remained a farm worker until he was seventeen and joined the Navy during World War II. Upon discharge he married his childhood sweetheart and returned to the fields to work again as a farm worker.

In 1952 he was offered a job at the Community Service Organization, a Latino civil rights group, as an organizer. He was very passionate and good at his job and led several successful campaigns to register Latino voters. He began to make speeches on Latino rights and became a very good speaker. In 1958 he became the organization's National Director.

In 1962 he left the Community Service Organization to concentrate on farm workers' rights and formed the National Farm Workers Association with Dolores Huerta. It was later called United Farm Workers. He became a national figure for organizing strikes to get farm workers a living wage and conducted a national media campaign to boycott grapes in support of this. He rallied national support for his farm workers and for Latino rights through strikes, boycotts and demonstrations. Robert Kennedy, the Black Civil Rights leader Ralph Abernathy, and Walter Mondale became friends and supporters of Chavez, further increasing his status as a national figure.

Chavez, like Dr. Martin Luther King Jr., was a follower of Gandhi and believed in non-violent civil disobedience, which was at the heart of his strikes and protests. He was also a vegan, believing it to be a healthier lifestyle.

He was against the use of the Bracero Program and lobbied to end it because he believed that using poor non-citizens as farm and factory workers only served to keep wages down for US citizens and kept these Mexican and Central American workers in poverty as well, but many critics used this to claim he was anti-immigration.

Chavez died in 1993. His familiar black union jacket is now in the National Museum of American History in Washington, DC. His portrait also hangs in the National Portrait Gallery. In 1992, a year before his death, Chavez was awarded the "Peace on Earth" Award from the Catholic Church for his lifelong work for Latino Civil Rights. In 1994, after his death, President Clinton awarded him the Presidential Medal of Freedom, which was accepted by his widow. There are numerous parks, schools and university buildings named in his honor. In 2012 President Barack Obama designated the Cesar E. Chavez National Monument in Kern County, California. Chavez is buried there.

Cesar Chavez Day, which is celebrated March 1, his birthday, is a state holiday in California, Colorado and Texas. His passionate work for Latino civil rights and his strong advocacy for workers' rights and unions will forever be linked to Cesar Chavez.

Unfortunately discrimination against Latinos still exists in America. Derogatory colloquialisms such as "wet backs" implying that someone swam across the Rio Grande to illegally enter the US, "greasers" and "beaners" applied to Mexican-Americans and "Spics," usually applied to Puerto Ricans, are some of the ugly racist terms used in the US to describe Latinos. Discrimination against Latinos usually comes out when immigration issues and legislation are discussed in the United States. It has also been prevalent as Anglo-Americans discuss such things as making English as the "official" language the United States. There is a great fear in White Anglo America that somehow their culture is being lost as other cultures, particularly Latino culture, is added to the mix.

But as Cesar Chavez said, "Preservation of one's own culture does not require contempt or disrespect for other cultures."

CHAPTER 4. AFRICAN-AMERICAN CULTURE

> I'd like to state that Spike Lee is not saying that African-American culture is just for Black people alone to enjoy and cherish. Culture is for everybody.
>
> —Spike Lee

> It is only in his music, which Americans are able to admire because a protective sentimentality limits their understanding of it, that the Negro in America has been able to tell his story.
>
> —James Baldwin

> Progressive art can assist people to learn not only about the objective forces at work in the society in which they live, but also about the social character of their interior lives. Ultimately, it can propel people toward social emancipation.
>
> —Angela Davis

The majority of African-Americans came to the United States after being enslaved. Most came from West Africa. However, a small percentage of African-Americans have traced their ancestry to Mozambique, Madagascar and Tanzania on the East. Slavery has been practiced by many cultures, but few were race based and in many cultures slavery was a temporary situation rather than a life-long (much less hereditary) condition. Slavery was practiced in the Mediterranean and in the Middle East and also among African tribes for centuries, but it still wasn't race based until the Europeans became involved in the West African slave trade. The horrors of slavery were magnified as it became racially based. The Europeans saw Black Africans as an inferior people or even as animals. They rationalized that since the Africans were not Christians, they had no souls and could be exploited freely. They were property and their condition was life-long, indeed multi-generational as their children were also considered property, even the children fathered by White men.

The first Black slaves brought to the British colonies in America were taken to a new colony in Hampton, Virginia, in 1619. They numbered nineteen. They were treated initially as indentured servants and received their freedom after a number of years. However, this practice was quickly replaced by the more harsh West Indies custom of permanent life-long slavery and severe racial discrimination. It also meant that the offspring of these slaves were also slaves. Slaves became private property under English common law and were treated similarly to cattle and horses. Between 1600 and 1820, some ten to twelve million Africans were brought to the Western Hemisphere, but only about 300,000 of these came to the American colonies. The importation of slaves was made illegal in 1820 in the US, but the breeding of slaves for sale became a large enterprise in the slave states.

If the importation of enslaved Africans became illegal in 1820, then clearly the ancestors of most African-Americans were here before that date. Meanwhile, a majority of White Americans' ancestors arrived after 1820, in fact, mostly during the last half of the nineteenth century or later. Thus, most African-Americans have a longer history in America than most Whites.

By 1700, Blacks made up about ten percent of the population of the British North American colonies. The slaves were not as docile as some would believe. There were numerous slave revolts and runaways were very common, so harsh laws were commonly enacted to block and retrieve runaway slaves. The first major slave revolt was the Stono Uprising, which occurred in South Carolina in 1739. The South Carolina colony had more than 56,000 slaves and they outnumbered the White population about two to one. Some 150 slaves captured guns and ammunition, killing twenty Whites in the process, and headed for freedom in Spanish Florida. Most were caught and killed but some escaped. How many is a mystery since successful escapes were never revealed — so as to not encourage more Black revolts and runaways. Spanish Florida harbored many escaped Black slaves who lived freely alongside the Seminole Indians and became known as the Black Seminoles; as mentioned above, some of these moved to the Bahamas when Florida became part of the United States.

It is commonly thought in America that only the Southern states had Black slaves. All the American colonies had slaves, but they made up only two percent of the population of the North. The northern colonies had small farms but no plantations, and therefore had fewer uses for slaves other than as domestic servants. There were, however, more free Blacks in the North, including some free Blacks of note. Crispus Attucks was a well-known free Black tradesman who was unfortunately the first American killed in the Revolutionary War, in the Boston Massacre. About 5,000 free Blacks also served in the Continental Army during the Revolutionary War.

During that war the British offered Black American slaves their freedom for running away and joining the British Army; about 25,000 slaves took advantage of this. After losing the war, Britain broke its promise and returned most of the former slaves to their owners. However, they did help about 4,000 Black soldiers escape to Canada, and some to Jamaica, rather than return them to their "owners" as they had agreed to do in the peace treaty. These 4,000 Black soldiers were given land to farm in Nova Scotia, but it was unsuitable for any crop or even to support livestock, and after they protested to the English government about this, they were given passage to West Africa and the British colony of Sierra Leone, where their descendants still live.

The American Abolitionist movement started in the northern colonies during the Revolutionary War when Americans began defining their concept of freedom. Benjamin Franklin was one of the earliest proponents. Between 1780 and 1804, most of the Northern States passed acts banning slavery and declaring Black slave residents free. But the South clung to and expanded its slave-based economy. After 1820, some Southern slave runners still attempted to bring Black slaves into the South illegally from Africa and the Caribbean. The US Navy was sent to patrol the South to prevent this (with partial success).

By 1810 there were 186,446 free Blacks, mostly in the Northern States. The Government also passed legislation banning slavery in the Northwest Territories, which would become the states of the American Midwest. However, even being a Northern free Black still had its limitations, and so a few free Blacks did return to Africa.

During the Antebellum period (before the Civil War), free Blacks began to develop the first Black communities. By 1830 there were over 319,000 free Blacks in the United States. They settled mostly in the Northeastern cities and began to start Black churches and fraternal orders, and Black businesses. Many of these failed over time due to lack of resources, but they did serve as a starting point for the rapid development and expansion of African-American culture. Free Black employment opportunities still remained second class to White employment opportunities. Free Black laborers were forced to work in the lowest paying, lowest skill jobs. Many Black women continued to work as domestics and nannies for White families, just as they had done as slaves.

Public education was not always available to free Blacks, and their education was mostly inferior to the education that Whites received. Despite these barriers a surprising number of free Blacks obtained advanced educations and had careers as ministers, nurses, teachers, doctors and other skilled professions, even if their services were frequently only requested within the free Black communities. There were of course small numbers of free Black farmers and business owners, and very slowly an African-American middle class began to grow.

The first Black College was Cheyney University of Pennsylvania, established in 1837. In 1854, two others were founded, Lincoln and Wilberforce Universities. In 1862, the Morrill Act provided for the establishment of land grant colleges in the former Northwest Territories which then established state universities in the Midwestern states. As part of the Act each state was required to provide a state university for Blacks if they did not open their public land grant universities to free Black students. As a consequence, most of these universities (which comprise what is now known as the Big Ten Schools) were open to free Black students. And because of the Land Grant colleges, public schools were also open to Blacks.

Most of the Black colleges in the South were formed after the Civil War. Southern White colleges and universities did not accept Blacks until the late 1960s when the US Courts ended segregation. Eventually 105 Black colleges were founded. Today about a quarter of a million students attend what are referred to as Historically Black Colleges and Universities. These institutions are open to all races and several of them now actually have a White student majority, but most have retained their Black majority. These colleges have served as the principal gateway for Black Americans into professions that had been traditionally open to Whites only. These institutions were a solid foundation for building a Black middle class.

In early America, Blacks were not welcome in White churches. Some slaves were given religious services by their masters, and much of this was geared to teaching the Christian duty of serving god and their masters well. The Christian Church was another way for Whites to justify their supposed superiority, as Blacks were seen as inferior heathens.

No wonder free Blacks began to form their own churches. They combined the basics of traditional European Christian services but were more open to expression and included many African spiritual traditions. This is where the Black spiritual songs were developed that have become the bedrock for much of American music. Black churches were not as formal or as stilted as the more traditional White churches (although some White churches changed, particularly among working class Whites after the Great Awakening).

It was the Black churches which first became the center of the African-American community. These churches were mostly accepted by religious White Americans and were for the most part safe and sacrosanct. Although some White Americans, frequently under the guise of the Ku Klux Klan, would attack or harass a Black church, this was abhorrent to most White Americans. And in more recent times when a Black church was attacked and bombed by Klansmen, such as the 16th Street Baptist Church in Birmingham, Alabama, in 1963 (killing little four girls attending Sunday school there), it not only united the African-American community but also stirred White consciences into supporting Black Americans.

The oldest Baptist Church in Kentucky and the third oldest in the United States was founded by a slave, Peter Durrett. The Black churches became community and cultural centers. They also became political centers which from their very beginnings sought to promote Black rights and civil liberties. The Black churches fostered Black music in the form of spirituals and also fostered the evolution of African-American cuisine as meals were shared at many social events. This is where news was heard, opinions were shared, and social services could be extended to help people in need. Black churches were active in educating their congregation and also in providing training in vocational and living skills. The Black church was a refuge and was ultimately a place for Black freedom of expression and of hope.

It was not a coincidence that the Black Civil Rights Movement was lead by the Rev. Martin Luther King Jr. and other prominent Black religious leaders. The Black church was always in the forefront of Black politics. Although Black churches were seen as liberal and progressive, and today vote Democratic, their congregations today are also frequently much more conservative than Whites liberals on certain social issues, such as their views on women's issues, gay marriage, and GLBT issues in general.

African-American culture is a complex mix of White Southern culture and African culture, and is also deeply influenced by the experiences of both slavery and generational poverty. And while slavery and poverty are horrifically negative effects, some unique cultural results also came out. Blues music is an excellent example of this. The music and lyrics of American Blues comes directly from the pain and oppression of slavery and poverty.

Oral tradition and storytelling is an African tradition that flourished among Blacks in America. It was the only way for Blacks to preserve their history, values, spirituality and culture and to share common experiences. The tales of Br'er Rabbit are an excellent example of this oral tradition, although the Uncle Remus stories written by Joel Chandler Harris don't do justice to the original complex traditional tales.

Other aspects of African oral tradition include the Dozens, a game of trading insults, signifying, and trash talk, which should always be taken in humor. Call and response in church services are also part of this oral tradition, as is interrupting to affirm a speaker's point. Rhyming has always been a part of the oral tradition and Rap music is just a more current version.

Black music and dance came into the mainstream in American culture when Whites began to imitate Black music and dance in the Minstrel Shows of the nineteenth century, where Whites would pantomime and imitate Blacks. These shows contained an abundant supply of negative racial stereotypes as they frequently depicted Blacks as simple and cartoonish, but the appreciation of Black music and dance was genuine—even though it was frequently a greatly watered-down White version of Black music.

The Harlem area of New York City was one of the earliest and most prominent Black communities. The Harlem Renaissance occurred in the 1920s and 1930s. Night clubs like the (originally Whites-only) Cotton Club became cultural spots where "everyone who is anyone" came to see and be seen. It was the Jazz Age and Harlem was the Jazziest—with Black performers. Black music like the Blues, Swing and Jazz, Black dance, and Black poetry and literature became prominent in New York art circles and nightlife. At the time even right-wing bigots like J. Edgar Hoover went to the Cotton Club, although he later disallowed his agents to go there because he saw Whites dancing with Blacks.

Harlem Renaissance poets who wrote of the Black experience, like Langston Hughes, Claude McKay and Countee Cullen, came to be recognized by mainstream American culture along with Black authors like Nella Larsen and Zora Neale Hurston, and Black artists like Palmer Hayden and William H. Johnson. But it was the musicians and singers that became the most noteworthy to White America, including some of the greatest ever American musical performers such as Lena Horne, Duke Ellington, Count Basie, Cab Calloway, Ella Fitzgerald, Fats Waller, Louis Armstrong, Dizzy Gillespie, Nat King Cole, Billie Holliday, and Ethel Waters. These talents defined not just Black but all American music.

Talented slave musicians had been prized in the South. Most were self-taught. The banjo was an instrument of West African origin and was originally played only by people of African descent. There is little doubt about the roots of African-American music. It is polyrhythmic like the music of West Africa. Call and response, syncopation, heavy percussion, improvisation, the use of falsetto and complex multi-harmonies are all musical roots most likely of West African origin. These elements were retained by the Black slaves in the "negro spirituals" they sang during their forced labor. The music was a way to free a person's soul from the realities of physical life. They strengthened Black America and are now the backbone of American music. The Blues, American Gospel, Jazz, Rock and Roll, Rap, Funk, Hip Hop, and even Country are American music forms that are most influenced by West African music.

American music is an amalgamation of African and Celtic elements, with Spanish guitar, and it has absorbed influences from many other cultures. American music has spread globally, in part because people hear the faint influences of their own cultures. But the heaviest stamp of American music was placed upon it by African-Americans.

Not surprisingly, American dance was also so inspired. Dance was a tradition among slaves and, like music, dance was a way to lift the spirit, free the soul and to connect with a person's roots. Free style and ring dances combined with African body language were elements of African dance brought to America. African-America inspired a variety of dance forms such as The Cakewalk, the Lindy Hop, the Charleston, the Jitterbug and Swing. Like music, African American dance achieved its first significant influence on the mainstream culture during the Harlem Renaissance. It is why J. Edgar Hoover saw Whites dancing with Blacks.

Black slaves also made significant contributions to the American fine arts. Black slave artisans and craftsmen were valued in the South. Quilting, ceramics and metal working were particularly appreciated skills. But free Blacks also made early contributions, such as the Baltimore portrait painter Joshua Johnson and the Boston engraver Scipio Moorhead.

American quilting, particularly Southern Quilting, was heavily influenced by Black slaves; some of their colorful patterns were inspired by memories of Africa and remind us today of modern abstract art. However, some Black artists went to Europe, particularly France, to work and to show their works, because of White American bias which persisted well into the twentieth century. It was again during the Harlem Renaissance that the first Black artists began to become part of mainstream American culture. The 1960s and 1970s was another period that gave rise to Black fine arts.

Although there were early pioneers in Black literature, like the poet Phillis Wheatley writing about slavery in the eighteenth century, it wasn't until the Harlem Renaissance that Black literature came into vogue. Poet Langston Hughes, Historian and essayist W.E.B. Du Bois (the founder of the NAACP), and Booker T. Washington's book *Up from Slavery* were early examples. In the 1960s poet and novelist James Baldwin, Richard Wright with his novel *Black Boy* and poet Gwendolyn Brooks entered the mainstream writing about the Black experience. Alice Walker with her work *The Color Purple*, and *Beloved* by Toni Morrison, are more current examples. But Alex Haley's book *Roots: The Saga of an American Family* and the subsequent television miniseries created a watershed, changing forever how the US would view and appreciate African-American experiences and contributions.

Most African-Americans are Protestants. The largest groups of African-American Christians are the Baptists with about ten million members, with seven and a half million in the National Baptist Convention alone. There are about three million Black Catholics in the United States. And about 150,000 Blacks practice Judaism. In 2010 the Pew Research Center estimated that there were 2,600,000 Muslims in the United States and that a quarter, or 600,000 of these are African-Americans.

In 1930 the Nation of Islam was founded by Wallace Fard. Elijah Muhammad became the head of the organization in 1934. While most African-Americans are Orthodox Muslims, it was the Nation of Islam that garnered most White and mainstream attention.

Malcolm X

Malcolm X was associated with the Nation of Islam but converted to Sunni Islam; it was his conversion that led to his assassination in 1965. Malcolm X was born Malcolm Little in 1925 in Omaha, Nebraska. He was the son of Earl Little, a Baptist minister and Black activist influenced by Marcus Garvey. Three of Malcolm's uncles were killed by Klansmen. The Klan also chased Earl and his family out of Omaha. They relocated to Milwaukee, and then went to Lansing, Michigan. Earl Little was frequently harassed by Whites for his outspoken Black advocacy. In 1931, Earl was killed by a streetcar when Malcolm was six years old. While his death was ruled an accident, some Black witnesses say he had been shoved in front of the streetcar by White bigots. Earl's wife Louise and her seven children suffered extreme poverty after his death. Because of this, in 1938 Louise had a nervous breakdown and was sent to a state mental hospital and Malcolm and his siblings were put in various foster homes. Malcolm was a good student and wished to become a lawyer, but he was told in junior high that it was "not a realistic goal for a nigger." He soon quit school.

He moved to Boston and lived with a half-sister. He then moved to Harlem and became a thief, drug dealer, pimp, and, some claimed, a gay male prostitute. He was declared "mentally disqualified for military service" when he told his draft board that he wanted "to steal some guns and kill some crackers."

He returned to Boston, was arrested for theft, and began to serve a six-to eight-year sentence at the Charleston State Prison, where he met John Bembry, who got him to start reading. Given a bit of direction, he developed a voracious appetite for the written word. He despised his father's religion; his open hostility to religion in prison earned him the nickname of "Satan."

His brother Reginald began telling Malcolm about the Nation of Islam, and he eventually converted him. Malcolm gave up pork, cigarettes and drugs. In 1950 he wrote to Elijah Muhammad and asked to join the Nation of Islam; afterward he corresponded regularly with Elijah Muhammad. In 1950 he began signing his name Malcolm X, stating that he renounced his White slave master's name and that the X represented his missing African name.

He was paroled in 1952 and went to Chicago to be with Elijah Muhammad. He eventually served the Nation of Islam in Detroit and Philadelphia and founded a Temple in Boston. In 1954, he returned to Harlem to lead a temple there. He was a powerful speaker and his speeches began to attract Black converts by the hundreds. He founded temples in several other cities. In 1955, he married Betty Sanders and they had six daughters.

White America first came to know Malcolm X when the police beat up one of the members of his temple for trying to stop the police from beating another Black person. Malcolm used his rage against the White community to rally a crowd of 4,000 followers. He forced the New York Police to allow him to speak to the jailed man and to arrange for him to be taken to the hospital in an ambulance. The police had given in due to the large crowd. When the incident was over, Malcolm X made a silent hand gesture and the crowd of 4,000 silently dispersed. A police officer later was quoted in the press saying, "No one man should have that much power."

Shortly, Malcolm X was being closely watched by the FBI and the New York Police. He was one of the first to proclaim and display the new "Black Power." This frightened White America. Malcolm X became an international leader in radical circles. In 1960, when Fidel Castro came to speak at the United Nations, Malcolm X was part of his welcoming committee. This fact not lost to the FBI. J. Edgar Hoover, who claimed he was a communist and used this to put Malcolm X under permanent surveillance. During this time, Malcolm X was also asked by the African nations at the U.N. to participate in many of their social functions as a representative of American Blacks. He was prominently featured in a New York television documentary about the Nation of Islam entitled *The Hate that Hate Produced.*

Unlike the other Black civil rights leaders, Malcolm X greatly disliked the idea of desegregation. He preferred a powerful separate Black Nation and he made few friends in White America; he called Whites "blue-eyed devils." He further angered White America when reporters seeking a sensationalist story pushed him for a comment on the assassination of President Kennedy: He responded that he didn't find it surprising, because "the chickens came home to roost." Because of these offhand bitter remarks, he was punished by the Nation of Islam and forbidden to speak in public for ninety days.

In 1964, Malcolm X met and posed for pictures with Dr. Martin Luther King Jr. during the debate of the Civil Rights Act in Congress. Although his meeting with King was brief, it had a significant impact on him as he greatly respected King.

In 1964, he began to disagree with Elijah Muhammad and objected strongly to his frequent affairs with women, which he felt were inconsistent with their religious beliefs. Influenced by King, he also began to moderate his views about Whites. He was encouraged by Black Sunni Muslims to make a pilgrimage to Mecca. He made his pilgrimage shortly after his break with the Nation of Islam and his conversion to Sunni Islam. His experience in Saudi Arabia caused him to further moderate his thoughts about race. He began to see that Whites and American culture had also been negatively impacted by slavery.

On his way home, he made stops in Paris and Britain. In Oxford, he was asked to participate in an Oxford University debate, *Extremism in the Defense of Liberty Is No Vice; Moderation in the Pursuit of Justice Is No Virtue.* Interest in the debate was so high that the BBC televised it live. Malcolm X spoke in the affirmative.

He became one of the most sought-after college and university speakers. Those close to him said that at this time he began to welcome the opportunity to speak to Black and White students, seeing them as the future he could positively influence. His racial hatred had all but disappeared, and most of his student followers were White.

The Nation of Islam was livid about his conversion to Sunni Islam and his abandonment of their causes; it is likely that they had ordered his death as early as 1964 when a member was to plant explosives in his car. That year *Ebony* magazine published a photo of Malcolm X with an M1 carbine, saying he would defend himself and his family from the death threats he was receiving from the Nation of Islam.

Although the FBI was aware of these threats and had been tipped off several times about attempts, they did little to prevent his assassination. J. Edgar Hoover was no fan of Malcolm X. On February 21, 1965, Malcolm X was assassinated. Three Nation of Islam members were later convicted of his murder.

In 1998, *Time Magazine* named *The Autobiography of Malcolm X*, written with

Alex Haley, "one of the ten most influential non-fiction books of the twentieth century." The 1992 movie *Malcolm X*, which starred Denzel Washington, was named one of the ten best movies of the decade by both film critic Roger Ebert and Director Martin Scorsese.

Perhaps the greatest gift that Malcolm X gave to White America was an understanding of the depth of Black hurt and rage. He founded the Black Power Movement and the Black is Beautiful Movement; he remains a powerful influence on both Black and White American culture. It is said that Malcolm X and his transformation from pain and hate to understanding and forgiveness represents the beginning of America's understanding and acceptance of the consequences of racism.

Muhammad Ali

Muhammad Ali, born Cassius Clay Jr. in 1942, in Lexington, Kentucky, is an American cultural icon. His father painted signs and billboards and his mother was a domestic worker. Although his father was Methodist, he allowed Ali's mother, Odessa, to raise him and his younger brother as Baptists.

Ali first became interested in boxing through a Louisville police officer and boxing coach. He won six Kentucky Golden Gloves titles and two national Golden Gloves titles, and won a Gold Medal at the 1960 Olympics in Rome. In the fall of 1960 he began his professional boxing career. By 1963 he had nineteen wins and no losses with fifteen knockouts, and he was given a title match against Sonny Liston. The odds favored Liston to win by seven to one. It was during the weigh-in that Ali taunted Liston with what would become a signature line, "Float like a butterfly, sting like a bee, your hands can't hit what your eyes can't see." In a surprise upset Liston could not answer the bell for the seventh round and Ali was declared the winner and the World Heavyweight Champion.

Not long after he won the title, Ali converted to Islam in 1963, joining the Nation of Islam. He was given the name Cassius X by Malcolm X, who had befriended him, but this name was then changed by Elijah Muhammad to Muhammad Ali. It was shortly after this snub that Malcolm X left the Nation of Islam and converted to Sunni Islam. Malcolm X's conversion ended his friendship with Ali. Ironically, in 1975 Ali would follow in the footsteps of Malcolm X and also convert to Sunni Islam.

The sport and newspaper reporters refused to call Ali by his new name and continued to call him Cassius Clay. The lone exception was Howard Cosell, and this act made for a lifelong friendship between the two men.

After a rematch with Liston, Ali defended his title against Floyd Patterson, who refused to call Ali by his new name. It was a brutal bout with Ali hitting Patterson and yelling at him all through the fight, "What's my name?"

In 1964, Ali failed his US Armed Forces Qualifying test because his reading and writing skills were very poor. However, in 1965, because of the need for troops in Vietnam, these tests were revised so that literacy was no longer a deterrent. Ali was classified 1A and fit for the draft. When notified of his status, he filed as a conscientious objector on religious grounds, stating that he was forbidden by the Koran to fight and kill. He also said, "I ain't got no quarrel with them Viet Congs," a statement most Americans took as unpatriotic. This was well before the large anti-war movement took off. Ali's actions against the war helped inspire many young people to question the war, and it also inspired Dr. Martin Luther King Jr. to finally express his growing concerns and opposition to the Vietnam War.

In 1967, Ali was inducted but refused to serve. He was arrested and charged with a felony. The New York State Athletic Commission suspended his boxing license and stripped him of his Heavyweight title. He was convicted quickly by a jury for his refusal to serve, but he appealed this decision. In 1971 the US Supreme Court ruled unanimously in his favor.

After four years of boxing inactivity, Ali was rusty; and although he won most bouts, he struggled and lost bouts to Joe Frazier and Ken Norton. However, he beat both of them in rematches and went on to win an upset over George Foreman to reclaim the title. Ali continued to box until just before his fortieth birthday with his last match in December of 1981. He had at that point lost three of his last four bouts and was in obvious physical decline. In 1984, a little more than two years after he retired from boxing, he was diagnosed with Parkinson's disease.

Ali offered and served his country in later years. He was active in the 1987 American Bicentennial Celebration of the US Constitution. In 1991, he went to Iraq to negotiate the release of American hostages. He also had the honor of lighting the torch at the Atlanta Olympics 1996. In 2002, Ali went to Afghanistan as a U.N. Goodwill Ambassador. And in 2005 he was presented the Presidential Medal of Freedom.

Dr. Martin Luther King Jr.

It would be difficult to find anyone who had more impact on the United States in the twentieth century than Dr. Martin Luther King. He was born the son of a Baptist minister in Atlanta, Georgia. He came from a middle class background; his parents were well educated and had traveled to Europe. It was at a Baptist conference in Germany where his father decided to formally change his name from Michael King to Martin Luther King after the man who had started the Protestant movement.

King Jr. was a good student and skipped two years of high school to enter Morehouse College at the age of fifteen. He graduated with a degree in Sociology. He then attended Crozer Theological Seminary in Pennsylvania and received his Divinity Degree. He then attended Boston University receiving a PhD in Divinity.

King became the pastor of the Dexter Avenue Baptist Church in Montgomery, Alabama, in 1954. In addition to his ministerial duties, King was a civil libertarian and was active in pressing for the rights of Blacks. He was convinced that the successful path to Black civil rights would be won by Gandhi's model of non-violent civil disobedience. In 1959, with financial assistance from a Quaker group, the American Friends Service Committee, he decided to make a trip to India to study Gandhi's methods.

In 1955, when Rosa Parks refused to give up her seat on a public bus to a white man and was arrested, King led the Montgomery Bus Boycott which made national headlines. During the boycott King's house was bombed and he was arrested by local authorities. These incidents made King a national leader. The incident caused the US District Court to review the rights of Blacks on public transportation, and they struck down segregation on public buses. King then became the leader of the Southern Christian Leadership Conference, and with this, King became the face and voice of the American Civil Rights Movement.

During this time Southern conservatives and J. Edgar Hoover began to assert that King was a communist. The FBI began to wiretap and tape his conversations. Hoover began to encourage the news media to write stories asserting that King was a communist. By 1958 there were so many newspapers alleging that King was a communist that a mentally-ill Black woman became convinced that King was conspiring with the communists against her. At his book signing for *Stride Toward Freedom*, she stabbed King in the chest and he had to have emergency surgery to save his life. Like Malcolm X, the FBI was aware of many death threats to King but took little action.

Attorney General Robert Kennedy had also warned King that his actions and words were being recorded by the FBI. Later J. Edgar Hoover tried, unsuccessfully, to blackmail King into stopping his civil rights protests by threatening to divulge his extramarital affairs to his wife and congregation. King refused and Kennedy warned Hoover to not carry out his threat. Hoover did not reveal the affairs until after Kennedy's death.

King's protests became national and even international events. The March on Washington in 1963, where he delivered his "I have a Dream" speech, was perhaps the highlight of his advocacy and received world-wide attention. In addition to Black civil rights, King became an anti-war advocate and also began The Poor People's Campaign to highlight poverty of all people in the United States and to advocate change. King was assassinated on April 4, 1968, in Memphis, Tennessee, while supporting a strike by poorly paid local sanitation workers.

Dr. Martin Luther King Jr. is the face of civil rights for Americans of all races and ethnicities. King's efforts would inspire women, Latinos, Native Americans and the LGBT community to seek their civil rights along the path that he paved for them.

Discrimination still persists in American culture against the African-American community, Derogatory colloquialisms such as "Nigger," which originally came from the Spanish word "negro," meaning "black," along with "Coons," "Darkies" and "Aunt Jemima," are still used to describe African-

Americans by the more crass, less-educated and unenlightened. The word "Nigger" is now considered unacceptable and its use a hate crime in general society. Unfortunately it is now used by some working class Blacks to describe each other, as either a gentle put down or as a way to recognize their bond.

CHAPTER 5. ASIAN-AMERICANS

I'm proud of my Asian-American heritage and being able to blend the two cultures together and to learn from each is fulfilling. I feel the values and traits of my Japanese ancestors have been instilled in me through my parents and grandparents, and I know their sacrifices paved the way for me to live the American dream.

— Kristi Yamaguchi, Olympic Gold Medalist

Being Asian American means wearing many layers of identity. At first glance, a man of Asian ancestry, at first spoken word an American, at deeper reflection, a person of color in America, at the core, a person who seeks peace and social justice.

—Eddie Wong, Executive Director, Angel Island Immigration Station Foundation, San Francisco

As a member of President Roosevelt's administration, I saw the United States Army give way to mass hysteria over the Japanese...Crowded into cars like cattle, these hapless people were hurried away to hastily constructed and thoroughly inadequate concentration camps, with soldiers with nervous muskets on guard, in the great American desert. We gave the fancy name of 'relocation centers' to these dust bowls, but they were concentration camps nonetheless.

—Harold Ickes

Asian-Americans number about 18 million, according to 2011 census estimates, just under 6 percent of the total population. They are currently the largest group of immigrants entering the country, surpassing Latinos in 2009.

Asian-Americans have the highest level of educational attainment with about 61% with of adults achieving a bachelors degree or higher, and they also have highest household median income of any racial or ethnic group in the United States. The US Census bureau defines Asians as any person who has origins in the Far East, Southeast Asia or the Indian Subcontinent. West Asians are considered a separate group. Asian-Americans include: Japanese, Koreans, Chinese, Indians, Filipinos, Vietnamese, Thai, Laotian, Burmese, Indonesians, etc. The term Asian-American has been in use since the late 1960s and replaced the terms Oriental and Asiatic. In the US Census and government records Pacific Islanders and Polynesians were part of this group, but now have a separate designation. West Asian people who are of Israeli, Arabic, Turkish, Iranians, and others of Middle Eastern origin are counted as "White" and are sometimes counted with European-Americans.

A demographic breakdown of ethnic Asian-Americans is as follows: Almost 4 million are of Chinese descent, 3.4 million are Filipino, 3.2 million Indian, 1.7 Vietnamese, 1.7 Korean, and 1.3 million Japanese. Other significant groups are Pakistani, Cambodian, Hmong, Thai, Laotian, Taiwanese Chinese, Bangladeshi, and Burmese. Although they are not strictly speaking Asian-American by Census standards, it should be noted that there are significant numbers of Americans from West Asia, with about 200,000 people of Turkish descent and about 3.5 million Arab-Americans, with most, 62%, coming from Syria, Lebanon, or Jordan, or they are Palestinians who have no country. Most of the others come from Egypt, Morocco, Iraq, Yemen and Libya.

Contrary to what many Americans think, Asian-American immigrants have been in the United States since the beginning, albeit in small numbers. For example, in the records of the Jamestown Colony in 1635 they list an "East Indian" as a slave. However, the first East Indian settlement of any note dates to 1763.

The Spanish, who had occupied the Philippines, built galleons there. On these ships the captains and officers would be Spanish, but the crews were most frequently Filipino. The treatment of these crews was very poor and many men served involuntarily. In 1763 the Filipinos crews from two large Spanish ships fled ashore in the bayous of Louisiana. Led by Juan San Malo, they established a colony which came to be called Saint Malo. These crews were called "Manilamen" by the locals. They married Cajun and Native women and became part of Cajun country. Descendants of the Manilamen are still present in Louisiana.

In 1778, Chinese sailors began arriving in Hawaii, the same year that the islands were discovered by Captain Cook. Many settled there, married Hawaiian women, and became part of Hawaiian culture. In the 1820s the Chinese also began regular immigration to the continental United States.

In 1841, an American whaler rescued a group of Japanese sailors and brought them to Hawaii. They too inter-married with the Hawaiians. However, one of these Japanese sailors changed American history as he continued with the ship to Massachusetts to seek fame and fortune. He later sailed with Commodore Matthew Perry as his interpreter in his historic trip to Japan. His interpreting began the first trade between the "Hermit Kingdom" of Japan and the outside world. From this began the trade with the land that was many for years America's largest trading partner.

By the 1840s and 1850s, the Chinese began a steady immigration into California as part of the Gold Rush. The Whites treated the Chinese harshly as second class citizens. They were relegated to laundry, cooking and other menial chores. Discrimination was so blatant that in 1854 the California Courts refused the admission of the testimony of a Chinese man against a White man in a murder trial. In 1862, California also placed a tax on all Chinese men of $250 per year.

In 1865, the Central Pacific Railroad Company began to import more Chinese laborers. They derisively called them "coolies." During the 1860s and 1870s, hundreds of Chinese workers would slave away and some would lose their lives building the railroads through the mountains and deserts of the United States.

The first Japanese colony in the continental US was Gold Hill in California, a tea and silk colony settled in 1869. That same year the Fourteenth Amendment declared that any baby, regardless of race, born in the United States was a full citizen. Despite this citizenship Asian-Americans were still viewed as foreigners and discrimination persisted.

The 1870s and 1880s were a particularly bad time for Asian-Americans. Hatred of the "Yellow Race" was rampant. In 1877, Dennis Kearney organized the Workingmen's Party of California that sought to prohibit the Chinese from working in the trades and professions. His group in 1878 helped persuade the government to disallow Chinese residents to become naturalized citizens. In 1882 the Congress passed the Chinese Exclusion Act, which prohibited more Chinese laborers from coming to the United States.

Violence against Asian-Americans was common. In 1886, twenty-eight Chinese miners were massacred at Rock Springs, Wyoming, in a labor dispute. In the following year in another labor dispute another thirty-one Chinese miners were killed in Snake River, Oregon. However the official records stated they were murdered by "robbers," and not the White miners who had committed this massacre.

By 1898, when the US annexed Hawaii by a stroke of a pen, US plantation owners had imported so many Japanese, Chinese, and Filipino laborers to the Hawaiian Islands that they now made up a majority of the population. Also in 1898, in the wake of the Spanish–American War and the Treaty of Paris, the Philippines became a territory of the United States and Filipinos, although not US citizens, were declared American nationals.

In 1907, San Francisco attempted to segregate Japanese students from Whites. However a strong protest by the Japanese Government and at the urging of President Theodore Roosevelt the City dropped this legislation.

In San Francisco, the primary immigration port of Angel Island is sometimes referred to as the Ellis Island of the West. This port saw approximately 175,000 Chinese and 60,000 Japanese come into the United States before 1924. However, the Immigration Act of 1924 began to ban immigration from many parts of Asia. This act caused a major dispute between the US and Japan, who saw it as a racial insult.

In 1930 an anti-Filipino riot occurred in Watson, California. The riots spread to Stockton, San Jose, and San Francisco, and even as far away as Los Angeles. The riots lasted five days and hundreds of Filipinos were stabbed, shot and beaten. The riot began when two hundred White men attacked a club where a few White women had danced with Filipino men. At the time, California had miscegenation laws that forbade inter-racial marriage between Whites, Blacks or Asians. Fermin Tobera, a twenty-two-year-old man, was killed in this riot and his body was sent back to the Philippines for burial. He became a martyr in the Philippines and became a national symbol of Filipino aspiration for independence from the United States. In September of 2011, the State of California formally apologized for their treatment of Filipinos and the riots.

In 1941, shortly after the Japanese attacks on Pearl Harbor, the FBI began to arrest and detain Japanese-American leaders. They feared they might be loyal to Japan, not the United States. About six weeks later, at the urging of the FBI and most military leaders, President Roosevelt signed Executive Order 9066. It was upheld by the US Supreme Court. It ordered the detention and relocation of more than 100,000 Japanese-Americans. This act would later cause Justice William Douglas to apologize and to state that it was the single greatest mistake of his entire life. Japanese-American families were sent to internment camps in remote places and guarded by armed military personnel. In the process the Japanese-Americans lost their land, farms, businesses, and homes. Disneyland was later built on land that had been shamefully taken from a Japanese-American farmer.

Canada also interned some Canadians of Japanese ancestry at this time, on the advice of the United States.

Throughout the war, Asian-Americans were suspect and discriminated against. In California and elsewhere, Chinese and other Asian businesses were vandalized and boycotted as White Americans had difficulty distinguishing Japanese from other Asians.

Japanese-Americans volunteered for service in World War II to prove their patriotism. However, the military suspected their loyalty and refused to allow them to serve in the Pacific and Asian theaters. Eventually they allowed the Japanese-American volunteers to join the US Army 100th Battalion in Europe, which merged with the 44th Regimental Combat Team. This was an all volunteer Japanese-American combat unit. They soon proved their loyalty and bravery. During the war the 44th became the most highly decorated military unit in American history, winning 18,143 decorations including 9,486 Purple Hearts.

In 1980, the US Congress appointed a commission to study the internment of Japanese-Americans during the war. In 1983, they published their findings, stating that the internments were not militarily justified and were done out of "hysteria, racial prejudice and a failure of political leadership." The Commission recommended an apology by the Federal Government and payments of $20,000 for each of the survivors.

Daniel Inouye, an American Hero

Daniel Inouye was born in 1924 in Honolulu, Hawaii. He was the son of a Japanese immigrant father and an American-born Japanese-American mother. He graduated from high school in Honolulu, where he was a good student. He began pre-medical studies at the University of Hawaii to become a surgeon. He acted as an emergency medical volunteer during the attack on Pearl Harbor, treating the wounded. His family was part of the Japanese internment in February of 1942.

In 1943, when the US Army allowed Japanese-Americans to volunteer, he enlisted and was sent to the all Japanese-American 44th Regimental Combat Team. In a short time he earned the rank of sergeant and was made a platoon leader serving in combat in Italy. He went to France and led an attack to save a battalion that had been cut off by the Germans. His bravery was rewarded with a battlefield promotion to second lieutenant. Later he was promoted to captain. He was severely wounded in Italy in 1945 and lost an arm, but remained in the Army until 1947.

During the war he was awarded a Bronze Star, two Purple Hearts and a Distinguished Service Medal, and he received an additional twelve medals and citations. The Distinguished Service Medal was later upgraded to the Congressional Medal of Honor at a ceremony held to upgrade the medals of 19 Japanese-Americans who had served bravely in the 44th but had been denied their rightful medals because of their ethnicity.

After the war, and the loss of his arm, he was forced to give up his goal of becoming a surgeon and instead resumed his studies at the University of Hawaii in political science. After graduation he attended George Washington University Law School in Washington, DC, and earned a law degree. He returned to Hawaii. In 1953 he was elected and served in the territorial legislature where he served two years in the House and was elected Majority Leader. He ran for the Territorial Senate in 1957 and was elected. He was then elected and served as Hawaii's first congressman when Hawaii was admitted as a State in 1959, and he was elected to the US Senate in 1962, serving there until his death in 2012.

One of Inouye's legacies was that he fought for and was successful in obtaining benefits for Filipinos who had served in the US Military during World War II. The Philippine government in 2009 awarded Inouye honorary citizenship for his efforts on behalf of Filipino Veterans.

Upon his death, Inouye became the first Asian-American and only the 31st American to lie in state in the Capitol Rotunda. President Barack Obama spoke at his funeral services along with Vice President Joe Biden and former President Bill Clinton.

Discrimination toward Asian-Americans is still prevalent. The derogatory terms of "Chink," "Slope," Slant eyes," "Yellow Devils" and "Gooks" are all American colloquialisms and hate speech to describe Asian-Americans.

West Asians or Arab-Americans also face discrimination, which has become very pronounced after the September 11, 2011, tragedies and the wars in Iraq and Afghanistan. In much of America, the word "Muslim" has a bad connotation, and the word was applied to President Obama during the 2008 Presidential campaign by the radical Christian right in an attempt to discredit him.

Asian-American Religion

According to the Pew Research Center, East Asian-American religious affiliation is as follows: 42% Christian, 14% Buddhist, 10% Hindu, 4% Muslim, 1% Sikh, and the rest unaffiliated religious practices or no religion. The religious make up of Arab-Americans and West Asians is as follows: 63% Christians, 24% Muslims, and the remaining 13% are Jewish or atheists.

Asian-American Contributions: Physics, Food and Health

Some of the largest contributions to science and medicine were made by Asian-Americans. Chien-Shiung Wu is known as the First Lady of Physics. Born in China in 1912, she came to the United States in 1936 to study physics at the University of California at Berkeley. After graduation she joined the faculty at Smith College, moving to Princeton and finally to Columbia, where she worked on the Manhattan Project developing the atomic bomb. She was a pioneer in particle physics. She was the first Chinese-American elected to the American Academy of Sciences. Her book *Beta Decay*, published in 1965, is a standard reference for nuclear physicists. In 1975, she became the first woman elected as President of the American Physical Society. That year she also was awarded the National Medal of Science. She won the Wolf Prize in Physics in 1978. Wu was also the first living scientist to have an asteroid named after her. She died at the age of 84 in New York City in 1997.

In 2011, the Smithsonian National Museum of American History arranged an exhibit called *Sweet & Sour: A Look at a History of Chinese Food in the United States*. The exhibition was an exclamation point on the fact that Chinese culture and food are now integral parts of mainstream American culture. Today Chinese restaurants cover America from the Atlantic to the Pacific. In her book *Fortune Cookie Chronicles*, Jenifer 8 Lee says there are over 41,000 Chinese restaurants in the United States, which means they outnumber McDonalds, Burger King, Wendy's, Dominoes, and Pizza Huts combined. Most of these are one of a kind and small family type restaurants, but there are also some notable chains.

The Panda Restaurant Group is the largest Chinese chain restaurant in the US including the Panda Express, Panda Inn and Hibachi-San, with 1,400 restaurants. In 2008, its Chairman Andrew Cherng was on Forbes' list of "Notable Chinese-Americans." The chain is so successful in the United States that Forbes reported in 2011 that they would be expanding to China, ironically bringing "American Chinese" cuisine to the Chinese. It is noteworthy that they already have restaurants in Mexico. In 2012, CNN listed the Fifty Best Chinese restaurants in the United States; they were located in twenty-three states and the District of Columbia, showing their impact across the entire continent.

Chinese-American food isn't really Chinese; it is a Chinese/American fusion. In 2011, *The Eater DC* reported on the "10 Chinese Dishes That Real Chinese People Don't Eat": crab wontons, General Tso's chicken, chop suey, the pu pu platter, sweet & sour pork, salad, egg rolls, beef broccoli, and fortune cookies. Real Chinese dishes include chicken feet, eels, jellyfish, pigs' ears, and century eggs — which most Americans don't eat.

In 2006 *The Washington Post* reported that there were about 10,000 Japanese restaurants in the United States, having doubled from 1996 to 2006. In 2012 the *Asia Pacific Journal* stated that there are 3,846 sushi restaurants in the United States, generating $2 billion in business each year and employing over 20,000 people. Sushi is one of the fastest growing foods in the United States.

The practice of yoga began some 5,000 years ago in the Indus valley. It spread throughout East Asia. Yoga came to the US in the nineteenth century, but it didn't become part of mainstream culture until the 1960s when young Americans and their counter culture became fascinated with Eastern philosophy and Americans also became more health conscious.

Acupuncture is traditional Chinese medical technique that dates to about 1600 BC. It became fashionable in the United States in the early 1970s as part of America's youth and health movements. The Eastern martial arts of Karate and Taekwondo, Kung Fu, Jujitsu, and Kali probably came to America in the nineteenth century, but they did not become well known until after World War II, when servicemen in the Pacific arena were exposed to it. And it wasn't until the 1960s, when the media, primarily television and movies, began to develop a genre around the martial arts that their practice became widespread. Since that time martial arts centers have sprung up across the United States so that men, women and children can participate in this sport.

Zen Buddhism has also had an impact on America. Although it came to the United States in the nineteenth century, White America wasn't very interested until after World War II. One of the first major exposures to Zen came from Jack Kerouac's 1958 novel *Dharma Bums*, which many claim was the spark for the 1960s Hippie and counter culture movement. In the 1970s, Robert Persig's book *Zen and the Art of Motorcycle Maintenance* made another Zen dent into American culture. Although many claim than Zen in America is a mile wide and just an inch deep, the concept is broadly recognized. You can now get books on Zen gardening, Zen cooking and Zen travel.

War and Pieces

American wars in Korea and Vietnam have greatly accelerated Asian influence on American culture, by both exposing American service personnel to Asia and through the immigration of those who were dispossessed by these conflicts. Koreans were very few in the United States before the Korean War. There are now just slightly under two million Koreans in the United States, including an estimated 200,000 undocumented Koreans. The United States has the second largest Korean population outside of Korea. (China has the largest Korean influx due its proximity and North Korean immigration.) Korean cuisine and culture have found their way into America. There are over 900 Korean restaurants in the United States.

The fall of Saigon in 1975 brought several large waves of Vietnamese immigrants to the United States. The US Census lists about 1.7 million Vietnamese, of which about a million speak Vietnamese, making it the seventh largest language in the country. Almost forty percent of Vietnamese-Americans live in California. Texas holds another fifteen percent, so that over half of Vietnamese-Americans live in these two states. Most Vietnamese have assimilated very quickly. In 2008, Anh "Joseph" Cao became the first Vietnamese-American elected to Congress. Cao represents Louisiana's second congressional district in New Orleans.

The Hmong

During the Vietnam War, the Hmong people were recruited in Laos by the US Military and the CIA to fight against the North Vietnamese and to disrupt their supply lines along the Ho Chi Minh Trail. The Hmong were promised a homeland supported by the United States if the US won the war. The Hmong were originally from China, but were driven out by the Chinese into Southeast Asia where the Vietnamese and other indigenous people were already living, and this forced the Hmong into the hills and jungles of Laos. The Hmong, under General Vang Pao's Secret Army, supplied by and sometimes led by US forces, made war on the North Vietnamese and Laotians on behalf of the US. When America left Southeast Asia, the Hmong were left to the hands of their enemies. Only a small group of about 1,000 were originally allowed to come to America.

Many Hmong escaped to refugee camps in Thailand, where treatment was not that much better than under their enemies. Congressman Bruce Vento of Minnesota was so outraged by the Americans' casual abandonment of the Hmong that he worked to save them and was successful in passing legislation to allow their immigration to the United States. As a result, about 250,000 Hmong live in the United States today, many in Minnesota, because of Bruce Vento. The metropolitan areas with the highest number of Hmong are the Twin Cities of Minneapolis and St. Paul, and Stockton, California. An interesting note: Walnut Grove, Minnesota, a small, very rural place best known for a book that was written about it and a subsequent television series, *Little House on the Prairie*, now has a population that is 50% Hmong.

Chapter 6. The European-Americans

> Somewhere in the troubling intersection between the American dream and the nightmarish patriotism engendered by Manifest Destiny, we sense their collective self-belief.
>
> — Point of View, BBC News Magazine, January 4, 2013
>
> The British walk through the world as if they own it; the Americans walk through the world not giving a damn who owns it.
>
> —Winston Churchill

Sometimes when White America talks about their European-Christian heritage, I wonder if they believe that Europe is a single country with a single culture. Combined, there are many more White Europeans in America than any other group, although the United States will soon have a majority made up of minorities. Obviously, there is not a single European culture, even in the United States. The diversity of European peoples, languages and cultures that have influenced America are another reason why American culture is so complex and rich. We have already looked at the Spanish influence on American culture, and now we will explore other Europeans.

The British

According to the 2000 US Census, there are about 36 million US citizens of British ancestry or about 13% of the population. But Britain hasn't got a single culture either. The British are made up of many peoples who have mixed together for a long period of time. As a whole, we see an "English" influence on American culture. However, the Celtic peoples of Wales, Scotland and the Scotch-Irish are also British. These British subcultures have also contributed their fair share to American culture. The British are the second largest European group in the United States, after the Germans, and comprise a slightly larger portion of the American population than the Irish. (I earlier asserted that the British cultural influence is the strongest; that is because at the founding, the leadership was primarily of British background and their influence remains strong.)

As the founding of Plymouth colony is fast coming up to its 400th anniversary, it is interesting to note the contributions of the English to American culture. The largest contribution of course is her language, although American English has changed radically with borrow words from many languages, especially Spanish, and has perhaps changed enough to be seen as its own dialect, with other English speakers worldwide (including the British) now more influenced by American English than "the Queen's English."

Equally important, British contributions include the American twin cultural universals: Puritan Christianity and "free market capitalism" as it came from the mind of the Englishman Adam Smith. It could even be argued that Adam Smith, author of *The Wealth of Nations*, had more impact on America than all the rest of English culture. During Ronald Regan's presidential inauguration in 1980, a significant number of the men attending wore ties with Adam Smith's likeness on them to show their reverence for "free market capitalism," as Reagan gave speeches about the "Shining City on the Hill" celebrating America's Puritanical Christian past.

American laws and her court system grew out of English courts and English common law. The concept of a constitution itself comes down from the Magna Carta. English tort law is the backbone of US civil law. The word "tort" comes from Old English (itself influenced by the French-speaking Norman conquerors) meaning injury. Behind the Old English Tort Law was the basic concept that you had the liberty to do most anything until you damaged your neighbor or infringed upon your neighbors' right to enjoy their liberties. Most American tort and civil laws come from this concept. US zoning laws are a good example of this: individuals may do anything on their property as long as it doesn't negatively affect the neighbors' enjoyment or the value of their property. Property laws, taxation, contract law and even alimony and licensing come from the English. It is fair to say that many if not most US civil institutions and bureaucracies were either inspired by or copied from the British.

The English Puritans were also the first to set up educational institutions in the colonies, teaching their children to read, to write and understand basic mathematics (jokingly referred to as " 'rithmetic"), known as "the three Rs," which are the core of American elementary education. In 1635, the Boston Latin School became the first American public school. In 1642, the Massachusetts Bay Colony made education mandatory for children, soon followed by other colonies.

The expression "as American as apple pie" is an oxymoron. Apples came to America from England, although they seem to have been cultivated first in Asia. Pies and pie recipes were brought from England on the Mayflower. The pie was a very common food in colonial and frontier America. Pies of fruits and meats were eaten daily and became cemented in American culture.

There were native apple varieties in America, but they were of the small crab apple varieties and were very sour. The Puritans brought their large, sweet fruit trees with them from England. They also grafted English varieties to the American trees, making new varieties. These varieties didn't do well at first because America lacked honeybees, so the colonists also brought honeybee hives from England — first to Virginia and then to Massachusetts. The Native-Americans called honeybees "White man flies." Peas were also brought from England to grow as a crop, and dried peas were also brought by the French for pea soup. According to old ship manifests, the foods brought in by the Massachusetts Bay Company in 1628 for the Pilgrims to grow in the new world included wheat, rye, barley, oats, peas, green beans, peaches, plums, filberts, cherries, pears, apples, quince, pomegranates, saffron, licorice seed, hops, hemp seed, flax seed, and currant plants.

British place names for states, counties, and cities are plentiful including New York, New Hampshire, New Jersey, Boston, and of course the region that is called New England. The Carolinas were named for King Charles I, Virginia after the "Virgin Queen" Elizabeth I, and Maryland after Queen Mary, the wife of Charles I. Even the colors of the flag, red, white and blue, were taken from the British Union Jack.

American Folk and Country music has roots in Celtic music ("Britain" traditionally included England, Scotland and Wales; and Ireland after 1801). In 1916, Cecil Sharp, the founder of the English Folk Music Revival, arrived in Appalachia and began recording the folk songs in the Mountains. Appalachia was a place where Celtic folk music in nearly its original forms and ballads could still be found. Sharp was an authority on Celtic ballads; he was able to identify sixteen hundred versions of five hundred songs from over two hundred and eighty singers, almost all having their origins in English/Scottish/Irish ballads. After his study in Appalachia, he published his book *English Folk Songs from the Southern Appalachians.*

The fiddle or violin was perhaps the most popular musical instrument in colonial America, and it came with the English colonists from England. A Scottish fiddler named Neil Gow is usually credited with developing the short bow stroke technique, in 1740, that defines American fiddling. The country fiddler Charlie Daniels provides a current example of the fiddle music developed by Neil Gow. Other instruments that were introduced to America by the British include the accordion, the bagpipes, the harp, the fife and flute, the bugle, the trumpet and trombone, clarinets and pianos.

David Hackett Fisher's 1989 book, *Albion's Seed*, states there are four principal sub regions in America's development that were deeply influenced by British culture in some different ways. In New England, it was the

Puritans and men like Ben Franklin. In the coastal South it was the upper class and aristocratic Cavaliers and men like Thomas Jefferson setting up plantations and the slave society. The frugal Quakers set up their society in the mid-Atlantic colonies. And the rural Scots-Irish and their Celtic sub-culture flourished in the areas of Appalachia, Kentucky and Tennessee and parts of the Deep South. Each of these groups brought British culture with some interesting subculture variations.

The plantation culture of Jefferson's upper class was first seen primarily in Virginia and the Carolinas but it spread throughout the South. The working class Puritan roots exemplified by Ben Franklin were widespread in Massachusetts and Pennsylvania. The two British cultures produced two founding fathers with quite different experience and outlooks, with competing viewpoints. Franklin, along with Washington and Adams, were federalists, while Jefferson, along with Monroe and Burr, favored strong state's rights. This is an argument that still persists, as Southern states in particular seek to implement local laws that challenge Federal law.

Benjamin Franklin

In 1998, newscaster Tom Brokaw published his book *The Greatest Generation*, which extols the virtues of the World War II generation, the people who were raised during the Great Depression and who fought in World War II. However, as much as this group suffered and as great as their contributions may be, they still fall far short of the greatest generation, that of the founding American fathers, such as Washington, Jefferson, Madison, John and Samuel Adams, and "The First American" who made some of the greatest contributions to the United States and American culture: Benjamin Franklin.

Franklin's father Josiah was born in Northamptonshire, England. His mother, Abiah Folger, was born a Puritan in Massachusetts. Josiah was a soap and candle maker. Benjamin was the last son of his father's fifteen children, seven with his first wife (who died) and another eight with Franklin's mother. Franklin was born in Boston in 1706.

Josiah wanted Benjamin to be a clergyman and he sent him to the Boston Latin School, but he could only afford to send him for two years. At the age of ten, Franklin began to work for his father, and at twelve he became a printer's apprentice in his older brother's print shop. In 1721, when Franklin was fifteen, he founded the *New England Courant*, the first independent newspaper in the colonies, which was printed by his brother James. Ben Franklin wrote under the pen name of *Silence Dogood* and one of his articles so inflamed the local authorities that his brother was jailed for a month for refusing to reveal the author. The *Courant* and Franklin's editorials set the model for newspapers and journalists in the Colonies and became an impetus for the First Amendment of the US Constitution, providing for freedom of speech and the press. Franklin helped write it. But the *Courant's* popularity along with its growing controversy eventually caused a rift between Ben and his brother James, and Ben left in 1723 at the age of seventeen to set up shop in Philadelphia. Franklin would found four other publications: The *Pennsylvania Chronicle*, *The Pennsylvania Gazette*, and *Poor Richard's Almanac* (which made him rich). The fourth was the first non-English newspaper in America: a German language publication, *Philadelphische Zeitung*.

Franklin's career also included serving in a number of government posts. In Philadelphia he served as the British Postmaster in the colonies, which led to him create the US postal system after the Revolutionary War. He served as America's first Postmaster General. He also served as the first American ambassador to France and then to Sweden. He was Speaker of the Pennsylvania Assembly and he also served as the Governor of Pennsylvania from 1785–1788.

Benjamin Franklin was also a scientist and inventor. His early work in physics and electricity made important advances in these fields. He was the first scientist to discover the electrical principle of conservation of charge and to define electrical currents as positive and negative. He was one of the first scientists to adopt and promote the wave theory of light. His publication *Maritime Observations* gave new designs for sea anchors and ships' hulls including Catamarans. Franklin was the first to chart and document the Atlantic Gulf Stream in 1768—the first study and publication on ocean currents. Together with his observations and lectures on volcanic eruptions in Iceland and their effect on temperatures, this was some of the first work in the fields of climatology and oceanography.

He was a proponent of lighter-than-air travel and was present when the first manned balloon flight took place in 1783. He signed the certificate of achievement as a scientific witness to document this event. He prophesied that humans would one day make war through the air.

His many inventions included the lightning rod, the *Franklin Stove* (which was one of the first efficient heating furnaces), bifocal glasses, the odometer (which he designed for carriages), swim fins, and the flexible urinary catheter. He was a pure scientist and never patented his inventions, writing in his autobiography that "as we enjoy great advantages from the inventions of others, we should be glad of an opportunity to serve others by any invention of ours; and this we should do freely and generously."

Franklin was also a social scientist and the creator of many social innovations. His population studies and his work *Observations on the Increase of Mankind* in 1755 influenced both Thomas Malthus' rule of population growth and Adam Smith's *Wealth of Nations* and his theories about free market capitalism.

In 1736, he created the Union Fire Company which became the model of modern fire departments. Out of this he also invented modern fire insurance, which became the model for American mutual insurance companies, and he is also credited with the innovations of life insurance, crop insurance, and annuities. He is in the Insurance Hall of Fame. He was also the creator of and was the first advocate for paper currency in Britain and the colonies; he lobbied for it in the British House of Commons in London in 1766.

The self-educated Franklin was an advocate for public education. He founded the College of Philadelphia which would later become the University of Pennsylvania. He also founded the American Philosophical Society. It was with the Philosophical Society that Franklin came up with concept of the public library, based upon the idea of allowing the public to subscribe to (check out) books for a promise of their return in good order. He was also a master chess player and reputed to be the best in Colonial America. In 1999 he was inducted into the US Chess Hall of Fame. Franklin was variously fluent in English, French, Spanish, Latin, Italian, and German, and he also spoke some Swedish and Native-American languages, all of which were self-taught. He was an avid swimmer and taught and coached others and advocated universal swimming lessons. He was inducted into the International Swimming Hall of Fame in 1968.

He was an accomplished musician and played the harp, viola, and harpsichord. He invented the glass armonica, whose unusual sound appealed to composers like Mozart and Beethoven, according to the Franklin Institute.

Franklin was a revolutionary and a radical who wanted to create a democratic republic modeled after the Iroquois Nation's democratic representative government. Franklin would later credit the Native Iroquois leader Canassatego for recommending this style of government to the founding fathers.

Franklin was an admirer of Native-American culture and society. He was an open critic of racism. After a White attack on Native-Americans (that the Whites later justified by saying that they had been attacked earlier by some other Indians), Franklin wrote in a fiery reply, "If an Indian injures me, does it follow that I may revenge that injury on all Indians?" He was a self-proclaimed enemy of authoritarianism. Although he came into the possession of two Black slaves, Franklin freed them and became one of the first prominent abolitionists in America. He served as the president of the Pennsylvania Abolitionist Society. Franklin advocated for the complete integration of Indians and Blacks into American society.

Franklin is frequently called "The First American" as he was the first publicly vocal radical calling for American independence. Franklin's radicalism started at age fifteen with his writings in the *Courant* and continued up to and throughout the Revolutionary War and into the Constitutional Convention. He along with Thomas Jefferson, John Adams, Roger Sherman, and Robert Livingston wrote the Declaration of Independence. He is the only person who helped write and signed all four founding documents of the Republic: The Declaration of Independence, The Treaty of Alliance with France, The Treaty of Paris ending the war, and the Constitution of the United States.

Franklin's politics and the US democracy he helped to form were based upon the idea that a society cannot exist without virtue. At the age of twenty he developed his *"Thirteen Virtues"* which governed his life and politics: Temperance (Do not eat or drink to excess), Silence (Only speak to benefit others), Order, Resolution, Frugality, Sincerity, Justice, Moderation, Cleanliness, Tranquility, Chastity, and Humility." Franklin was also a realist and said he could only work diligently on one of these virtues each week, "leaving the others to chance."

Ben Franklin is the finest example of British-American heritage.

Thomas Jefferson

Thomas Jefferson was born in 1743 in what is now Albemarle County, Virginia. His father, Peter Jefferson, was English gentry and a wealthy planter and surveyor. His mother, Jane Randolph, was the daughter of a wealthy ship captain and planter. Where Franklin was the epitome of the English Yankee working-class colonist, Jefferson was the epitome of the Southern English aristocratic upper-class planter. Unlike the self-taught Ben Franklin, Jefferson had tutors and clergymen as his teachers from an early age. He learned Latin, Greek, and French, history, mathematics, science and the classics. At fourteen his father died and left him a fortune, which included his plantation of five thousand acres of land and approximately forty Black slaves. At sixteen, he entered the College of William and Mary in Williamsburg. He studied under the law professor William Wythe and became his law clerk. Jefferson was admitted to the Virginia Bar in 1767.

Jefferson was a man of leisure and as such became a voracious reader and amassed a library of more than six thousand books, some of which were bequeathed to him from William Wythe upon his death. In the War of 1812, when the British attacked Washington and burned the Library of Congress in 1814, Jefferson sold his large collection to the government for a tidy sum to begin the new Library of Congress.

He married Martha Wayles, the daughter of a large planter, in 1772. The following year the couple inherited another eleven thousands acres and another 135 slaves when her father died, but the estate also came with a large debt that Jefferson, who was never very good with money, would struggle to pay — especially in later life as he continued to borrow and take on more debt to pay for his aristocratic lifestyle.

As a lawyer, Jefferson's clients were the wealthiest and most prominent families of Virginia. In 1769 he began a career in politics and began serving in the Virginia House of Burgesses, and served until 1775. In 1774 Jefferson began to openly advocate for American independence. In 1775 he served in the Second Continental Congress, where he met the two cousins John and Samuel Adams. He and John Adams became close friends. On the recommendation of John Adams, Jefferson was asked to write the first draft of the Declaration of Independence, with revisions and changes to be made by Franklin and Adams. It was completed in June of 1776. On July 4, it was ratified and signed.

During the Revolutionary War he continued to serve in the Virginia Legislature and then was elected and served during the war as governor. He was a very poor wartime governor and fled the capital at Richmond to hide in the West. He was widely criticized for this perceived cowardice and he was not re-elected as governor. After the war, Jefferson was appointed by the Virginia planters as a Virginia delegate to the Continental Congress. Although Jefferson was a slave owner, under the influence of his friend John Adams, a strong abolitionist, he advocated and wrote a US ordinance banning slavery in all the nation's territories, but it failed to pass.

Shortly after the death of his wife, Jefferson was appointed Minister to France, where he found it extremely difficult to follow his predecessor, Ben Franklin. He later brought his youngest daughter to France, accompanied by one of his slaves, Sally Hemings, whom he lived with as his wife while in Paris. Hemings was an illegitimate daughter of Jefferson's father-in-law with one of his slaves; thus she was a half-sister to Jefferson's wife. Jefferson was thought to be the father of Hemings' children and a 1998 DNA test confirms this to be true. Jefferson freed all of Hemings' children as they came of age and they all later lived and "passed" as Whites. Oddly, Jefferson did not free Sally Hemings from slavery, but she was freed by Jefferson's daughter shortly after his death and she lived the rest of her life with one of her sons.

Upon his return from France, President Washington asked Jefferson to serve as his Secretary of State. Jefferson soon got into a disagreement with Alexander Hamilton, the Secretary of the Treasury, about fiscal policy. Jefferson falsely accused Hamilton of being a "royalist." He then became angry with Washington's attempts to create a federal government. Jefferson was in favor of a confederation of individual states which he thought would protect the Southern planters and their plantation society. Washington became angry with Jefferson and would have sought his resignation, but Jefferson knew this and quickly resigned on his own. Washington, also a Virginian, considered Jefferson an aristocrat and a traitor to his new nation and he never spoke to him again.

Jefferson along with James Madison formed an "anti-administration party" which became the foundation of the old conservative Southern Democratic Party. He remained anti-federalist and developed the argument for "States' Rights" to preserve the aristocratic plantation society. This stance would define Southern politics for the next two hundred years, and now it defines the modern Republican Party.

In 1796, Jefferson was elected as the Vice President under John Adams. Although the two were friends, Jefferson also began arguing with his mentor Adams over federalism and the rights of states. Jefferson promoted the concept that only large land and business-owners should have the right to vote, to which Adams greatly disagreed.

In 1800, Jefferson and Aaron Burr ran for President and were tied. Therefore the out-going Federalist Congress could decide the winner, and they chose Jefferson as the lesser of two evils: they distrusted the overly ambitious Aaron Burr even more. Jefferson became the third president, with Burr as Vice President according to the rules at the time. Even so, Jefferson had won the election principally because of the inflated number of electors given the Southern states in the Electoral College: non-voting slaves were counted as 3/5 a person, thus weighting the slave owners' votes disproportionately. Northern critics complained that Jefferson had "won the temple of liberty on the backs of slaves."

Jefferson attempted to undo the work of the previous two federalist administrations by seeking to dismantle the Federal Bank and the new federal tax system in favor of the individual states, but was only partially successful. Vice President Burr and Alexander Hamilton's hatred for each other grew, and after Hamilton insulted Burr, he challenged Hamilton to a duel and fatally shot him. This made Burr very unpopular. After leaving the Vice Presidency, the ever ambitious Burr tried to lead a secessionist movement in the Western territories against the federalist government to create his own nation. Burr was tried for treason, and although he was acquitted he was greatly hated and disgraced, and he left to live in Europe.

Jefferson was elected to a second term, again because of the advantage the South held in the Electoral College, but his popularity waned dramatically as his disastrous economic policies plunged the nation into economic chaos, particularly after he passed the Embargo Act of 1807 which effectively killed most American trade. In 1809, the Congress repealed the Act just before Jefferson left office, dealing a blow to his political career from which he never recovered.

After his presidency, Jefferson founded the University of Virginia and was active there until his death. Politically, Jefferson set the stage for the politics of the South and the old Democratic Party and their mantra of states' rights. Jefferson was the epitome of the upper class British-American from the aristocratic plantation South.

The Germans

There are about 43 million Americans of German descent according to the 2000 US census, or 15.2% of the entire US population. They are the largest ethnic group of continental Europeans in the United States. The Germans did not colonize the Americas, but rather came as immigrants to the first British colonies and then later to what had become the United States. The first German immigrants began to arrive in New York and Pennsylvania in the 1670s. Overall, most German immigrants were Catholics, but some Lutherans came too, and a small number of other Protestants. They were attracted by free land and religious freedom; and many Germans came to America to escape compulsory German military service.

There were also some organized German atheist immigrants who came to America. The City of New Ulm, Minnesota, was settled by German atheists. However, the city is now populated mostly by German Catholics. North

Dakota was another place for settlement for German atheists.

The Germans introduced kindergartens to the United States, and the Christmas tree. The harmonica is also from Germany. Americans listen to German classical music along with German polkas. Hot dogs ("Frankfurters") and hamburgers are also of German origin, named after the cities of Frankfurt and Hamburg, Germany. In addition strudel, sauerkraut, bratwurst, braunschweiger or liverwurst, knockwurst, and pretzels are now American foods of German origin. Americans drink wine from the Rhine and Mosel regions of Germany and have imported German wine grapes to grow these wine varieties in the United States.

Most of American brewing and many of the American beers came from German immigrant families such as Anheuser, Busch, Coors, Hamm's, Miller, Pabst, Schell's, Stroh's, and Schlitz.

The first German settlement was Germantown, Pennsylvania, founded in 1683. Many Germans paid their passage to America by selling their labor for a fixed period of years as indentured servants. Most of the earliest German immigrants were Lutherans followed by small sects such as the Amish, Hutterites, Moravians, and Mennonites. German Catholics, the largest group, didn't begin arriving until after the War of 1812; the same is true of German Jews. The largest numbers of German immigrants came in the period 1840 to 1880; they were the largest incoming group during that time and these were mostly Catholics.

Many Germans were also socialists and some were communists. Germans were early advocates of unions and workers rights. At the same time, a famous capitalist, America's first millionaire, was the German-American John Jacob Astor, who became rich from New York real estate.

Prior to World War I, German and Yiddish (largely based on a Germanic dialect) were spoken by large numbers in the United States, but the use of these languages has largely died out in the United States as the Germans and German-Jews have assimilated. The assimilation was hastened by anti-German sentiments during World War I, but the German and Yiddish speakers were already following the traditional pattern of European-American foreign language speakers who generally see their language disappear by the third generation. However, as the number of German and Yiddish speakers has drastically declined, they have left their impact and American English has many borrow words from both German and Yiddish.

A majority of the German immigrants were farmers, but there were also many skilled tradesmen like printers, glassmakers, brewers, carpenters and cabinet makers, doctors, clock makers, musical instrument makers and butchers who came to America and enormously improved these trades in America. For example American butchering uses both German and English cuts of meat, and most Americans have a particular taste for German meats.

German-Americans live in all fifty states, but the upper Midwest states of Iowa, Wisconsin, Minnesota, Nebraska, and North and South Dakota have the highest concentrations with 35% to 47% of their total state populations being German-Americans. Midwestern culture, with its foods, churches and polka music, was influenced heavily by its German population. American presidents with partial German ancestry include Washington, Hoover, Eisenhower, Nixon and Barack Obama.

The American German Bund, Charles Lindbergh, and Father Coughlin

Although the Germans assimilated quickly into America, there was some anti-German sentiment in America leading up to and during World War I. While a small number of German-Americans were pro-German before the Great War and a smaller number during the war, most German-Americans were loyal to the United States. The US Justice Department arrested and detained about 4,000 German-Americans including a small number of Germans who had actually spied, but most others had just openly supported Germany. And while the treatment of German-Americans wasn't nearly as hysterical, harsh or sweeping as the treatment of the Japanese-Americans during World War II, there was some strong anti-German sentiment in World War I, but very little by World War II. During World War I some German-American towns were even renamed to show their patriotism. Berlin, Michigan, was renamed Marne, Michigan, after the World War I battle of Marne. During World War I the small city called Teuteburg, Minnesota, named by the German-Americans who were the dominant ethnic group, was formally renamed Young America in World War I.

During World War I in Minnesota, a state with one of the largest German-American populations, briefly banned German language instruction in the schools and sought to disallow uniforms and religious dress in schools in an attempt to close German Catholic parochial schools (these schools required student uniforms and were taught by nuns dressed in their habits).

In reaction to these suspicions, Minnesota German-Americans became one of the largest volunteer groups to join the US Army in World War I, in order to prove their patriotism and Americanism. There were so many Minnesotan casualties in World War I, with the largest group being German-Americans, that one of the nation's new federal veteran's hospitals was located near Minneapolis, at Ft. Snelling in Minnesota.

The years between World War I and World War II saw a rise of German nationalism and sympathy if not out-right support of the Nazis. Not all of this support was from German-Americans. American conservatives and anti-Semites also approved of Hitler and many American businessmen viewed Hitler favorably for his anti-communist and anti-labor views.

Father Charles Coughlin, an Irish Catholic and a rabid anti-Semite, was a supporter of Hitler; he gained enormous power and influence in the US as the first religious media personality. He was the model for American televangelist and right-wing radio talk show hosts. He had widespread credibility among German-American and Irish-American Catholics. He was known as the "Radio Priest." At his peak he was broadcast over a large national network of radio stations with listeners estimated at thirty million. He preached anti-Semitism, and against socialists and communists — whom he claimed were part of an international Jewish conspiracy to enslave White Christians. In terms of monetary policy, he was against the gold standard which he insisted was a "Jewish metal." Coughlin promoted silver as the Christian alternative and was a large silver speculator. He was supported politically and financially by Henry Ford and a growing group of anti-Semitic Conservative Christian Republicans, including Minnesota Congressman Charles Lindbergh. He insisted that President Roosevelt was secretly Jewish and that his real name was "Rosenfeld." At one point Father Coughlin advocated that Roosevelt should be assassinated. He created a right-wing fascist newspaper ironically called *Social Justice*. A line from a Woody Guthrie folk song of that time, titled *Lindbergh*, sang of Coughlin: "Yonder comes Father Coughlin wearing the silver chain, gas on the stomach and Hitler on the brain."

Coughlin's efforts helped inspire the creation of the German American Bund, a group of American Nazis supporting Hitler, and his radio ranting and anti-Semitism greatly aided in the recruitment of their members.

A surprising number of well-known Americans, including Henry Ford (who was given the Commander Cross of the Order of the German Eagle by Hitler), gave their support to anti-Semitism, Nazism and other right wing causes, but none was a more famous supporter of Hitler than Charles "Lucky" Lindbergh, who was the first person to fly non-stop across the Atlantic Ocean from the United States to Paris. He was at the time an "American hero."

Lucky Lindy, Not So Lucky and Not So Great?

Lindbergh's father, Charles A. Lindbergh Sr., was elected a Congressman from Minnesota. He was strongly supported by the German-Catholic community which had a solid majority in that Congressional district. Lindbergh Sr. was of Swedish birth but changed his name from Carl Mansson to the more German-sounding Charles Lindbergh. During World War I he led the "America First" movement, which sought to side with Germany during the war, and then sought to promote American isolationism once the war had started. He was an anti-Semite and an early admirer of Hitler, as was his son Charles Jr.

Charles Jr. became obsessed with flying and airplanes. He learned to fly and became one of the first US mail pilots. In 1927 Lindbergh became the first person to cross the Atlantic by flying from Long Island, New York, to Paris in a plane called *The Spirit of St. Louis*. He was an instant hero for this accomplishment and received world-wide recognition. In America he became known as "Lucky Lindy" for his aeronautical feat. He also became fairly wealthy.

As a result of this fame and fortune, Lucky Lindy's infant son was kidnapped and accidently killed in a botched ransom scheme. Lindbergh took his family to live in Europe to escape the press and because of his wife's fear that it would happen again.

In 1938 he became good friends with Herman Goering, who had just been named as the Commander of the German Luftwaffe. The Nazis knew that Lindbergh was a supporter and he was given clearance to tour secret German airbases and was even allowed to fly the newest German military aircraft. Goring, on behalf of Hitler, also presented Lindbergh with the Commander Cross of the Order of the German Eagle for his support of Germany, the same award Henry Ford had received earlier for his support of the Nazis and Hitler.

Lindbergh's acceptance of the award caused controversy in the United States when the Nazis conducted the anti-Jewish pogrom of Kristallnacht very shortly afterward. The American press was filled with editorials saying that Lindbergh should return the medal, but Lindbergh publicly and stubbornly refused. In 1938, he also urged in a letter that England and France should ignore Hitler's violation of the Munich agreement and urged their governments to ally with Germany and to persuade Hitler to attack the Russian communists. He openly stated many times that he would rather see America allied with Nazi Germany than with Communist Russia.

In 1940 he returned to the United States to lead the America First Movement and urged America to not attack Germany. Most Americans prior to Pearl Harbor wanted to stay out of the war. In 1941, in testimony to Congress he argued against Roosevelt and his Lend Lease Policy of sending arms to the English and French in the war against Hitler. Roosevelt openly questioned whether Lindbergh's loyalties were with Germany or the United States, and Lindbergh in a fit of anger resigned his US reserve army officer commission. A few months before Pearl Harbor, the event that finally dragged public support soundly behind the war effort, Lindbergh made a speech in Des Moines, Iowa, that was called "Who are the War Agitators?" In the speech he said that there were three groups that wanted war: Jews, the British, and the Roosevelt administration. In another speech he blamed Jewish ownership of the American media and film industry for agitating and causing war.

Lindbergh, like Hitler, believed in White supremacy. In 1939 Lindbergh wrote in a *Reader's Digest* article, "We can have peace and security only so long as we band together to preserve that most priceless possession, our inheritance of European blood, only so long as we guard ourselves against attack by foreign armies and dilution by foreign races."

He also said that European Whites "demonstrated superior ability in the design, manufacture, and operation of machines," a statement that rang true to many at the time but has now been pretty thoroughly discredited. Lindbergh also said that "The growth of our Western civilization has been closely related to this superiority."

Despite his frequent speeches about morals and the corruption of

American values, it was revealed after his death that in addition to the six children he had with his wife Anne Morrow Lindbergh, Lucky Lindy had affairs with at least three German women who gave him seven illegitimate children. Two were sisters: Bridgett Hesshaimer and her sister Marietta gave him five children, and the third was his private secretary, an East Prussian aristocrat named Valeska, who bore him two more illegitimate children.

The American Fuhrer

Fritz Kuhn, a German born American Nazi, was the leader of the German American Bund. The Bund was financed by the Third Reich and its primary activities were to recruit American Nazis, encourage American support of Nazi Germany, to foster White superiority, and to spread anti-Semitism. Kuhn was a guest of the Third Reich in Berlin during the 1936 Olympics.

Like Lindbergh, Kunz gave impassioned speeches about American morality and Christian values that he claimed were being destroyed by Blacks and Jews. Like Hitler, he despised jazz and said it was a "Negro mongrelization of White music." At his peak he played to a crowd of over 20,000 at Madison Square Garden in February of 1939, lecturing on the loss of Christian morals in America. As leader of the German American Bund, Kuhn was seen as the moral leader of this White Christian movement. Not long after the Madison Square Garden speech he was convicted of theft of funds from the German government and from the Bund, and income tax evasion. During his trial it was revealed that he had spent enormous sums on prostitutes and sex parties. He had a long term and on-going relationship with a German prostitute and had spent a significant amount of German government funds supporting her. The testimony at his trial also revealed that Kunz, a married man, had been seen at a New York jazz night club dancing and drinking with a former Miss America and had spent large sums on liquor for her and others, money that he had illegally taken from the German government. The Bund dissolved after his trial.

It is interesting to note that although Minnesota and her German Catholic residents on the whole are a very liberal, that the Minnesota Congressional district that supported Charles Lindbergh Sr. is much the same German Catholic district that now supports the Christian-conservative Republican Michele Bachmann. It should be noted that there were a number of German-Americans of the left as well as the right. It should be pointed out in fairness that German –Americans were also early leaders in the American peace, labor and socialists movements.

Irish-Americans

The number of Irish-Americans is almost seven times larger than the population of Ireland (4.68 million). According to the US census in 2000, some 31 million Americans list their heritage as Irish. This does not include the Scots-Irish Protestants who came from Protestant Ulster and are of English and Scottish ancestry and are therefore considered British. Irish is the third most common ancestry among European Americans, falling behind German and slightly behind British. New York is the state with the largest Irish-American population, while Boston is the "most Irish" city with more than twenty percent of the population tracing their roots to Ireland. Irish-Americans live all across the United States and most US counties have a population of 5% or more.

The first Irish in America were indentured servants. About 100,000 came in the 1600s and another 100,000 in the 1700s. In the Southern colonies the Irish came in small numbers, and were confused with the large number of Protestant Scots-Irish and settled in mostly rural areas and didn't build a significant amount of Catholic churches and were not seen as either different or as a threat to the local Protestant populations. However in the Northern colonies the Irish Catholics settled in groups in the cities and built their Catholic churches and schools. They also competed as laborers with working class Yankees in the labor market. Irish discrimination was significant in Northern colonies, but anti-Catholicism generally was prevalent throughout the colonies. As the numbers of Irish Catholics increased in the US, discrimination became more pronounced and it was common to see signs in public places in American cities that said, "No Irish or Catholics Allowed."

The largest wave of Irish immigration came in the nineteenth century, particularly during the Potato Famine. Ireland was starving to death because of potato blight and the harsh economic conditions imposed by the English, who were actually exporting available food out of Ireland to England. Millions of Irish crossed the Atlantic to the United States. Lacking resources, the Irish were forced to come as passengers or crew on the "coffin ships" and many died during the journey. A coffin ship was an old decommissioned ship, some of them actually raised and repaired after being sunk in harbors, patched up to try the Atlantic crossing. The ship's captains were mostly common sailors who managed to find an old boat to repair, and the crews were mostly inexperienced Irishmen and boys who could not even pay the paltry fare.

These Irish immigrants struggled to get to America only to find hostile cities where they were not wanted and discrimination was prevalent. The Irish were called "Papists" and stereotyped as stupid, drunks, violent and lazy. The derogatory American colloquialism "Mick" is term applied to the Irish. It is thought this term was because many Irish surnames start with Mc, such as McCormack and McMillan.

The Irish began living in concentrated communities in the northern parts of America and soon Irish ghettos were a part of many Eastern cities. A large number of Catholic immigrants, including the Irish, changed from Catholicism to Protestantism. The Catholic Church developed what was called the "Ghetto Policy" in which the Catholic Church sought to limit contact between American Catholics and Protestants to prevent possible conversions. They told the Irish and other Catholics that they were forbidden to date or marry Protestants, or to attend public schools, and encouraged the Irish and Catholics to live in Irish or Catholic neighborhoods, attend Catholic schools and to shop only in Catholic businesses when possible. Of course, many Protestants also opposed marriage with Catholics. This policy kept the Irish in their ghettos and prevented them from assimilating into mainstream America. The Ghetto policy also affected the large number of German Catholics, but unlike the Irish the German Catholics settled in the Midwest on farms and in small cities that were largely German settlements, and they did not clash as much with the Protestants or other Americans.

The Catholic Church began developing their parochial school system because of the Church's policy and because they felt unwelcome in public schools. In many public schools at the time Protestant religious instruction was part of the regular instruction. When attempts were made to change this, violence and riots frequently occurred.

Since most of the Irish came as unskilled workers, they became low paid millworkers and factory workers. One of the highest ambitions for these new arrivals was to become firefighters and police officers, which they did in large numbers. The Irish-Americans soon dominated these professions in many Eastern cities. They also sought power through politics and developed powerful political organizations like Tammany Hall in New York. The Catholic Church was also a large employer of the Irish with many becoming priests and nuns. The Irish were good politicians. They soon came to dominate the American Catholic Church, even though German Catholics were larger in numbers.

The Irish-Americans were one of America's few ethnic groups that remained tied to the politics of their country of origin until recent times. The Irish Republican Army (IRA) which sought Irish independence from Britain received much of their financial support from Irish Americans. It became an issue in US and British relations. In 1984 the United States Justice Department went to court to force the Irish American groups to stop funding the IRA in Ireland.

Irish culture is still a major part of American culture. St. Patrick's Day is celebrated by mainstream America as well as by Irish-Americans. Irish music and pub culture is still strong in America and millions of Irish-Americans have made a return pilgrimage back to the home country.

In 1928, New York Governor Al Smith became the first Irish Catholic to run for President. He was unsuccessful because at the time America was not ready to accept a Catholic in the White House. During the election the Ku Klux Klan actually burned a cross in front of Smith's home. In 1960, John Kennedy, of Irish heritage, became the first Catholic elected president, but only after assuring Protestant ministers, particularly the Reverend Billy Graham, that his Catholicism would not overshadow his duties as president.

Other important Irish-American contributors to American politics include Mary Harris Jones, known as "Mother Jones," and Elizabeth Gurley

Flynn, who were important leaders in the American labor movement and with social justice issues. Irish-Americans were very prominent participants in the American labor movement.

Italian-Americans

The Italian-Americans are the fourth largest group of European Americans. There are about sixteen million according to the US Census, which is just under 6% of the total US population. Many of America's early explorers were Italian: Columbus, John Cabot (Giovanni Caboto), and Giovanni Verrazano was the first to discover and sail into New York Bay. Alessandro Malaspina explored and mapped the West Coast of the Americas from Cape Horn to Alaska. Enrico Da Tonti, a Catholic priest, explored the Great Lakes region with the French explorer La Salle. He later co-founded New Orleans with La Salle and served as governor of the Louisiana Territory for the next twenty years. Father Eusebio Kino explored and mapped California for the Spanish.

The Italians started coming to settle in America in 1620 and music was their earliest contribution. Thomas Jefferson, during his presidency, recruited a group of Italian military musicians who became the core of the US Marine Corps Band. The first music conservatory was created in Boston by Filipo Taretta in 1801. The first opera house was built in New York by Lorenzo Da Ponte in 1833. American opera was developed by Italian-Americans, and later American pop music was greatly enhanced by Italian-American "crooners" like Frank Sinatra, Dean Martin, and Perry Como adding to this Italian-American musical tradition. Early Rock singers included: Dion, Fabian and Frankie Valli of the Four Seasons.

A number of Italian sculptors and artists were recruited to build the buildings and monuments in the nation's capital. Constantino Brumidi was one of the most noteworthy, creating the frescoes in the Capitol Dome and staying in America to spend his life working on other American monuments. The largest Italian immigration occurred from 1880 through 1920. Italians, mostly from southern Italy and Sicily, came to America. Unlike the early craftsmen and artisans, this group was poor, mostly unskilled, very religious and clannish. The Ghetto Policy fostered by the Catholic Church greatly hindered their assimilation just as it did the Irish Catholics and kept them poor, and soon "Little Italy" was also a part of many large Eastern American cities.

Most of the Italian immigrants were hard-working, religious people, but they also brought "La Cosa Nostra" ("Our Thing") to the United States. They called themselves "men of honor" ("Mafiosi"), and their organizations became known in America as the Mafia.

The Mafia started in nineteenth century Sicily and came to the US with these poor Italian immigrants. They were at first very small crime organizations called "families" which presided over a territory. Selling "protection" to the Italian immigrants was the original crime, but they soon moved into gambling and prostitution. During Prohibition these organizations flourished with the sale of illegal liquor and grew from small urban neighborhood organizations to national crime organizations. They also began to trade in drugs, fix sporting events, engage in smuggling, construction-bid rigging, and murder for hire. They also infiltrated and sometimes took over unions. But perhaps the most damaging aspect of the Mafia has been bribery of public officials, vote-rigging, the buying of politicians, jury rigging and witness intimidation. Through these activities the Mafia has made a lasting negative impact on American society and has caused doubts about American government institutions and justice. Even the Central Intelligence Agency has used and been used by the Mafia. It started in World War II when the CIA used them for their connections in Italy, and continued into the post war period when at one point the Mafia was hired in an attempt to assassinate Cuban President Fidel Castro.

Not all organized crime was or is Italian; other ethnicities such as Jews and the Irish have also been involved. Mickey Cohen, who started Las Vegas, and Isadore Blumenfeld, better known as Kidd Can, were part of what became known as the Jewish Mafia. Many American businessmen had or have connections to organized crime and the Mafia. Joseph Kennedy, the father of Jack, Bobby, and Ted, made his money during Prohibition by importing illegal liquor with the Mafia. Another example: Richard Nixon's first Congressional campaign headquarters was in a free office provided by mobster Mickey Cohen and he received Mafia funds for his campaign. He was also was funded by the Mafia in his election to the Senate. Nixon's best friend, Charles "Bebe" Rebozo, was known as the Mafia's banker. Rebozo laundered funds for organized crime. He and Nixon also jointly owned a small hotel and casino in Mafia-controlled Havana before the Cuban Revolution.

The Mafia lost millions in the Castro-led Cuban revolution, along with Nixon, the Bush family and other prominent Americans. The Mafia owned the hotels, gambling, prostitution and other related businesses in Cuba prior to the revolution and controlled much of Cuba, particularly Havana. So it isn't surprising to find that they were involved with the CIA in the Bay of Pigs fiasco or were later used by the CIA to attempt to kill Castro.

It has also come to light in recent years that the head of the FBI, J. Edgar Hoover, was bribed by the Mafia. His notorious gambling at the horseracing tracks was financed by the Mafia, and even on his annual vacation he went to a California hotel owned by the Mafia. It was also rumored, and likely true that this association started by the Mafia obtaining pictures and other evidence of his homosexual affairs and cross-dressing, which the Mafia used to control the Director of the Federal Bureau of Investigation.

This dark legacy of corruption and violence has permanently changed the political culture of the United States.

Italian-American Cuisine

One of the most delightful Italian contributions to American culture has been its food, and like the Italian immigrants, most of this food is southern Italian. Pizza and spaghetti are considered as American as they are Italian. The National Restaurant Association states that Italian cuisine was one of the most important influences on American food. The red Marinara sauce, the white Alfredo sauce and Bolognese sauces are used in Italian-American and American fusion cuisine. The many varied pastas from the short risotto and gnocchi, to long spaghetti and vermicelli, the twisted fusilli and tube-like cannelloni to wide lasagna noodles all have found their way into American cuisine.

In addition to pizza and spaghetti, other common Italian-American dishes include: Lasagna, Baked Ziti, Frittatas, Cioppino, Italian Wedding Soup, Calzones, Stromboli, and even the famous Muffuletta sandwiches of New Orleans fame are Italian cuisine. Italian cheeses from both northern and southern Italy are used in American cuisine, the more common of which are: Asagio, Bircchetto, Caciotta, Gorgonzola, Mozzarella, Provolone, Ricotta, and Romano. Deserts and sweets include: Tiramisu, Cannoli, and Biscotti.

Italian-Americans have also made very significant contributions to American viticulture and winemaking. Many of America's wineries were started by Italian-Americans. During America's prohibition years from 1919 to 1933, American wineries began to rapidly disappear. The Italian-American wineries, particularly those in Napa California began producing sacramental wines for the Catholic Church which was still legal. They also began to produce grape juice and developed a new market for this with consumers. Through these two products they were able to save the American wine industry from Prohibition.

The Italians did face some discrimination in America. The derogatory terms "Wop," "Dago," or "grease ball" are sometimes applied by Americans to Italian-Americans. Many honest Italian-Americans are also unfairly characterized as being criminal and part of the Mafia. Ironically Italian neighborhoods and communities and businesses were some of the most negatively impacted by the Mafia, particularly with their protection, gambling and loan sharking schemes.

The French

Some eleven million people or 3.9% of the total population of the United States are of French ancestry; and there are roughly 2 million French-speakers. However, the French have made many more contributions to American culture than their numbers would indicate. The largest contribution was the sale of Louisiana, known as the Louisiana Purchase, in 1803. For $15 million dollars the United States bought 828,000 square miles of land which included all of the states of Arkansas, Missouri, Oklahoma, Iowa, Nebraska, and most of what are now the states of Louisiana, Minnesota, North Dakota, South Dakota, Montana, Colorado, Wyoming, and part of northeastern New Mexico, Northern Texas, and smaller portions of what is now the Canadian provinces of Alberta and Saskatchewan that were later traded to Britain to settle the western border between the US and Canada. Historian Eric Hobsbawm in his book, *The Age of Revolution*, stated that after France's failure to re-conquer Haiti in 1803 after a slave revolt in 1791–1793, that France decided to give up most of their claims in the New World. As a consequence they sold these lands to the United States to help the US against the British, with whom they had long been in conflict.

The French began exploring and settling North America in the 16th century under King Francis I, who furnished Jacques Cartier with ships supplies and men to explore and settle North American lands and claim them for France. Unlike the English, not many French women made the trip to the new world. French settlers mostly inter-married with Native Americans which also gave them advantages as explorers and fur trappers. Later they were also able to use these Native ties to persuade some tribes to side with France in their battles with the British. These wars became known as the French and Indian Wars. Early French settlements were small forts for supplying and protecting their fur trapping and trading empire. The most prominent settlements were Quebec and Montreal in Canada, and New Orleans, Mobile, Biloxi, Baton Rouge, St. Louis, Cape Girardeau, Detroit, and Green Bay in what is now the United States. The French lost many of their settlements to the British in the French and Indian Wars.

The French explorer La Salle named the French claimed lands Louisiana after King Louis XIV in 1662. The first settlement was a fort at what is today Biloxi, Mississippi in 1699. The French colony of Nachitoches located in present day Louisiana was settled in 1714 and sugar cane became the primary economic activity. The settlement was at the Northern end of El Camino Real (The Royal Highway) the Spanish colony trail in New Mexico. The French established a colony here to foster trade with the Spanish and to set a boundary to ensure that the Spanish didn't encroach on French territory. New Orleans was established in 1718 and became the capital of Louisiana Territory replacing Biloxi as the capital.

In addition to sugar cane the French also began to cultivate cotton. In 1719, a year after settlement, two French ships arrived in New Orleans with cargos of Black African slaves to work the sugar cane and cotton plantations. New Orleans became known as a place of rogues, slaves, runaway slaves, and pirates. It also had the worst French soldiers, who were often sent there as a punishment. The settlement was described by a priest-historian as wretched hovels under a thicket of willows, with waterways infested with alligators and snakes.

In 1722, a hurricane stuck the colony, nearly destroying it. As a response, the French Administrators developed a grid pattern for the city's development which they determined would greatly diminish damage from future storms.

This grid pattern was used to develop what is now the City's French Quarter, which has indeed survived many hurricanes. After the French failure to re-take Haiti in 1803, many of the French and their Haitian sympathizers fled from Haiti to New Orleans and brought their Creole culture. It is a mix of French and West African influences and they also brought African Voodoo religion to New Orleans and Louisiana.

Another group of French people, called the Acadians, were expelled in 1755 from Canada's Maritime Provinces when the British took them from France in the French and Indian War. The Acadians migrated to the French colony of New Orleans and Louisiana territory, where they became known as Cajuns. They have a unique culture that is a mix of French culture with Canadian and Native-American influences.

With these migrations of French people from France, Canada and Haiti, with Blacks, Native Americans and with some Spanish and Americans coming to live, New Orleans developed a polyglot culture and racial mix which is evident in the city today.

The original colonies of France in Missouri and Illinois, that were part of the Louisiana Territory, still have some evidence of French influence today. However the French-Missouri dialect that was widely spoken in these areas for more than a hundred and fifty years has all but died out.

In addition to the Louisiana territory there are also French influences in northern New England, especially Maine, where some of the expelled Acadians and other French-Canadians settled and have left their marks on the culture. A few other small French colonies have also contributed to the French influence in America.

The French in America are mostly Catholic. However a number of French Protestants, the Huguenots, came in the 1600s to the New Dutch Colony of New York, and they were welcomed, becoming prominent members of the colony. They also established a Huguenot colony called La Rochelle, which has become known as New Rochelle. In 1700, several hundred Huguenots also settled in the Virginia colony.

In the 1600s Huguenots (who were then unwelcome in France) petitioned the British crown for land and were granted it in near Charleston, South Carolina. Paul Revere and Francis Marion, known as the Swamp Fox during the Revolutionary War, were Huguenots. The Huguenot Church and people were slowly assimilated into the American culture. Most Huguenot churches became affiliated with Episcopalian or other American mainstream Protestant denominations.

The French sided with the American colonists during the Revolutionary War. This wasn't so much out of a love of Americans as it was a result of rivalry with the British. France gave money and arms to the Americans along with military guidance and advice. However, some valuable French soldiers also joined the Americans, such as Charles L'Enfant, and the Marquis de Lafayette who served as an American general. Americans were so grateful to France and so disliked the British that at the conclusion of the War the leaders of the American colonies briefly entertained the idea of making French the official language of the United States. However this notion was short-lived as most colonists could not speak any French. In four New England states, June 24 is an official holiday— Franco-American Day.

Ironically during the American Civil War both France and Britain supported the South and sent money and arms to the Confederacy against the United States. It had little to do with slavery as both had economic reasons for doing so, but this support soured America's relations with the two nations for some time afterward.

Because most French-American ancestors left France before the French Revolution, the royal Fleur-de-lis, rather than the modern French tricolor, is considered the symbol of French-Americans. The royal Fleur-de-lis still adorns many things in New Orleans including the helmets of the New Orleans Saints football team.

The French did occasionally face some discrimination in America. Americans would sometimes use the English derogatory term "Frog" for the French. In St. Paul, Minnesota the "Frogtown neighborhood" is called so because it was originally a French-Canadian and Catholic neighborhood. The term "Frog" for Frenchmen came originally from the English, who said disdainfully that the French were "Frog Eaters" —the French eat frog legs, a delicacy, it should be noted, that is also enjoyed by many Americans.

Polish-Americans

The largest group of Eastern Europeans in America are the Polish. There are nine million Americans of Polish descent or about 3.2% of the entire population. Most came to the United States during the large European immigration from 1870 to 1914. They were primarily Catholic, but there were also Polish Jews and Polish Eastern Orthodox. The Catholic majority was impacted by the Ghetto Policy of the Catholic Church and many settled in "Polonia," as the Polish neighborhoods in large American cities were sometimes called. Most of the original Polish immigrants were different than other American immigrant groups in that most of them came to America with the idea of making money and then returning to Poland. However, they came in family groups, and second and third generation Poles did not share their parents' or grandparents' desires to return to Poland.

Because of this original desire to remain Polish, and the effects of the Catholic Ghetto Policy, the Polish assimilated very slowly into American life. Up until the 1950s and 1960s, Polish was still spoken regularly in their neighborhoods and in their churches. Some Polish businesses thrived, but most Poles were recruited into heavy industry such as steel and auto making. The Polish mostly settled in large cities. American cities that have large Polish neighborhoods include Chicago, New York, Detroit, Milwaukee, Minneapolis, Cleveland, Pittsburgh, Boston, Baltimore, Los Angeles, San Francisco, Portland, South Bend and Duluth.

Poles also faced discrimination in America. "Polack" became an ethnic slur derogating the Polish and rendering them second class citizens. A variety of "Polack Jokes" were used to imply that all Poles lacked intelligence.

However, Polish influence on American culture has been significant. Polish-Americans have made large contributions to American literature and poetry. The Polish wedding with polka music has been emulated by many other ethnic groups, particularly in the Midwest where the "Chicken Dance" is a must at many weddings. Foods like Polish sausage, Kielbasa, Pierogi, and Babka Cake are eaten by many Americans, along with bakery goods and bread like the dark Polish rye. The Poles have the second largest household income among all European ethnic groups in America. (Russian-Americans have the largest household incomes.)

Russian-Americans

There are just over three million Americans of Russian descent. There are still over 800,000 who speak Russian as their primary language. Many of these are new Russian immigrants since the breakup of the Soviet Union, but Alaska, Washington. Oregon, and California were once part of Russian America and some of the earliest European settlements, particularly in Alaska, were Russian colonies.

The Russian American company settled Fort Ross, just north of San Francisco, in 1812. And it was the center of the Russian American Company that served as the official trading and colonization agency of the Russian Federation in America. There were considerable disagreements with Spain, as they, too, had claimed these Pacific coastal areas. But the Russian Fort Ross was well armed and equipped and Spain lacked the means to expel them, so a sort of undeclared truce developed. In fact the Spanish settlements just to the south never would have survived without Russian supplies, particularly after some Spanish supply ships were lost to storms over their long journey to re-supply their California colonies. The Russian colonies continued until the mid nineteenth century, when the growing costs associated with the long-distance support became burdensome, and the Russians were worried that Britain would eventually seize their holdings from British Canada. Bowing to the inevitable, the Russian Czar sold his holdings, including Alaska, to the United States in 1867.

Secretary of State William Seward took a great deal of harassment from Congress and the press for this purchase, which they called "Seward's Folly" and "Seward's Icebox." Next to the Louisiana Purchase, it was the best land acquisition in US history. Seward was also negotiating to buy Siberia from the Russians, but the Congress would not allow that purchase to proceed. World history might have been very different if the United States had owned and colonized Siberia. Although many of the Russians returned to Russia after the sale of their colonies to the United States, a few stayed in place and wove their way into the tapestry of American culture.

The largest wave of Russian immigration took place from 1881 to 1922. The first group came in 1881 and 1882; these were mostly Russian Jews who were escaping the horrific pogroms under Alexander III of Russia. They came to New York and other large Eastern cities.

Leading up to and especially after World War I, large groups of Russians began to come to America as people fled the devastation of World War I, the Russian Revolution, and the ensuing civil war. Those Russian émigrés loyal to the Czar were known as "White Russians." They were mostly middle and upper class Russians fleeing the communists; the White Russians would help solidify the anti-socialist and anti-communist spirit in the United States.

The Soviet Union permitted a wave of emigration by Jews in the 1970s, many of whom chose to come to the United States; this trend continued at an accelerated pace after the break-up of the Soviet Union. These waves of Russian Jews were followed later by many non-Jewish Russian professionals after the break-up of the Soviet Union and the collapse of the economy.

Russian-Americans have made many contributions in America. One immigrant, Vladimir Zworykin, was the inventor of television. Igor Sikorsky, who came to the States in 1919, invented the helicopter. The composers Stravinsky and Rachmaninoff, Irving Berlin, and George Gershwin were immigrants from Russia along with many other composers and musicians. American ballet has been greatly impacted by Russian-Americans, and the actors Yul Brynner (Russian-born) and Kirk Douglas (born to Jewish immigrants from the Russian Empire) are leading examples in the American entertainment industry.

A negative element of this third wave Russian immigration to the US has been the introduction of organized crime from Russia into the US, which has been dubbed "the Russian Mafia." Here the term "Russian" is actually us used to designate a variety of groups of different backgrounds, many of them not ethnically Russian: Jews, Armenians, Ukrainians, Lithuanians, and from the Caucasus region Chechens, Dagestanis, and Georgians. Although this is a relatively new element in the US, by the 1990s it was already having a major economic impact.

The Dutch in America

There are about four million Americans of Dutch ancestry or about 1.6 % of the American population. In 1609, the Dutch East India Company hired Henry Hudson to explore and find a suitable location for a colony in America. In 1613, a few Dutch villages, including New Amsterdam, which would become New York City, were settled in what is now New York State. However, most of these early settlements were abandoned. In a now famous tale, Peter Minuit bought Manhattan Island from the Native Americans for the New Amsterdam Colony for about $24 worth of trade goods, and New Amsterdam became the capital of the Dutch colonies.

The Dutch colonies grew from a population of under 2,000 in 1648 to about 10,000 by 1660. About half the people were Dutch, a quarter were Walloons (French-speaking Belgians) and a quarter were French Huguenots (French Protestants). The British captured the colony in 1664, renaming it New York. The Dutch recaptured the colony and briefly held it, but traded it to the British for Suriname in South America. After the British occupation, Dutch immigration to New York ceased. However, the Hudson River Valley, parts of New Jersey, and other nearby areas continue to be home to many families of Dutch extraction.

In 1683, about 200 Dutch colonists settled in Germantown, which is now a neighborhood in Philadelphia, with most of these being Quakers as was their patron, William Penn, the founder of Pennsylvania. German immigration soon overwhelmed the area and the Dutch were assimilated. These Dutch are not to be confused with the Pennsylvania Dutch, who are actually German. The term Pennsylvania Dutch is thought to have two possible origins. The first was that "Dutch" is a corruption of the German word Deutsch, meaning German. And second, that the term Pennsylvania Dutch was coined about the time of the American Revolution when the British used German Hessian troops against the Americans. The Hessians were hated and were seen as foreign invaders. The hatred of these Germans ran so high that some people theorize the Germans of Pennsylvania decided to mask their German roots by calling themselves "Pennsylvania Dutch."

The Dutch were allies of the Americans in the Revolutionary War, supplying arms to the colonists. The Dutch were also the first country to recognize the United States on November 16, 1776, officially making the United States a country. The Dutch also helped America finance the Louisiana Purchase.

While the Reformed Church in America was founded by the Dutch in New Amsterdam in 1628, the main wave of immigration among Dutch Catholics and members of the very conservative Dutch Reformed Church occurred in the mid-nineteenth century. Most were farmers and settled into the rural Midwest. Western Michigan has a large number of these immigrants.

The idea of Santa Claus came from the Dutch as did the Legend of Sleepy Hollow, which is an Americanization of a Dutch tale. There are many famous Americans with Dutch ancestry including five presidents: Martin Van Buren, Theodore and Franklin Roosevelt, and both George Bushes. Many place names in New York and New Jersey are Dutch, like Brooklyn, the Bronx and Harlem, and Hasbrouck Heights.

The Scandinavians: Norwegians, Swedes, Danes and Finns

In the United States the descendants of Scandinavians include about four million Norwegians, about 1.2 million Swedes, 1.5 million Danes, and about 700,000 Finns, or about seven and a half million total Scandinavian-

Americans. Except for Finnish and Sami (Laplanders) their languages are similar and are Germanic languages. The concept of Scandinavia comes from their common Viking and Norse heritage and the Kalmar Union which united Norway, Sweden and Denmark and Finland under one monarch. The union lasted from 1397 until 1523, when the Swedes declared their independence because of disagreements with the Danes. The Scandinavians, particularly the Swedes, were the last Europeans to become Christians. These hardy people clung to their Norse religion until the Swedish civil war of 1066 ended the Norse religion and they were forced to convert.

There is enough evidence to show that the Vikings were the first European explorers and settlers in what is now the Newfoundland, in Canada, which they called Vineland; they also colonized Iceland and Greenland along the way. However, the first cold wave of the Little Ice Age which lasted from about 1350 to 1650 (the entire Little Ice Age is generally given as the period 1350 to 1850) caused the climate to cool so that in these Northern areas there were some years of permanent winter without a summer growing season; anthropologists and historians now believe this caused famine among the Viking colonists, and these colonies were then abandoned. It is also believed that in this period, increased shore and drift ice also hampered their travel to and from the colonies.

In Minnesota a Swedish-American farmer supposedly discovered a large slab of rock with runes (ancient Viking writing) on one side that for many years was thought to prove the existence of ancient Viking explorers in Minnesota. It is called the Kensington Runestone. Swedish scholars have pretty much shown the rock to be a hoax, but many Swedish and Norwegian-Americans in Minnesota still believe in its authenticity and the stone is proudly displayed in Alexandria, Minnesota.

Authorized by Queen Christina, the first Swedish colony was started in America in 1638 in the Delaware Valley, which is now a part of Delaware, Pennsylvania and New Jersey. The colonists were both Swedish and Finnish settlers (Finland was a part of Sweden from the thirteenth to the nineteenth century). By 1655, the colony could not be supported by Sweden and so it joined the New Dutch colony and was given autonomy. The Swedes and Finns built log cabins, as they had done in Scandinavia, and this along with the Iroquois and Ojibwe long huts are the supposed inspiration of the American log cabin. The original Swedish colony was quickly assimilated into the other American colonies.

In the middle of the nineteenth century, Swedes began to immigrate again to the United States, settling in the Midwest, where many became homesteaders and farmers in the new American territories. Minnesota became home to many of these Scandinavian settlers. A Swedish historian, playwright and author, Vilhelm Moberg, during the years 1949 to 1959, wrote a series of novels called *The Emigrants* documenting these early pioneers in Minnesota.

By 1900 Chicago was the largest city populated by Swedes outside of

Stockholm. However Minneapolis was not far behind. Minnesota also has the largest population of Swedish-Americans in the United States, with almost 600,000 descendants. Other states with significant Swedish-American populations are Wisconsin, New York, Pennsylvania, Michigan, Iowa, Nebraska and Illinois. At the turn of the twentieth century many Swedish immigrants also went to the state of Washington.

Although some early immigrants were Catholics, Swedish-Americans are mostly Lutherans.

Norwegians came to America in 1825. These immigrants were Quakers and were generally discriminated against in Lutheran Norway. They settled first in New York, but a majority moved on to new lands opening up in Minnesota, Illinois and Wisconsin. The next arrivals went to North Dakota. Like the Swedes, Norwegian immigrants also went to Washington in the early twentieth century. Also like the Swedes, more than half of the Norwegian immigrants settled in the Midwest. Minnesota has the largest population of about 850,000 descendants. At a very distant second, third and fourth place come the states of Wisconsin, California, Washington and North Dakota.

There are about one and a half million Americans of Danish descent. They settled mostly in the Midwest and Western parts of the United States. There were also small numbers of Danes who came to the American colonies in the early years, mostly as single men and they were quickly assimilated. However in 1640 they did briefly make up about 50% of the population of New Amsterdam.

In 1666, the Danes took control of the island of St. Thomas in the Caribbean and shortly later the islands of St. John and St. Croix. They imported Black slaves and used the islands to produce sugar. These islands regularly traded with New England and developed some common cultural customs. In 1917, Denmark sold the three Islands to the United States, and they were then re-named as the US Virgin Islands.

In 1850 the first significant Danish immigration came to the United States. About 17,000 Danes converted to Mormonism to gain their passage to America; they settled in Mormon Utah. The largest Danish immigration occurred between 1860 and 1930. Most Danes came to the United States as farmers. States with the highest populations are California, Utah, Minnesota, and Wisconsin.

The Finns are considered Scandinavian primarily because of geography and because they were part of the Kalmar Union and then part of Sweden from the thirteenth century up to the twentieth century. However, the Finnish language and their cultural roots are not European. Finnish is a Uralic language and is Asian, as are the Sami, Estonian and Hungarian languages. (The Sami who live in the northern and Arctic parts of Scandinavia are sometimes called "Laplanders" by Europeans; many of the Sami people consider this a pejorative term.) The Finns originally came from northwest Asia and then migrated and settled in the northern forests that are now part of

Finland and Russia. Finland was fought over and claimed first by the Kalmar Union, then the Swedes, and then the Russians, until the Finns achieved their independence in 1917. The Finns are culturally very intertwined with the Swedish and Sami peoples. Recent Finnish genetic studies have shown modern Finns to have both European and Asian genetics and that the Finns likely originated in an area of Northern China.

The largest Finnish immigration to the United States was from 1870 to 1930. Most Finns settled in the Upper Peninsula of Michigan and in Northern Minnesota. The primary religion is Finnish Lutheran. Finns tend to be very liberal politically and were early advocates of the American labor and leftist political movements. The sauna is the best known Finnish contribution to American culture.

Minnesota's Finnish community was instrumental in the American labor movement. Finns formed a sizeable portion of the Industrial Workers of the World (I.W.W.) membership, the first national American labor union. They were also known as the Wobblys. The number of Minnesota Finns belonging to the I.W.W. was somewhere between five and ten thousand, according to the Finnish language newspaper of the I.W.W., *Industrialisti*, which was published in Duluth, Minnesota. It was also the union's only daily paper. At its peak, it ran 10,000 copies per issue. Another Finnish-language Wobbly publication was the monthly *Tie Vapauteen* (The Road to Freedom). The Finns also established the I.W.W. educational institute, The Work People's College, in Duluth,

It should also be noted that there are also about 32,000 Scandinavian-Americans who are also of Icelandic descent.

Gus Hall

Arvo Kustaa Halberg was born in rural Northern Minnesota in 1910; he later changed his name to Gus Hall to appear more American. His parents were Finnish immigrants. Like most Finns, he and his parents were members of the International Workers of the World, sometimes called "the Wobblies." He spoke both Finnish and English. He came from a large poor family with ten children, and at the age of fifteen he went to work to help support his family by working in the northern Minnesota lumber camps and iron mines.

In 1927 at the age of seventeen he was recruited into the Communist Party USA (CPUSA) and became an organizer for the Young Communist League. In 1931, he was given the opportunity to go to Moscow and study at the International Lenin School.

Upon his return, he moved to Minneapolis and became a union activist. In 1934, he was jailed for six months for his part in the Minneapolis Teamster's Strike, which became violent when the Minneapolis Police used force to break it up.

Afterward he moved to Ohio to organize steel workers there. He became involved with John L. Lewis and helped organize the Congress of Industrial

Organizations (the CIO), which would later merge with the American Federation of Labor to become the American labor organization the AFL-CIO.

In 1937, Hall became more active in the CPUSA and became the Communist Leader of Cleveland. He ran for Governor of Ohio as a communist and received a small number of votes. On the basis of what many believed were trumped up charges, he was sent to jail for election fraud in 1940 and spent 90 days in Jail.

He joined the Navy in World War II, just after Pearl Harbor, and was honorably discharged in 1946. After the War he was elected to the National Executive Board of the Communist Party USA.

In 1948 under the Smith Act, Hall was convicted of advocating Marxism, which the government said was the same as "the act of teaching the violent overthrow of the US Government." He served five years in prison and was released on bail while the Supreme Court reviewed the Smith Act. In 1951, the Court upheld the Smith Act and his conviction, and Hall skipped bail with three other convicted communists and went to Mexico. They were caught and sent to prison for another three years. The Supreme Court later reversed their decision, finding that Hall's conviction was unconstitutional, and he was released.

After his release Hall became the General Secretary and Chairman of the Communist Party USA. In the early 1960s the government was again attempting to send Hall to prison, now under the McCarran Act, which the Supreme Court again found unconstitutional. However, the State of New York used the McCarran Act to revoke Hall's driver's license and to otherwise harass him. He was awarded the Order of Lenin, the highest civilian award in the Soviet Union for his courage, suffering and contributions to communism.

In the 1960s Hall attempted to democratize the Communist Party USA and to merge it with the growing new American left movement and the anti-war movement, but he was unsuccessful. He also advocated peaceful co-existence between the United States and the Soviet Union.

In 1964, Hall and the Communist Party USA supported Lyndon Johnson because Hall feared that a Goldwater presidency would have brought war with the Soviet Union. Hall also visited the Soviet Union on many occasions in the 1960s and 1970s, and many people thought he had become a Soviet apologist. Hall endorsed the communist governments of Cuba and Vietnam but severely criticized the Communist governments of China and North Korea.

Starting in 1972, Hall ran four times for President of the United States on the Communist Party USA Ticket. In 1980 and 1984, Angela Davis, the Black Power advocate, was his running mate. The most votes he obtained in these elections was about one percent of the total vote in 1976, and most of this was a Watergate protest vote rather than a vote for the CPUSA.

After 1984, the state election laws were made more demanding and it became financially impossible to raise the money necessary to be on each state's ballot and to run a national campaign. Because of these financial requirements all American minor parties were soon excluded from national politics.

In 1987, it was revealed that Morris Childs, Hall's long time deputy and trusted friend, was working as an undercover agent for the FBI. The revelation devastated Hall. Then in 1991, Angela Davis led a large number of members to split from the CPUSA to form their own socialist party. Hall and the CPUSA would never recover. Gus Hall resigned as party chairman in 2000, shortly before his death.

Famous Scandinavians in America

Famous Swedish-Americans include the poet Carl Sandberg, actors Greta Garbo and Uma Thurman, Justice William Rehnquist, and former Michigan Governor Jenifer Grandholm. Famous Americans with partial Norwegian ancestry include actors Marilyn Monroe (her actual birth name was Norma Jean Mortenson) and Priscilla Presley, the musician Beck (born Bek David Campbell), and politicians Michele Bachmann and John Ashcroft. Famous Americans with Danish heritage include the social reformer journalist Jacob Riis and actress Scarlett Johansson (Danish father, American Jewish mother). And famous Americans with at least partial Finnish background include not only Labor and political leader Gus Hall but actors Marian Nixon, Jessica Lange, Christine Lahti and Matt Damon, and musician Mark Hoppus from the punk rock group Blink 182.

Minnesota, a Scandinavian Regional Sub-Culture

There are many sub cultures in the United States. Louisiana and the City of New Orleans, with its French, Cajun and Creole culture, is but one obvious example. Minnesota is another. Nearly two thirds of Minnesota's population are descended from Scandinavia or Northern Germany, and Minnesota culture and language strongly reflect this. Most Americans can discern a distinct "Minnesota accent," which is a Scandinavian accent that came to national attention in the Cohen brothers' movie about Minnesota, *Fargo*. The Cohen brothers are also Minnesota natives.

In the Minnesota accent, vowels are pronounced much harder and longer, almost like a double vowel so that the exclamation "oh" is pronounced "oooh." The familiar Minnesota phrases of "Ya," or "Oh Ya!" which means yes or is also used as an affirmation of a speaker's point and are pronounced "yaaah," and "oooh yaaah!" It is also used as a question "Yaah?" meaning, are you sure? Another common phrase, "You betcha," meaning "you are right," is frequently used, along with the cryptic "See ya!" which is pronounced as a single word, meaning "I will see you later." Another Minnesotan speech oddity is ending a sentence with the word "with," as in "Want to go with?" or in "Do you want your hamburger with?" meaning, would you like either tomatoes or onions on your burger? There are a number of Swedish and Norwegian borrow words used in Minnesota English, the most noteworthy and common is the word "uffda" (pronounced auffduh) which is a Norwegian word meant to show surprise or emphasis as in "Uffda, that was a very large fish!" Minnesotans also use the word "hairs" to mean "hair" as in "His hairs were not combed," because in the Germanic languages hair means just a singular strand, not the collection on a person's head or body. Howard Mohr, a writer for the PBS radio show *A Prairie Home Companion,* wrote a book called *How to Talk Minnesotan: A Visitor's Guide,* lampooning the Minnesota dialect.

Liberal Minnesotans were somewhat disturbed during the 2008 election as they listened to the Vice Presidential candidate, Sarah Palin, speak. Although most Minnesotans didn't care for her, as was made obvious by the election results, they found her strangely familiar. She sounded Minnesotan, even using the phrase "You betcha!" The reason for her different speech pattern is that Palin comes from a part of Alaska that was settled by Minnesotans during the 1930s and their Minnesota accent has endured there.

Minnesota culture is also very Scandinavian. The Minnesota summers are very short and the Minnesota winters are very long, as they are in Scandinavia, and winter in Minnesota, as in Scandinavia, is used for cultural pursuits. Minnesota has a vibrant theater scene including the world-class Guthrie Theatre (which is thought to be the best off Broadway theatre in the United States). Minneapolis also has two of the best art museums in the country: The Minnesota Institute of Arts is one of the largest public funded art centers in the United States and the Walker Art Center with its sculpture garden is one of the top five modern art museums in the United States. The American Swedish Institute in Minneapolis is another example along with the Minnesota Orchestra, whose recordings over many years are considered some of the best in American classical music.

Other Scandinavian influences are the prevalence of the Finnish Sauna which came to Minnesota and spread throughout the United States. Many in Minnesota eat "sauce" for breakfast, which is a Finnish custom of eating canned fruit as part of the breakfast meal. The Finns are also known for their love of very dark humor, which is also a Minnesota trait. It is perhaps the inspiration of the Cohen brothers' movies that are frequently very dark yet funny. The German word and concept of "schadenfreude," which has recently become a popular American borrow word from German, which means "pleasure derived from the misfortune of others," has long been common practice in Minnesota culture—particularly if it is someone you dislike or you think deserves it or "should have it coming."

Scandinavians are also very civic minded, liberal and progressive, and Minnesota politics and civics are reflective of this. In Presidential elections, Minnesota has the highest percent of voter turnout of any state in the nation. Minnesota also leads the nation in volunteering. Minnesota politics is by large measure mostly liberal and progressive with deep roots in the labor movement. Minnesota's Finnish community was instrumental in the

American labor movement, as described above. The number of Minnesota Finns belonging to the I.W.W. made Minnesota one of the chief battlegrounds in the American labor movement, and although labor culture has subsided elsewhere in the United States, it is still important in Minnesota. Minnesota was also important in the organization of farmers and the Farmers Union.

Minnesota was fertile ground for multiple political parties. Minnesota was also home to communist and socialist political parties and was also home to the separate Labor and Farmer parties. The Farmer and Labor parties in Minnesota merged into the Minnesota Farmer Labor Party, which dominated Minnesota politics through the twentieth century. In 1948 it merged with the minority Minnesota Democratic Party to become the Democratic Farmer Labor Party (DFL), which is the only independent state or minor party to be allowed to affiliate with either major national party. Noted DFL politicians include former Vice President Hubert Humphrey, who served under President Johnson and ran for President in 1968 (he lost to Nixon), former Vice President Walter Mondale, who served under Carter as Vice President and ran for president in 1984, losing to Ronald Reagan, and former Senator Eugene McCarthy who ran for President in 1968 as an Anti-War candidate. It was McCarthy's surprising showing in the early 1968 presidential primaries that caused President Johnson to not run for another term. Minnesota usually votes Democratic in presidential elections, including 1984, when it was the only state to vote for Mondale against Ronald Reagan's re-election.

Minnesota was one of a half dozen states that voted for Teddy Roosevelt and his Bull Moose Progressive Party in 1912 elections. They also elected an Independent professional wrestler, Jesse Ventura, for Governor in 1998.

Other quirks about Minnesota's Scandinavian culture include the sport of ice fishing, as shown in the movie *Grumpy Old Men*. Minnesota is known as the land of 10,000 lakes (there are actually well over 15,000). Although some people just walk out on the frozen winter lakes and cut a hole in the ice to fish, many people use a shelter which is known as "the fish house" or "the ice house." These are usually small square wood-frame buildings with a little heater that can be towed onto the ice by car, truck or snowmobile to a suitable location for fishing. Many Minnesota lakes have whole cities of these fish houses, and some have actual streets that are located in the same place each year and are snow plowed for easy access. They can also be problematic. A very large lake, Lake Mille Lacs, developed a problem with fish houses as these little hovels were stored in the summer for a few dollars per season on private property along the shorelines. Their working-class owners, who couldn't afford real lake cabins or homes, began to use and live in their fish houses as summer lake cabins. As there were no bathrooms or other facilities to serve these unwanted squatters, the Mille Lacs County Board outlawed their summer and shoreline use on the grounds of sanitation and other health concerns. Many ice fishermen are also known for heavy drinking, especially given that local sheriffs lack the equipment to patrol on ice.

Another cultural quirk in Minnesota, which was also shown in the movie *Fargo*, is the almost cult like appreciation that many Minnesotans have for wildlife art. Throughout the state limited edition wildlife prints are lavishly displayed in homes and businesses. In Minnesota, wildlife artists compete fiercely each year to have their art chosen for the federal and state duck hunting stamp, and many Minnesotans with no artistic talent wait each year for the chance to buy the signed prints of this chosen art, as the duck stamp is thought to be the epitome of greatness for this kind of art.

"Minnesota Nice" is another feature of Scandinavian culture. Minnesotans are found to be both friendly and very polite. It is a cultural taboo, unacceptably rude, to confront, anger, or hurt another. Minnesotans will go out of their way to not be rude to anyone. Many times this behavior is more habit than friendliness, and it is not always what it appears to be. It is also sometimes passive aggressive. One of the more amusing things about Minnesota Nice is that at a four-way traffic stop, drivers will motion other drivers to go, whether they have the right of way or not, and frequently there will be a delay in the traffic as everyone is too polite to go for fear of being perceived as rude. This has changed somewhat in the Twin Cities metropolitan area where many residents are no longer Minnesota natives. Part of Minnesota Nice is the long goodbye. It is rude to just say goodbye once and leave too quickly, so a departure in Minnesota can take some time and several good-byes.

Cleanliness and neatness is another German and Scandinavian trait. Visitors to Minnesota will notice the lack of litter, the cleanliness of public buildings and bathrooms and the neatness in most homes.

As is true of most subcultures in America, Minnesota's Scandinavian subculture is starting to fade as mobile Americans move from place to place bringing their language, culture, and habits to Minnesota. The Twin Cities of Minneapolis and St. Paul and their suburbs serve as an economic magnet attracting workers and new residents from the surrounding states of Wisconsin, Iowa, and North and South Dakota, and beyond. Minnesota culture is also changing as new immigration groups particularly large groups of the Hmong, Somali, Canadians and Russians, along with some Latinos, have come to live and work in Minnesota.

Other European Americans

There are also many Americans who are descendants from other European countries. These descendants are as follows: about 1.7 million Czechs, 1.5 million Hungarians, 1.5 million Portuguese, 1.3 million Greeks, about 900,000 each, Ukrainians and Swiss, about 700,000 Lithuanians and Austrians, 500,000 Romanians, 400,000 Armenians, 300,000 Belgians, 200,000 Serbs and Georgians, about 100,000 Bulgarians and Latvians, about 57,000 Basque, 38,000 Albanians, 31,000 Maltese, and 25,000 Estonians.

Chapter 7. Canadian-Americans, Jewish-Americans, Polynesians and Mixed Races

Canadian-Americans

There are about a million people in the US of Canadian descent and many more Canadians who live in the US legally and illegally, plus many Canadian "snowbirds" who leave Canada to winter in the southern Sun Belt each year. Much of Canadian culture is very similar to the United States, which gives Canadians in the US a cultural invisibility, and because most Canadians are of White European ancestry (unlike the Latino population), many people in the US have no objection to their immigration, legal or not. In Minnesota and northern New England, there are likely as many or more illegal Canadians as Latinos, but there is little concern about this. Governor Tim Pawlenty of Minnesota made a speech about illegal immigration which he said was negatively affecting Minnesota, and he said he would contact the Mexican Ambassador to voice his concerns. He did not express any concern about Minnesota's illegal Canadian population nor did he want to contact the Canadian Ambassador, perhaps because the Canadians come every weekend into Minnesota to shop in Minnesota stores and gamble at the Indian casinos.

Under appreciated by many in the US, Canada does have a separate culture. Canadians are very sensitive to these cultural differences and sincerely wish to not be seen as just a northern appendage or suburb of the United States. It has become such a concern in Canada that in 2000 the Molson Beer Company, noting this sensitivity, televised an ad called "I am a Canadian" which featured an actor who became known as "Joe Canada."

In this ad Joe stands in front of a movie screen showing images of Canada and

Canadian culture, as he delivers a rant which includes: "I am not a lumberjack or fur trader, I believe in diversity not assimilation, peacekeeping not policing, the last letter of the alphabet is zed, not zee; I have a prime minister not a president, I don't live in an igloo, I say 'about' not 'aboot,' and the beaver is a proud and noble animal. I speak English and French, not American. We are the first nation of hockey and we are the best part of North America." It ends with and "And my name is Joe and I am a Canadian!"

It was done with humor, but it became wildly popular overnight, striking a nerve in Canada with thousands of Canadians reciting it and cheering patriotically when the ad was seen or recited in public places. It touched a vein of subterranean anti-Americanism as Canadians resent being perceived as a second class US culture. This unexpected Canadian jingoism caused a Canadian reporter to lament: "Imagine if an American beer company did an anti-Canadian commercial and how much this would offend Canadians; but then Americans would never think that much about Canada." In an ironic twist the commercial was ended by its commercial sponsor when the Canadian Molson Beer Company was acquired and merged into the American Coors Beer Company.

The British, French and Native Peoples' cultural influences are perhaps deeper and much more noticeable in Canada than in the US. One of the impacts Canadian culture has on American culture is that it enhances and renews US ties to these three cultural roots.

One of the more interesting Canadian influences was caused by what is known as the Canadian Shield or the Laurentian Plateau. It is an area of tough, exposed igneous rock that runs down the middle of Canada from the Arctic to the Lake Superior and into the US in northern Minnesota. It was such a barrier that travel from eastern to western Canada was greatly inhibited, so much so that well into the twentieth century much of the east–west Canadian travel dipped into the United States under the Canadian Shield and along US Highway 2 through Minnesota, which humorously became known as "The Queen's Highway" because of this Canadian traffic. "The Queen's Highway" also encouraged Canadians to settle in Minnesota and people from the US to settle in western Canada in significant numbers. This Canada–US east–west traffic was also enhanced along the Soo Line and the Duluth, South Shore, and Atlantic Railroads which were subsidiaries of the Canadian Pacific Railway running from Sault Ste. Marie, Canada, through Michigan's Upper Peninsula, northern Wisconsin, and northern Minnesota, then turning sharply north to Winnipeg, Canada.

Minnesota has a particular bond with Canada. Minnesota was the land of the Voyageurs, the French fur trappers and traders who were plentiful throughout Minnesota in its early history. Pig's Eye Pierre Parrant was a Canadian trapper and bootlegger who founded Minnesota's capital city of St. Paul.

Jean-Baptist Faribault was another French Canadian fur trader in Minnesota in the late eighteenth and early nineteenth centuries. In the War of 1812, the British required Canadian men to serve and fight the Americans. Faribault was not fond of the British rule in Canada and he refused to serve, and as a consequence all his possessions were confiscated by the British-Canadian government. He then became a US citizen and resumed his trapping and trading in Minnesota; he became one of the state's founders. He founded the present day city that has his name, Faribault, and in southern Minnesota a county was also named for him. He donated a house that became the first Catholic Church in Minnesota. He was a generous man and much of his trading success was due to his good relations and fair dealing with the Native population. He was admired equally by the Native Americans and the White settlers.

Canadians have made their impact in New England and many cities have sections that were or are still called "Little Canada." While most of these have been assimilated, the Canadians, particularly the French Canadians, have made their impact.

Some famous Canadian-Americans include actors John Candy and Dan Aykroyd and writer Jack Kerouac (who was very proud of his French Canadian background), and Thomas Edison. That's right, Edison. Although he was born in the US, his father was a Canadian revolutionary and patriot who was forced to flee to the US because of his participation in the McKenzie Rebellion of 1837 which sought to overthrow the British-Canadian government. Edison's father insisted that he and his children were exiled Canadians forced to live in the United States.

Jewish-Americans

In the US, "Jewish-American" is less a religious designation and more a cultural ethnicity. Jews were present in the American colonies as early as the seventeenth century, but in small numbers. Jewish-Americans are primarily Yiddish speaking Ashkenazi but come from many nationalities. In the early days of the American colonies, a small number of Sephardic Jews of Portuguese and Spanish nationalities came to settle. Because of discrimination against their religion they could not hold office, but by the end of the eighteenth century they were allowed to participate in most civic activities. During the Civil War the Union Army even employed a Rabbi Chaplin for the first time.

The numbers of Jewish-Americans remained small until the nineteenth century when large numbers of Ashkenazi Jews began arriving from Germany due to rising anti-Semitism. Many Ashkenazi emigrated and some who stayed in Germany, like Karl Marx's father, converted to Lutheranism to avoid persecution. Most of these new American immigrants were middle class shopkeepers or had skilled professions. There were 250,000 mostly Yiddish speaking Ashkenazi Jews in the US by 1880. They faced a good deal of discrimination.

In 1880 Jewish immigration to the US increased dramatically as persecution and economic woes in Russia and Eastern Europe pushed many Jews to emigrate. Many of these were Yiddish speaking Ashkenazi. About 2,000,000 came in the years from 1880 to 1924. After 1924, US immigration quotas began to tighten significantly. New York City has the largest concentrations of Jews of any major world city, as the Jewish population mostly settled the large cities of the Northeastern US. Jewish-Americans are now residents of many US cities. The Jewish population of the United States of over five million people is either the largest in the world, or second to that of Israel, depending on the definitions of who is Jewish. The state of New York has by far the largest population of Jewish-Americans, followed by New Jersey and Florida.

Although many Jews were highly literate and skilled when they came to the US, there is a myth that they all were skilled and had money. Some of this has to do with European biases against Jews as "moneylenders" because until the Reformation the Jews were the only moneylenders and bankers in Europe. Money lending for interest was forbidden by the Catholic Church.

In America there were many poor and working class Jews. New York's Garment District prior to World War II was but one good example of poor and working class Jewish-Americans. Before World War I most Jewish-Americans, 80%, were factory workers. However, some of this was due to discrimination and a ban against Jews in many professions and discrimination barring Jews from attending many major universities, particularly the Ivy League.

Jewish-American writers and leaders encouraged assimilation into the American culture, and they assimilated rapidly. The second and third generations quickly gave up Yiddish and their other national languages. Many of these Jewish immigrants, regardless of class or profession, were educated. In Jewish culture there is a strong demand for literacy that dates back many generations. As American professions and universities opened to Jews, they educated and pushed their children into the professions, particularly in the fields of medicine, law and finance. This high literacy rate is one reason for Jewish-Americans to be one of America's most financially successful ethnicities. However, this financial success may also be due in part to the fact that the Jewish-American population as a whole is older than the American average. The aging Jewish population and the declining Jewish-American birthrate currently indicate that the population could soon start to decline, as the birthrate below the replacement level.

American Jews during the late 19th and early 20th centuries abandoned a racial definition of Jewishness in favor of one that embraced ethnicity. This ethnicity has become more important as many Jews have intermarried, have given up their religion or are passive in religious matters, but still seek out and retain their cultural identity. By tradition, to be a Jew you had to have a Jewish mother or had to convert, but as many Jewish-Americans have intermarried it is common for the children of these marriages—with or without religious belief—to claim Jewish ethnicity and culture.

Politically, Jewish-Americans have been aligned with liberals in the Democratic Party. Many Jewish-Americans were instrumental in the American labor movement and were attracted to leftist causes. This attraction to the left also occurred because of the considerable bias against Jews which persisted well into the twentieth century. They (like many other immigrant groups) were discriminated against in many civic and professional fields. However, they received the support of liberals and progressives like President Franklin Roosevelt, who included Jews in his administration, and Governors Al Smith of New York and Floyd Olson of the Minnesota Farmer Labor Party, who did likewise in their state governments. As a result Roosevelt received 90% of the Jewish-American vote in his presidential elections in 1940 and 1944 and Smith and Olson received similar support in their elections.

Recently some Jewish-Americans have begun to affiliate with the right and Republicans. Much of this is because of the strong military posturing from the right and Republicans for the support of Israel and for military action in the Mideast. It was these issues that caused Jewish-American and Democratic Senator Joe Lieberman, who was Al Gore's running mate in 2000, to switch sides and back Republican Senator John McCain for president in 2008 against Barack Obama. Lieberman even considered the idea of running with McCain as Vice President on the Republican ticket, but the idea was vetoed by conservative Republicans who threatened to split the party if Lieberman was on the ticket.

The Jewish-Americans were instrumental in the civil rights movement, the women's rights movement and the gay rights movement. A number of Jewish leaders have suggested that support for these human rights movements have their foundation in the history of discrimination against the Jews, particularly the Holocaust, which has made them more empathetic to these causes. Jewish-Americans were supporters and help found the NAACP. They were advocates in the civil rights demonstrations in the 1950s and 1960s. Betty Friedan and her 1963 book, *The Feminine Mystique*, launched the second women's rights movement in America.

Because of this sustained long term multi-generational devotion to universal literacy among Jewish-Americans, they have also been very prominent in the American arts. Although Jewish-Americans have been a strong influence in all the arts, their strongest contributions have been in the performing arts and entertainment fields. The list of Jewish-American musicians and songwriters, singers, comedians, and actors is impressive, but perhaps the most impact they have made has been in the film and television industries. Jewish-Americans were some of the earliest pioneers in this industry. Hollywood and New York are filled with Jewish-American writers, producers, directors, agents. Many of the early moguls of Hollywood were Jewish-Americans. Some have speculated that the new film and television industries emerged so quickly that discrimination never had a chance to become institutionalized and Jewish-Americans seeking opportunities quickly filled these new arts. Others have suggested that the arts and entertainment industries were more open to different people and groups. Regardless of cause, the American film, television and entertainment industry owes much of its heritage and success to Jewish-Americans.

One of the darker professions that some Jewish-Americans took up was organized crime. Jewish-Americans like Italian-Americans felt shut out of the mainstream economy. Because of this, it has been argued, some Jewish and Italian-Americans gravitated to the illegal economy where discrimination was not an issue. Jewish-Americans like Meyer Lansky, Bugsy Siegel and Mickey Cohen (who helped create Las Vegas), Arnold Rothstein (who allegedly fixed the 1919 World Series), and even Midwesterners like Isadore Blumenfeld, better known as Kid Cann, were prominent figures in American organized crime. In more recent years, Jewish-American organized crime has reappeared in the forms of both Israeli and Jewish-Russian Mafia criminal groups. Jewish-American organized crime has also supplied financial support for Israel, creating diplomatic tensions between the US and its ally. It was recently leaked that the US and Israel were at odds over visas because the US was restricting some Israeli visas due to concerns about organized crime.

In addition to arts and entertainment Jewish-Americans have made significant contributions to American cuisine, particularly with what has become known as "deli cuisine." Foods like bagels, blintzes and hummus, common foods in Central Europe and the Mideast, primarily came into American cuisine through Jewish-Americans. Many Yiddish words have become common in American English such as cockamamie, boy-chick, kosher, tucas, mensch, chutzpah, nosh, schlep, along with the expression oy vey! In New York City, up until the later part of the twentieth century there were so many people speaking a mixture of English and Yiddish that some people called the mixed language "Yinglish."

Polynesians

The Hawaiian Islands are a volcanic chain of hundreds of islands stretching over 1500 miles; they are part of the Pacific Ocean region known as Polynesia. The Kingdom of Hawaii was an independent nation from 1810 until 1893, when the Hawaiian monarchy was overthrown by America; it became an independent republic until 1898, when it was formally annexed by the United States.

Archeological evidence estimates the first human habitation occurred when Polynesians settled the islands sometime between the years AD 300 and 500. Europeans did not discover the islands until British explorer James Cook found the islands in 1778 and named them the Sandwich Islands after his financial benefactor, the Earl of Sandwich. Cook made a second visit in 1779 and got into a fight with the native Hawaiians; Cook was killed when he tried to kidnap the Hawaiian Chief to hold him for ransom, a tactic he had used successfully in Tahiti.

After the accounts of Cook's visits were published, British vessels began to visit Hawaii on a regular basis. Their visits were disastrous for the Polynesians. Like the American Indians, the Hawaiians had no immunity to the European diseases, and influenza, small pox and measles killed as much as half of the Hawaiian population. In one outbreak of measles in the early 1850s, nearly one out of every five Hawaiians died.

In 1819, Protestant missionaries from the US began to arrive in Hawaii and soon other missionaries and colonists arrived. As the American colony grew, so did American influence. The colonists eventually persuaded the US government to formally annex Hawaii in 1898, and Hawaii became a state in 1959.

In the 1780s and 1790s, a series of Hawaiian conflicts consolidated power under one ruler, Chief Kamehameha. Hawaii became a kingdom, which lasted until the American revolt in 1893. One hundred years later, in 1993, Congress and President Clinton made an apology to Hawaii for the illegal American revolt which ended the Hawaiian monarchy.

Today Hawaii has a population of about a one and a half million people of which only about ten percent are Native Hawaiians. The largest ethnicity are East Asians, which are about 39% of all Hawaiians. (The first East Asians, Chinese immigrants, came on American and British trading vessels to Hawaii in the 1780s. By now, however, most of the East Asians in Hawaii have either Filipino or Japanese ancestry.) This is followed by about 25% European Whites called "howlies" by the Native Islanders, which is a corruption of the Hawaiian word "haole" meaning stranger. Another 25% are listed as mixed race, with the small remainder being Hispanics, as a large Puerto Rican population was imported to start the Hawaiian sugar industry in 1899. Another group includes other Polynesians like Tahitians and Samoans.

Hawaii is a place with its own unique identity and strong local culture. Hawaiian culture has made an impact on American culture disproportionate to its population and size. Hawaiian words such as aloha, luau, lei, hula and poi, have crept into American English. Hawaiian music and dance have found their way into mainstream American culture. The steel guitar and the slack-key guitar style are Hawaiian influences in American music. And since December 7, 1941, there are few places in America that have had more impact on the American psyche than Pearl Harbor.

American Samoa

American Samoa in the South Pacific is the southernmost territory of the United States. It is very distant and very small. It is much closer to Australia than to North America and has a population of only about 56,000. However Pago Pago is an important naval station and port.

The first European discovery was by the Dutch in 1722 followed by the French 1768 who named them the Navigator Islands. The Samoans and the

French fought and a good number of French were killed and afterward the Samoans were feared for their ferocity for many years.

In the 1830s European missionaries began to arrive and by the late nineteenth century American, English and German trading vessels began to come regularly to the port of Pago Pago. (Pronounced Pango Pango.) In March 1889, the American and German navies almost went to war over Samoa, but a typhoon destroyed or damaged the warships of both navies and a truce was forced. In 1899 Germany and the United States agreed to divide the Samoan Islands, with the Germans obtaining the western half and the Americans the eastern half, which is now called American Samoa, with its capital at Pago Pago. Unlike Puerto Ricans, American Samoans are not citizens but are considered American Nationals; as such they may freely travel and live anywhere in the United States. However, if they have one parent born in the United States, Samoans are then considered citizens and can vote in US elections.

After the Allies defeated Germany in World War I, Western Samoa became a territory of New Zealand and remained so until 1962, when it became the first independent Pacific Island nation.

Samoan language and culture is about 3,000 years old; it is the oldest of the Polynesian cultures. Samoans have added to American Polynesian Culture. Rugby and American football is extremely popular in American Samoa and a number of Samoans have played college football and a good number have become professionals and earned their way into the National Football league.

Mixed Race

Race is a controversial subject. In pure biological terms there is no such thing. Humans are too close and intermixed to have significant differences; we all come from a common ancestor less than 200,000 years ago and have been inter-marrying since. Any geneticist will tell you there are too few differences to significantly matter. If you take the darkest skinned person on the planet with all their friends and relatives and put them in the arctic for a hundred generations, they will likely be light, and if you take the lightest skinned person with all their friends and relatives in the tropics for a hundred generations they will likely be dark, and that is race. Race, as we humans tend to divide ourselves, is much more about cultural groupings. And even considering these man-made cultural groupings, far too many of us are of mixed cultural backgrounds and in common terms are considered "mixed-race" or "bi-racial."

The US Census has struggled with racial designations as the population is continuously crossing these cultural divisions. Most African-Americans are of both European and African ancestry and many have some Native-American ancestry. Many European-Americans have some Native-American ancestry, and some African ancestry. There are a growing number of non Asian-Americans who have some Asian ancestry. It became such a difficult issue that the Census needed some definitions. In 1997 the Office of Management and Budget developed some guidelines to tabulate race and ethnicity. They established five groups: White, African-American or Black, Native American or Alaskan Native, Asian, and Native Hawaiian or Pacific Islander. In the 2000 Census for the first time a person answering the Census was also allowed to respond that they were of two or more of these races. However, since it is a self-identifying response, and since many Americans actually have little idea about their racial or cultural ancestry, it is really more of a general preference than an ethnic or cultural identifier.

It was for many years a taboo and a disadvantage to describe a person as being "bi-racial" or having a multi-cultural background. Even the common words and descriptions used to describe bi-racial were considered negative. Words like mulatto, half-breed, and miscegenation, all have negative connotations—and up until the 1960s there were laws against miscegenation in many places. In 1954 President Eisenhower explained Southern sentiment to Chief Justice Earl Warren, the author of the *Brown vs. Board of Education* decision that desegregated schools, by saying: "All they are concerned about is to see that their sweet little White girls are not required to sit in schools alongside some big Black bucks."

The thought of inter-racial sex was enough to send even moderates to extremes in the 1950s. American culture has grown and changed very rapidly in the last half of the twentieth century. Now many people are acknowledging their multi-ethnic and racial ancestry. Keeping in mind that there are many more multi-racial people than were reported in the 2000 Census, because this is a voluntary self-reporting, here are the following results:

People who reported that they are mixed White and Native-American were about seven million, which is about two million more than are Native-American. People who identified themselves as White and African American were about 700,000, a number we know to be much, much lower than the reality. Those who claimed to be White-Asian were also about 700,000. Those claiming Black–Native American ancestry were about 180,000, and White-Native Hawaiian and Pacific Islander (Polynesian) were about 125,000. All these numbers are very low and not very reflective of the actual realities, but it is beginning to show the real diversity of the United States. According to geneticist Mark Shriver at Morehouse College, fifty-eight percent of African-American people have the equivalent of at least one great-grandparent who was White European.

Black Indians

Certain tribes in the Southern part of the United States had very close contact with the Black African slaves, particularly the "Five Civilized Tribes": the Creek, the Chickasaw, the Cherokee, the Choctaw and the Seminoles. All of these tribes had Black slaves, but unlike the White slavery,

Native slavery was usually considered a temporary state before release or adoption into the tribe. Native slavery came from battles won, whereby conquered tribes, particularly the women, spent a certain time as slaves with the victors before being either adopted, or inter-marrying, or being released back to their original tribe. The Native Americans did this with their Black slaves as well. And Blacks captured in raids either became part of the tribe or were released or freed, or at least as free as an African-American could be in pre-Civil War America. Frequently the "freed" would stay with the tribe, as there were few other places to go without re-enslavement by Whites or even other tribes.

The consequence of the Native ownership of Black slaves was that there were a lot of Native-Black children born and raised as Native Americans. They became known as "the Black Seminole" and the "Black Cherokee," etc.

In 1866, the US Army ordered the Five Tribes, who had been loyal to the Confederacy, to free their Black slaves and to grant them membership in their tribes. Some were more welcoming than others. The Seminole accepted the Black Seminole, while the Cherokee were racially biased against the Black Cherokee and accepted them only because they were forced to do so.

As the US began to develop her policies about Native peoples, the Dawes Act of 1887 was created to divide communal reservation land of the Five Tribes into private property. So a legal rule defining who was Native and who would get this land was developed. It was designed to exclude the Black Cherokee, who did not receive land and where deprived of any federal benefits; and they lost their legal designation as Native Americans. Oddly enough, the act really didn't benefit the Indians on the whole. Those Native Americans on the government roles were given very small parcels of land, and the majority of the "Indian land" was then sold at auction to Whites. The Act sought to limit the number of Native Americans so as to limit the amount of land given to them. The federal government gave the Native Americans land on reservations in exchange for moving off their original lands that Whites wanted, and then the Whites stole this new land from them as well.

In 2011, in an election supervised by the Carter Center, the Black Cherokee were allowed to vote and participate in Cherokee tribal elections and assert their rights. The federal government has finally recognized and allowed the Black Cherokee to begin to claim their Native heritage.

Rosa Parks, the early civil rights leader who was arrested after she refused to give up her seat on a bus to a White man in Montgomery, Alabama, was a descendant of the Black Cherokee.

Chapter 8. The American Language

The proposal to formally make English the official language of the United States is ironic, if not idiotic. The movement has to do with xenophobic American fears that one day we will wake up and everyone will be speaking Spanish or Chinese. Preserving an "official language" raises the poignant question, just what is it that you are trying to preserve? English has many dialects and American English is a composite of many languages, including a lot of Spanish loan words. And like all languages it is constantly changing and borrowing words from other languages. If you have doubts about how fast it is changing read the following sentence: "LOL, M @ the apt. Wear R U? ☺" As illiterate as this sentence may seem, most of us can read it, and for a younger generation it is becoming the norm. Even how we write and what we write upon is rapidly changing because of electronics. This book will be written with very little use of pens, pencils and paper, and many if not most of its eventual copies will be electronic and not paper.

American English is changing in many ways. It is changing because of technology, as in email and texting, as well as in new scientific and technological innovations and discoveries requiring new words. The word "television" is a good example of this. Prior to its invention and then use in the middle of the twentieth century, there was no word for television. Now this word is not only common in English, but it is used in many other languages. Many thousands of new words were created in the last half of the twentieth century just to accommodate new technology.

American English is also constantly changing through its exposure to other languages and cultures, and this is not a new or recent phenomenon. As stated earlier, "American" English is a good part Spanish, as many of our words for Western culture come from Spanish, such as ranch, corral patio, lasso, along with hundreds of others. American English also evolved under the influence of French,

African, Polynesian, Asian and Native American languages and many other borrow words and concepts that come from many other languages.

Slang and colloquialisms are constantly changing the English language, especially as spoken in America. The word "okay," or worse, "okie-dokie," is not exactly the language of Shakespeare. And that is the point: American English is not the language of Shakespeare. All languages evolve over time, some more rapidly than others.

Even the English language of Shakespeare was a polyglot. English is a Germanic language, as are German, Dutch, Swedish, Danish, Norwegian, as is the Jewish language of Yiddish. They all came from a common linguistic ancestor. The closest thing to old English as it first came to the British Isles is the Dutch language of Frisian. In the British Isles, English picked up vocabulary from the Celtic languages, especially "four letter" Celtic words which are considered taboo, more because they are Celtic than because they are "swear words." The Latinized or Greek-based English version of these words is not taboo. They are considered to be the usable and the "polite" forms of these words with which we describe body parts, body functions and procreation. Even the out-dated custom of not "swearing" in front of a lady came from middle class English fears of that if a woman heard these "filthy" Celtic words she might then teach them to her children. It was a class thing, and still is, as these "four letter" words are the language of the working class. While people of all classes in America use these words, it is their frequency and their public use that divide the classes. American working class language is informal and includes these four letter words, while middle class and leisure class use more formal English and eliminate these words as well as most slang and other colloquialisms.

Formal language is also the language of American business and schools, which is why the American working class sometimes struggles to fit into these situations. If you want to understand these class differences in American language, then think of the language that is used by laborers, or in the military, in a working man's bar and at construction sites, versus the language used at banks, churches and universities.

In addition to Celtic words and phrases that found their way into English, the Romans came and conquered England during the years AD 43 to 409, and the "barbarian" language of English was further enriched, or corrupted, by Latin — as much or more than a quarter of the modern English language is derived from Latin. Written English is Latin script with an alphabet that replaced the old Anglo-Saxon runes. It was very similar to the Scandinavian runes.

The constant invasions of the Viking Norsemen also changed the English language, with at least two percent of modern English coming from words of the Norse languages. In 1066 the Normans invaded England and the English language was dramatically changed with the addition of many words from Old French, which was also Latin-based. Modern English has more than a quarter of its words from Old French. (There is some overlap with some

English words from Latin which were changed or modified by French words.) These French language changes also came with some new linguistic concepts like surnames. Prior to the Norman invasion, an Englishman said he was Robert from Trent, or used the Norse identifier that he was Robert, Michael's son. After the Norman invasion, the English took their surnames or "last" names from their occupations, like Cook, Smith, Fisher, Potter, Farmer, Lawyer, Carter, Mason, Carpenter, etc., which is why these are such common English surnames.

American English as we have seen has been changed dramatically from sixteenth century English with the addition of at least 10,000 Spanish words, along with many Native-American words, and adding even more French words, along with African, Asian and Polynesian and other words.

African languages were all but forbidden in America, and slaves were usually beaten for speaking their native tongues. Furthermore, they spoke so many different languages and dialects that it is not surprising that these languages died out in America except for what are called pidgins, which are simplified versions of mixed languages, such as Gullah, which was spoken in Georgia and South Carolina, and Creole in Louisiana. However, some West African language patterns have survived and have influenced American English.

African American Vernacular English, AAVE, is now recognized by many linguists as a dialect of English because of its specific logical structure. A majority of Americans consider AAVE to be slang or a poor or uneducated version of Standard American English, and while AAVE is primarily an African-American dialect, it isn't exclusive to Blacks. In fact many Southern rural Whites also use the dialect. The Southern accent shows strong influences from African languages and AAVE. And while AAVE originated in the South, many Northern Blacks with Southern roots still use AAVE despite having lived for multiple generations in the North. It is also common for AAVE speakers to "code switch," meaning in the workplace or a formal setting they will use Standard American English while using AAVE in more informal, friendly and family settings. Elements of Black slang and AAVE have found their way into modern mainstream American culture through music, television and movies.

Although English was first spoken and contained on a little group of British Islands unconnected with the rest of Europe, the English language was never destined to be culturally monolithic. Defining the size of English is rather like describing the size of a rapidly inflating balloon. With the Oxford English Dictionary (Second Edition) listing over 600,000 definitions, English may well be considered the largest language in the world.

The idea of inventing a universally spoken world language, like "Esperanto," has died largely because English is now the world language. English has quickly become the language of science and business because of its ability to precisely describe scientific and technical concepts. Over 375 million people speak English as their first or only language. However a whopping 500 million to a billion, depending on how fluency is described, speak English as their second language. Combining native and secondary speakers makes English the most widely-used language of the world. Chinese may be a close second, depending how their many dialects are classified. American English is also the fastest growing language in China, as many Chinese are now learning it as their second language.

American English magazines, books, internet traffic, movies, television, and music, have inundated the world market and can be found in the remotest places on the planet. Other dialects of English such as Australian, British, Canadian, New Zealand and South African English, and even small sub-dialects like Cockney English, are being swamped by their exposure to American English and they are changing to conform. However, some of these dialects are also having an impact on American English, such as the incorporation of Australian words like "bloke" and "outback" which have come into American usage.

English is also the official world language of aeronautical and maritime communications and is the most taught foreign language in the world. As it is used in other countries, it is also constantly being changed and added to with borrow words from other languages along with new words describing scientific and technological advances coming from the United States as well as from the other English and non-English speaking countries.

The thought that an act of Congress is necessary to insure the continuation of American English when, in fact, this language has gained such worldwide usage, would be laughable if it wasn't so tragically rooted in American White bias and xenophobic fears against Latinos and Americans who speak Spanish, Asian or other languages.

CHAPTER 9. AMERICAN RELIGION AND BELIEF SYSTEMS

> Puritanism was hewed out of the Black Forests of feudal Europe and the American wilderness.....Puritanism, therefore, is an American heritage to be grateful for and not sneered at because it required everyone to attend Divine worship and maintain a strict code of ethics.
>
> —American historian Samuel Eliot Morrison

> Recognition of the Supreme Being is the first, the most basic, expression of Americanism
>
> —President Dwight D. Eisenhower

> We have to keep our god placated with prayers, and even then we are never sure of him. How much higher and finer is the Indian's god? Our illogical god is all-powerful in name, but impotent in fact; the Great Spirit is not all-powerful, but does the very best he can for the Indian and does it free of charge.
>
> —Mark Twain

> Islam is a religion of hatred. It's a religion of war.
>
> —Reverend Franklin Graham in the August 30, 2010, issue of Time Magazine, "Does America Hate Islam?"

> I don't think atheists should be considered citizens or patriots. We are 'one nation under god.'
>
> —President George Herbert Walker Bush

According to the American Religious Identification Survey (ARIS), in 2008 American's religious affiliation is as follows: 76% are Christians, 1.2% Jewish,

0.6% Muslims, 0.5% are Buddhists, 2.1% other religions, and 15% gave the response as having no religion, or were atheists or agnostics. The remainder refused to answer. Of the Christians in the ARIS Survey, 51.5% were Protestant and 24.5% were Catholics.

Americans are many times more religious than other peoples. The historian Alexis De Tocqueville wrote: "Religious insanity is very common in the United States." A 2011 Gallup Poll found that 92% of Americans believe in god, with more than 9 in 10 Americans still saying "yes" when asked the basic question "Do you believe in god?" According to a 2005 Eurostat Eurobarometer Poll, only 47% of Germans, 34% of the French, and 38% of the British believed in god. In Catholic Italy and Ireland, the numbers were much higher than the rest of Europe, with 74% of Italians and 73% of the Irish believing in god. But that's still much lower than in the United States. In Scandinavia, belief is much less, with 32% of Norwegians, 31% of Danes and only 23% of Swedes saying they believed in god. American religious fervor can be compared to the Islamic fervor in many countries today. Although many people in the United States would greatly disdain this comparison, their disdain has more to do with the fact they are biased against Muslims. For example Americans, particularly conservative Christian America, have a much higher tolerance level for Christian misogyny than Muslim misogyny.

There are regional differences in religion in the United States. According to a 2013 Pew Forum on Religion and Public Life, the Midwest most closely models the overall religious makeup of America. The South, by a large margin, is the most deeply religious and has the heaviest concentration of evangelical Protestant churches. The Northeast, while known as a "WASP" stronghold (White Anglo-Saxon Protestants), also has the greatest concentration of Catholics and Jews. The West is the least religious and has the largest proportion of unaffiliated people; a larger percent of Westerners are atheists and agnostics.

The Pew Forum also reported that African-Americans are the most religious group in America. Hindus and Jews are the most educated, with half of all Hindus and a third of all Jews having advanced degrees compared to one in ten in the general population. Not surprisingly, these groups also report higher income levels than the other religious groups. Jews and Buddhists also report the lowest percent of followers having an absolute belief in god or a higher power, with only 39% of Buddhists believing in a higher power and only 41% of Jews believing in god. Other religions that have an absolute belief in god or a higher power are as follows: 93% for Jehovah's Witnesses, 90% for Protestant Evangelicals, 90% for African-American Churches, 82% of Muslims, and 72% of Catholics. The largest groups of American Christians are the Baptists, which make up 20% of the total population and two thirds of all African-Americans.

American Buddhists are primarily White European converts and only a third are Asian-Americans. Three out of four American Buddhists are converts from Christianity.

All American religions have retention problems as people leave their faith for other faiths or become atheists and agnostics, but the Pew Forum reports that Jehovah's Witnesses have the lowest retention rate of all: only 37% of those raised as Jehovah's Witnesses retain their religion in adulthood. The Catholic Church also has significant problems retaining those raised Catholic, with about a third leaving the Catholic Church.

Religious Americans tend to be much more conservative than those who are agnostics, atheists, or have weaker religious beliefs. The Pew Survey shows that 50% of Americans who attend church weekly state they are conservative, 31% say they are moderate and only 12% say they are liberal with the rest not answering. Those that say religion is not important affiliate as follows: 19% conservative, 38% moderate and 36% liberal.

American Religious Bias

Americans do not like atheists. In 2011 Gregory Paul and Phil Zukerman wrote in an opinion piece in the *Washington Post*: "Long after Blacks and Jews have made great strides, and even as homosexuals gain respect, acceptance and new rights, there is still a group that lots of Americans just don't like much: atheists. Those who don't believe in god are widely considered to be immoral, wicked and angry. They can't join the Boy Scouts. Atheist soldiers are rated potentially deficient when they do not score as sufficiently "spiritual" in military psychological evaluations. Surveys find that most Americans refuse or are reluctant to marry or vote for non-theists; in other words, nonbelievers are one minority still commonly denied in practical terms the right to assume office despite the constitutional ban on religious tests."

A 2007 Gallup Poll found that 54% of Americans would not vote for an atheist for President. However a 2012 Gallup Poll showed somewhat less with 43% stating they would not vote for an atheist. Some of this erosion of anti-atheist belief is likely due to Barack Obama's election which appears to have broken political barriers for many groups, not just African-Americans, however atheists still remain the group most discriminated against. Until a Supreme Court decision in 1961, atheists were restricted from holding public office, serving as witnesses in court, or serving as jurors by many state constitutions. And atheists are still required to say they belong to "one nation under god" in the Pledge of Allegiance and to "solemnly swear" to god in taking some public oaths of office. In addition to the discrimination against atheists with 43% of all Americans refusing to vote for them, the other groups are as follows: 40% would not vote for Muslims, 30% for gays and lesbians, 7% for Latinos, 6% for Jews, 5% for women and 4% for African-Americans.

The KKK and Other Religious Intolerance

The Ku Klux Klan (KKK) is a White Christian militant group that was founded to protect White-European Protestant Christian culture in the United States and to obstruct the civil liberties of African-Americans and other people of color. They are also against Catholics and Jews. It was sometimes said by Klan members that the initials KKK was to show they were against "Coons, Kikes, and Catholics." It has been one of the most powerful of all American hate groups.

The Klan was founded in 1866 by six former Confederate Army officers at Pulaski, Tennessee. In 1867, Nathan Bedford Forrest, a former Confederate general, took control of the organization and was named "The Grand Wizard." Many former Confederate soldiers soon joined the "invisible army." Clashes and power struggles among Klansmen and local political disagreements soon infected the Klan, and Forrest resigned in disgust in 1869. US federal troops aided in this decline as they sought out and disbanded the local Klan militia units or sent them into hiding. However, local units of the Klan continued to operate in secrecy in many areas.

In 1915, William J. Simmons reorganized the Klan and brought the local units into a national organization and developed many new chapters, particularly in the North. It proved to be a fruitful period for bigotry as new immigrants, especially Catholics and Jews, were arriving in large numbers—much to the consternation of many biased White Protestants. African-Americans had also begun their northward migration to Northern factory and transportation jobs, raising concerns among the Northern White working class. These new immigrants and Black migrations fanned the fires of hatred soon to be lit by the Klan. By 1921, the Klan had more than 100,000 publicly declared members and many more undeclared supporters. In 1924, over 40,000 Klansmen paraded in Washington, DC, in their hooded robes, during the Democratic National Convention. In the 1920s many politicians in the South and the Midwest felt compelled to join the Klan to get elected. The Klan was headed by the Governor of Indiana during this time.

In the late 1920s and early 1930s, the Klan had a series of horrendous scandals and committed acts of horrific violence, and this along with political in-fighting destroyed its national unity. Other Christian-Right groups like the German American Bund and the followers of Father Coughlin competed with the Klan for members, and while the Klan remained dominant in the South, it slowly lost its hold on the North to these other groups.

In the 1950s and 1960s Civil Rights era, the Klan was again rejuvenated in a fight to preserve racial segregation. But it was slowly destroyed by federal law enforcement and further decimated by groups like the Southern Poverty Law Center.

The Klan's symbol, the burning cross, is a Christian religious symbol, and the Klan was a White Protestant Christian organization—despite some Christian denials. The American Nazis and the German American Bund also had religious inspiration, taking their cues from Adolf Hitler who wrote in his book, *Mein Kampf*, "I am convinced that I am acting as an agent of our creator by fighting off the Jews, I am doing the Lord's work!"

Hitler even chose the swastika, the bent cross, as the Nazi symbol to link the Nazis to Christianity.

Anti-Semitism and anti-Catholicism have been prevalent throughout US history. Anti-Catholic riots were common prior to the twentieth century. For example in 1843, when the Catholic Bishop persuaded the Philadelphia School Board to allow the Catholic students in public schools to skip required Protestant religious exercises, the next day the Philadelphia newspapers ran headlines saying, "The Pope Reigns in Philadelphia!" The majority Protestant population became enraged and the wave of religious intolerance and violence that followed was horrific. A Protestant mob invaded the Catholic neighborhood of Kensington and burned and destroyed St. Michael's and St. Augustine Catholic Churches. They burned thirty Catholic homes and businesses to the ground and damaged and looted over one hundred other homes, leaving well over two hundred people homeless. The mob was so intent on killing all the Catholics in the city that the Federal government, fearing a wholesale slaughter, sent the Blue Jackets from the USS. *Princeton* to defend the Catholics. In the clash that followed thirty people were killed and over a hundred and fifty seriously wounded.

Jews have not always been treated well in the United States. Christian bigots have for years claimed that there was a Jewish conspiracy to dominate "Christian Whites." The United States also has a shabby track record in its treatment of Jews. An example of this frequently violent anti-Semitism occurred in 1902 on New York City's Lower East Side when a large funeral procession for a popular rabbi was halted by a group of construction workers who began hurling debris down upon the three hundred Jews in the procession. Soon many others joined in and blocked the procession, and the police were called. The police joined the rioting mob and also began to beat the Jews. Two hundred Jews, both male and female, children and adults, were severely beaten and many were hospitalized.

Religious intolerance remains a problem in the United States today. In 2011 the FBI reported that one in five hate crimes reported in the United States were due to religious bias, most of them stemming from anti-Jewish or anti-Islamic prejudice.

Popular right-wing Christian Conservatives such as Ann Coulter have become cheerleaders in an attempt to stoke the fires of religious bigotry. "We should invade their countries, kill their leaders and convert them to Christianity," Coulter said of Muslim nations. The former Attorney General John Ashcroft, the man whose duty is to enforce the laws that protect religious freedom in the United States, said in 2002, "Christianity is a faith where god sends his son to die for you, (while Islam) is a religion in which god requires you to send your son to die for him." Even the Reverend Franklin Graham, the son of Reverend Billy Graham, has come under criticism for defending his and other Christian intolerance toward Muslims; he says: "There is no tolerance under Islam." Graham also incredibly and falsely claims that Christianity is more unfairly treated in America than Islam and said, "When you mention Muhammad in a room, everyone says, that's nice, but when you mention Jesus, it polarizes the room." He has also said, "The Qur'an is inherently violent." And he defended this comment in interviews by saying: "You buy the Qur'an and read it for yourself. It is in there. The violence that it teaches is in there." In response to these American fears of Islam, the former President of Pakistan Pervez Musharraf said, "Islam teaches tolerance, not hatred; universal brotherhood, not hatred; and peace, not violence." Muhammad Ali who lost five years of his prime boxing career because he was a Muslim conscientious objector said, "I believe in the religion of Islam, because I believe in Allah and peace."

Recently the proposed construction of a new mosque in New York City became nationally controversial because many felt it was too close to the site of the planned 9/11 memorial site, even though the monument and the 9/11 tragedy have nothing to do with American Muslims.

In June of 2013, the American Muslim Advisory Council organized an event in Manchester, Tennessee, after some anti-Muslim activities. These activities included a Coffee County Commissioner who posted a picture on Facebook showing a man pointing a shotgun, with the caption, "How to wink at a Muslim." The event was to promote understanding about the American Muslim community. Featured speakers were US Attorney Bill Killian and FBI Agent Kenneth Moore. The event planners expected a crowd of 100 and were completely surprised when 600 anti-Muslim Christians showed up to protest the program. Outside the convention center Robert Spencer of Jihad Watch and Pamela Geller of "Stop the Islamization of America" made anti-Muslim hate speeches and said the government was silencing their freedom of speech by not inviting them to speak at the Muslim event.

Jihad Watch, an extremely biased anti-Muslim group, is financed by the Bradley Foundation based in Milwaukee, Wisconsin. The Bradley Foundation is a right-wing conservative group with about half a billion dollars in assets. According to the Foundation's 1998 Annual Report, it gives away more than $30 million per year. The Bradley Foundation was a supporter of an Iraq invasion in the 1990s and sent letters urging President Clinton to invade. Later they assisted Vice President Cheney and Defense Secretary Rumsfeld in a campaign to persuade Americans to support an invasion of Iraq. Stop the Islamization of America is a sister organization co-managed by Geller and Spencer. The Southern Poverty Law Center and the Anti-Defamation League list both as hate groups.

These two groups fired up the 600 attendees; their behavior became so threatening and disruptive that neither the US Attorney nor the FBI Agent could speak. The crowd's behavior became so heated that violence against the Muslims and the speakers was feared, and the FBI stopped the event to prevent violence. A local attendee, Elaine Smith, told the press that the audience was so menacing that she was afraid for her safety. Smith said, "I came here because I wanted to learn something ... but I couldn't hear because the audience was so disrespectful. I cried when I got here. It makes me really sad especially because these people say they're Christians. The god I worship doesn't teach hate."

Contrary to the freedom of religion that Americans like to preach, US culture and history is littered with religious intolerance.

America is also not very secular despite its claims, nor is there any real separation of the Christian churches and the state. American society requires adherence to the Christian religion in the military, in government oaths, by having military and government chaplains, and by placing religion on the currency and in the Pledge of Allegiance. Even the body which protects freedom of religion, the Supreme Court, opens its sessions with a Christian prayer. Until recent legal action by the American Civil Liberties Union, many local governments had the Ten Commandments and other Judeo-Christian religious symbols physically enshrined and displayed in their institutions. American culture has been dominated by Protestant Christian culture, but it is changing as new religions are taking a larger share and as the great number of American atheists and agnostics continues to grow. It is these changes that are causing right-wing Christian rhetoric to get louder and more adamant as they continue to demand to remain "America's religion."

American Religious Extremism

> Religious frenzy often passed into sexual orgy, and as dusk came on, the preacher played on the emotional nature of his hearers, he would be surrounded by a mass of humanity in which all intellectual control had been released, some falling insensible, some writhing in fits, some crawling and barking like dogs, some having the 'jerks' and others throwing themselves as couples on the ground or among the trees in frenzies of passion.
>
> —Historian James Truslow Adams describing 19th century evangelical Christian tent revivals.

As stated by the historian Alexis De Tocqueville, "Religious insanity is very common in the United States." And religious extremism is a significant part of American history and culture. Like the revival of radical Islam, American Fundamentalist Christians share many basic beliefs that have serious negative impacts. Advocates of both beliefs will frequently show a disdain for, disbelief in and suspicion of science; they are frequently anti-intellectual, placing "faith" above reason and evidence. They often display religious intolerance which can sometimes manifest itself as racism.

The Puritan ethic was in fact a fairly extremist religious movement, which is why they left England in the first place. In a point that is generally overlooked, the Puritans came seeking religious freedom, for themselves, but they were not seeking universal religious freedom. They were interested in finding a place to practice their own strict religion and to exclude all others. They regularly burned, branded and hanged dissidents as witches and were so superstitious as to make medieval Europe appear rational and moderate. They were also rigid, cruel and lacked basic empathy. If you were poor or sick, it was because you deserved it and god meant it to be. If you were wealthy, it was because you were more deserving and god wished it upon you. The Puritans accepted the European concept of the Divine Right of Kings, and Predestination said if you were a king then you deserved to be, because god wanted you to be, and if you were a poor peasant then you deserved that, because god wanted it to be. It is a concept that by and large has stuck in American culture.

A *Time* magazine article published in 2006, *Does God Want You to Be Rich?* found that 61% of Americans believed god could make you rich, with almost a third of Americans believing that if you gave your money to the church, then god would make you rich. Sociologist Robert K. Merton called this phenomenon the Matthew effect, from a Biblical verse in the Gospel of Matthew (25:29) in the King James Version. It states: "For whosoever hath, to him shall be given, and he shall have more abundance: but whosoever hath not, from him shall be taken away even that he hath." Originally this verse was used as a socialist criticism of capitalism, but it has now become the opposite as Christian-Conservatives of the religious right now cite the Biblical verse to justify their harsh world outlook. Ironically these Christian conservatives are also creationists and disavow Darwin's theories and the concept of evolution, but incredibly they will use the phrase "survival of the fittest" to justify their beliefs. They also falsely attribute the phrase to Darwin. Darwin didn't advocate "survival of the fittest"; his theories were about "natural selection." The concept and phrase "survival of the fittest" originally came from the English sociologist and conservative political theorist Herbert Spencer, but it has been also falsely credited to American sociologist Robert K. Merton.

America's bias against the poor started in colonial times with the Jamestown precept, "If any shouldn't work, neither should he eat" (2 Thessalonians 3:10). It was reinforced by the Puritan Work Ethic. It is now used as a conservative and Republican standard for welfare and the care of the poor and helpless. The interesting thing about this phrase is that when it was first spoken it had nothing to do with the poor. During the early Jamestown days, wealthy and middle class colonists spent most of their days out searching for gold, and as a result not enough food was being grown to feed the colony. In response, the leaders demanded everyone do his/her fair share of planting and growing and said, "If any[one] shouldn't work, neither should he eat."

The promotion of the Work Ethic philosophy and survival of the fittest has led many to believe that the poor and sick are deserving of their fate and to believe the government should not "interfere" by providing social programs or assistance. This philosophy is now the bedrock of Christian-Conservatives and the Republican Party and why they fight programs like Social Security, Medicare, National Health Insurance, Food Stamps, Welfare, Public Housing, Senior Housing, Head Start, Senior Nutrition and Meals on Wheels, and even Student Loans. And it likely explains why, at the same time, they have no problem subsidizing big business, oil companies and agriculture while keeping taxes low on the wealthy and their corporations. As one of America's most noteworthy historians, Samuel Eliot Morrison, said, "Puritanism appealed to merchants because they taught that man could serve god as well in business or a profession, as by taking Holy Orders."

The Revivalist Movement

The Puritans were not the only extremist religious movement influencing America. The American Revivalist Movement led by Jonathan Edwards began in 1734 at North Hampton, Massachusetts. In 1736 Edwards published a book entitled *A Faithful Narrative of the Surprising Work of God in the Conversion of Many Hundred Souls in North Hampton,* and the American Revivalist Movement swept the nation. Copies were printed in Boston, London and Edinburgh. It was also translated into German and Dutch.

This inspired John Wesley to break away from the Church of England to form the Methodist Church. And although revivalism was slower to gain traction in the cities, it soon became the dominant religion of rural America. At this time more than eighty percent of America was rural. Soon the road revivalist and the camp and tent revival meetings and Fundamentalist Christianity became a common thread in the rural American fabric. This was how people socialized. This was where they heard music and where they developed friendships and met their marriage partners.

In the nineteenth century, a rural area of upstate New York along the Erie Canal known as "The Burned Over District" became infamous for its creation of new and different extremist religious groups. This name came from Charles G. Finney, the Presbyterian minister who led the Second Great Awakening. Finney claimed that the area was so well evangelized that there were no more souls to convert or "burn." One new religious group that was born in the District was the Church of the Latter Day Saints, also called the Mormons. Its founder Joseph Smith was a "ne'er do well" who had bounced around New England, having moved ten times before landing back on his parents' farm in Palmyra, New York. Smith claimed that an angel of the Lord visited him one night and told him where some magic golden plates were buried on his parent's farm. Smith claimed they were written in a strange and ancient Indian language, but fortunately he claimed to have a magic pair of spectacles in his pocket at the time which allowed only Smith to see and read them. Smith then wrote the contents of the golden plates on paper and they were published as the Book of Mormon. The book became the foundation for an odd polygamist cooperative theology. Smith declared himself the "Head Prophet" of the new religion. He claimed god spoke through him. The new religion allowed Smith to acquire twenty-seven wives over the next five years, some as young as ten years of age. The religion attracted many men with the same ambitions and desires.

Although the Mormon Church officially banned polygamy and child brides in the 1890s as part of an agreement with the federal government, the practice has secretly continued. In 2002 Tom Green, a thirty-seven year old Mormon, was convicted of statutory rape, polygamy, welfare fraud, and failure to pay child support. At the time he was living with five wives and twenty-nine children in a compound in Utah. He had just taken his thirteen-year-old step-daughter as a new wife. The only reason he was caught and prosecuted was that he appeared on a national television show to talk about his life and the Mormon life-style. Mormonism is today alive and well in America, as is demonstrated by the fact that one of the elders of the Mormon Church, Mitt Romney, became the Republican Party's presidential candidate in 2012.

In 1843, the Burned Over District produced another prophet. William Miller of Hampton, New York, received a vision from god that told him that on October 22, the Second Coming of Christ would occur. Miller gained thousands of followers who believed his vision. Miller told them they must give away all their land, money and possessions by that date and find the highest spots near the sky so that god would recognize them. On the night of October 22, 1843, Miller's thousands climbed trees and hills, stood on the tops of barns and buildings awaiting the Second Coming; when it didn't occur, they climbed off their high perches and rioted.

In Lebanon, New York, also in the District, two women who called themselves Mother Ann Lee and Jemima Wilkinson founded the Celibate Shakers Communities. These were cooperative Christian communities that were anti-sex, believing that sex was the original sin. These communities died out after a generation, for obvious reasons.

In 1848, the District produced one of the few anti-capitalist socialist Christian groups. It was founded by John Noyes and they were called the Oneida Communities. These communities emphasized craftsmanship and became quality producers of silverware, steel traps and other craft products. By 1881, they were doing so well that they gave up socialism, embraced capitalism and reorganized as a joint stock company.

In 1866, Mary Baker Eddie claimed she had made a miraculous recovery from an undiagnosed illness by reading and studying the Bible and praying. She began to advocate this method over medicine and gathered many followers. In 1875, she published her book called *Science and Health*, which claimed Bible study and prayer were superior to modern medicine. Her new religion was called Christian Scientists, perhaps an oxymoron.

In 1848, in the Burned Over District, the Fox sisters introduced "Spiritualism" by claiming the ability to speak to spirits, including the dead in "Séance Sessions." During the next ten years over sixty-seven newspapers and magazines in America would be exclusively devoted to this subject.

The District wasn't the only place to find new religions. In 1870 in Pittsburgh, Pennsylvania, Charles Taze Russell became convinced the earth was in its last days and the Second Coming of Christ was imminent. He also doubted many mainstream Christian beliefs such as immortal souls, hellfire, the Trinity, and predestination. He wrote a book, *Three Worlds*, which defined his views including his "end of time" prophesy, and said that these were the last days and that a new age of earthly and human restitution under the guidance of an "invisible Christ." He claimed this new era was imminent. Initially called Zion's Watch Tower Tract Society, his new religion would later become known as the Jehovah's Witnesses. Russell founded a publishing empire based upon his Bible study and his teachings. By 1910, he had 50,000 followers in America and elsewhere as his followers were prolific in their missionary zeal.

After Russell's death the organization was taken over by Joseph Rutherford. His rise to power was controversial and many left the organization at that time. Rutherford was controversial and accused Catholic and Protestant clergy of gross misdeeds. He spoke out against the US government; Rutherford and his religious directors were jailed during World War I and charged with espionage on behalf of Germany, but the charges were later dropped.

Rutherford also made grand claims that in 1925 the end of the world would occur with the resurrection of Abraham and Isaac and other Jewish patriarchs. When this did not happen, the Jehovah's Witnesses began to leave the religion en masse. By the end of the 1920s the religion had lost about two thirds of their total members.

Rutherford reorganized and re-named the religion the Jehovah's Witnesses in 1931. Rutherford declared that only 144,000 original followers would be granted into heaven and declaring celebrations like birthdays and all holidays to be idolatry. He was still anti-government and declared government oaths, and the Pledge of Allegiance, as idolatry. He also discouraged his followers from voting or participating in government or obtaining a worldly education. This refusal to take oaths would later mean death in the concentration camps for his followers in Nazi Germany. Rutherford encouraged this martyrdom and built a cult of exclusion with his followers. The organization grew to over 100,000 by the time of his death in 1942.

The "end of days" has been predicted a number of times, and each failure has cost the Jehovah's Witnesses many adherents. Their last claim for the beginning of the end was in 1975. In 1980, the Jehovah's Witnesses magazine, *The Watch Tower*, admitted the failure of predicting the end and they have made no definitive prediction about an end date since. Jehovah's Witnesses is a small religion with about seven million followers world-wide. The Pew Forum reports that Jehovah's Witnesses have the lowest retention rate of

American religions. This will likely remain a small religion as they lose as many as they seem to recruit, despite their active missionary zeal.

Black Supremacy Religious Movements

There are also some religious Black supremacy movements in the United States. The Nation of Islam, which started in the 1930s and became significant in the 1960s, was a Black Supremacy movement under Louis Farrakhan. He preached a doctrine of Yakub, which held that the original men were Asiatic Blacks, and said that Whites were devils created 6,000 years ago by a scientist called Yakub. They believed in sacrificial killing and ritualistic murder as a part of the early Nation of Islam doctrine. They taught that it was the duty for every Muslim to offer as sacrifice four "Caucasian devils." This teaching also culminated in the creation of the "Death Angels," a small splinter group of the Nation of Islam. Between 1972 and 1974, the Death Angels murdered 14 white people in the San Francisco Bay area. The Nation of Islam later disavowed these teachings saying they were only metaphoric. They also preached black self-reliance, black separatism, cooperative economics, strict moral and physical discipline, and opposition to Black-White miscegenation. They also tend to be very anti-Semitic.

Another group, The Nation of Yahweh, is a black supremacist religious group that is an offshoot of the Black Hebrew Israelites, a group that believed they were the direct descendants of the ancient Israelites. Followers believe that the only true Jews are Black and that the lighter colored Jews are the spawn of Satan. The Nation of Yahweh also formed a secret group called "The Brotherhood." To become a member of The Brotherhood, applicants had to kill a "white devil" and bring their leader an ear, nose or finger of the victim as proof of the murder. Several Nation of Yahweh members were convicted of conspiracy in more than a dozen murders, among these convictions was Robert Rozier a former college and pro football player and member of the secret Brotherhood, who admitted to killing seven White people.

Jim Jones, Moonies, and the Branch Davidians

In the 1970s, an explosion of radical religious, quasi-religious or spiritual groups became such a concern that a new occupation, "deprogrammers," was created to assist people whose family members had been converted to the new cults who would then be bilked of their wealth and possessions and isolated from their families. Two of the more notable sects of this era were the Unification Church of the Reverend Sun Myung Moon (whose converts were pejoratively called "The Moonies") and second, The People's Temple, of the Reverend Jim Jones. Where the Moonies took severe advantage of their converts, they were not killers, but unfortunately the same could not be said of Jim Jones.

Jones was a charismatic dictator who soon came to the attention of

California law enforcement because of the extreme abuse of his followers. To avoid the authorities he moved his entire church and congregation to Guyana, in South America, where the abuses of his flock continued and complaints of this abuse from families who had lost relatives became so severe that California Congressman Leo Ryan and his staff went to Guyana to investigate. Jones and some of his followers killed the Congressman and his staff upon their arrival. They then ordered the adult adherents to commit suicide—but not until he had ordered the murder of all of the children, who were forced to drink poisoned Kool-aid. Jones and 909 followers died, including 303 children. It was one of the worst mass killings in American history.

In 1993 Texas law enforcement received complaints of child sexual abuse and the illegal stockpiling of military type weapons by a radical religious group called the Branch Davidians. They were a sect the of the Mormon Church formed in 1959 by David Koresh, who had set up a religious compound near Waco, Texas. The Federal Bureau of Alcohol, Tobacco and Fire Arms went to investigate and were greeted by armed men who refused their entry into the compound. A siege developed and FBI officers were brought to the scene and forced their way in. Violence began and in the aftermath four FBI agents, Koresh, and seventy-six of his followers were dead. In the aftermath some blamed the FBI for excessive violence as many were killed in a fire of unknown cause during the confrontation. A 2000 government investigation found that Koresh and his followers set fire to the building to commit suicide rather than be overtaken by law enforcement officials. Right-wing gun advocates and religious extremists have martyred Koresh and his followers. In 1995 the Federal Building in Oklahoma City was destroyed by two bombers who told authorities they did it in part to avenge the deaths of the Branch Davidians in 1993.

Other Religious Organizations

Two other significant religious organizations whose contributions to American culture are rather more positive are the Young Men's Christian Association (YMCA), created in 1851, and the Salvation Army, an English import that came to America in 1877. Ballington Booth, the son of the founder of the Salvation Army in England, who brought the organization to America, was also the founder of Volunteers of America, which is a nonprofit corporation and is now the largest owner of federal subsidized housing in the United States.

American Christian Fundamentalists Against Science

One of the most destructive and negative influences on American culture has come from Christian fundamentalists and their fear and loathing of science and reason. Although this bias goes well back before the Scopes

Monkey Trial, there are many modern examples as this bias continues to do damage to America's ecology, science and educational systems. In 2003 the US Justice Department at the direction of Attorney General John Ashcroft and the Bush White House began an investigation of Professor Michael Dini, a biology professor at Texas Tech University. It was alleged by the Liberty Legal Institute, a group of Fundamentalist Christian Lawyers, that Dr. Dini was violating the civil rights of his students. His crime was that he required any student who wished a letter of recommendation from him for a career in biology or to enter medical school to have a basic knowledge of, and belief in, the theory of evolution.

The fact that a US president and his attorney general would find this to be a crime is a stunning revelation about the American intellect and religious bias.

Tom DeLay, a fundamentalist Christian, was the Republican House Majority Leader until his departure following revelations of money laundering and illegal campaign contributions. On November 24, 2010, DeLay was found guilty by a jury in Austin, Texas, of conspiracy to commit money laundering and making an illegal contribution. He was sentenced to three years in prison and 10 years probation on January 10, 2011. In 2005, when DeLay was asked as the Republican Majority Leader to comment about the Columbine School shootings, he summed up Christian bias against science when he claimed that the tragedy occurred "because our school systems teach our children that they are nothing but glorified apes who have evolutionized out of some primordial mud." Paul Krugman characterized DeLay's comments in the *New York Times* by writing that according to DeLay, "Guns don't kill people; Charles Darwin kills people."

Religious and Conservative Denial of Climate Change

One of the most damaging aspects of American religious denial of science is the denial of climate change. In 2008 Congresswoman Michele Bachmann who ran for President in 2012 said, "(Nancy Pelosi) is committed to her global warming fanaticism to the point where she has said she's just trying to save the planet. We all know that someone did that over 2,000 years ago; they saved the planet — we didn't need Nancy Pelosi to do that."

In 2010 Sara Palin, the former Alaskan Governor and 2008 Republican Vice presidential nominee said, "These global warming studies (are) a bunch of snake oil science." In 2009 the conservative columnist George Will wrote in the *Washington Post* that, "According to the University of Illinois' Arctic Climate Research Center, global sea ice levels now equal those of 1979." Will's statement was a lie. The Arctic Climate research center doesn't exist and the scientists who do climate research at the University of Illinois said that Will and the *Washington Post* should be reprimanded for this blatant falsehood.

According the US Environmental Protection Agency and the major scientific agencies of the United States, including the National Aeronautics and Space Administration (NASA) and the National Oceanic and Atmospheric Administration (NOAA), they all agree that climate change is occurring and that humans are contributing greatly to this change. In 2010 the National Research Council also concluded that "Climate change is occurring, and is very likely caused by human activities, and (climate change) poses significant risks." World-wide most independent scientific organizations have concurred.

The limits that fundamental Christianity places upon science and culture are serious impediments to American development and continued prosperity. Unfortunately Christian Fundamentalism is growing and they will continue to impede progress.

Atheists, Agnostics and Humanists

According to Religious Tolerance.org, a 2003 poll shows that 58% of Americans say that a person must believe in god to be moral. A *Time* magazine poll showed the same results. In addition to the forty-three percent who would not vote for an atheist for president, a significant number of Americans just don't like or trust atheists. The results vary from state to state, with far higher numbers in the so called Red Republican states: in fact the Pew Public Forum in 2009 ranked the states by the importance of religion and the top twelve contain no surprises. In order, they are: Mississippi, Alabama, Arkansas, Louisiana, Tennessee, South Carolina, Oklahoma, North Carolina, Georgia, Kentucky, Texas, and Utah. This is the reason the Deep South is called the "Bible Belt." In all of these states at least two thirds of the population ranked religion as "very important" in their daily lives. The national average is 56% and two states, Vermont and New Hampshire tied for the lowest with only 36% saying religion is important in their daily lives. One out of four Democrats report having no religion, while only one out of ten Republicans do so.

In 1959, Madalyn Murray filed a case, *Murray v. Curlett*, on behalf of her son, William J. Murray, who was being forced to attend Bible readings in school and was being harassed by teachers and school administrators for refusing to participate. The case was consolidated with a case filed by Edward Schempp against a Pennsylvania school district that had forced his son to pray in school. The consolidated case is usually cited as *Abington School District v. Schempp*, although arguably *Murray v. Curlett* became the more famous of the two. The case was argued before United States Supreme Court on February 27 and February 28, 1963. The Court decided eight to one in favor of Murray and Schempp, declaring school-sponsored Bible reading and prayers in public schools in the United States to be unconstitutional. The reaction from the religious right was immediate and angry. Congressman George W. Andrews of Alabama said of the Court, "They put Negros in the schools and now they have driven god out!"

Chapter 10. Regional Cultures

> When the Oakies left Oklahoma and moved to California, it raised the I.Q. of both states.
>
> —Will Rogers

> Everyone from the South knows who Jefferson Davis was, and this is one thing that distinguishes the South from other parts of the country.
>
> —William F. Buckley

> When the taste changes with every bite and the last bite tastes as good as the first, that's Cajun.
>
> —Paul Prudhomme

As stated in the Introduction, subcultures are complicated and their study has become dominated by empiricists using replicable sets of mathematical and statistical algorithms. And sometimes in the length of time it takes to research and develop these complex models, the culture and subculture have already changed. So it becomes necessary in a work like this to describe these in more general terms.

The forty-eight contiguous states are generally divided into four regions, New England, the South, the Midwest, and the West. We also have a few states and territories that are set apart and recognized as culturally different: Hawaii, with its Polynesian/Asian culture, Alaska because of distance and isolation, and Puerto Rico with its Spanish/Carib culture, not to mention the other US territories in the Pacific and the Caribbean. Appalachia and the Pacific Northwest are frequently defined as cultural regions, as are the Mid-Atlantic states, and the

Rocky Mountain states. California and Texas are generally seen as having their separate cultures. Cities like New Orleans and Los Angeles (commonly known as "LA") and of course "the City" or "the Big Apple," New York, are considered as having their own cultures. And even neighborhoods of large cities such as the French Quarter in New Orleans, Greenwich Village in New York, the Cuban culture of Miami, along with the many Chinatowns, all the places called Polonia and Little Italy, and other ethnic neighborhoods across the nation have their subcultures. Even rural areas may be distinguished by their sub-cultures; think of Amish country, the Mennonite colonies, Bayou country, Utah's Mormon country, the Minnesota Lake country, the Florida Keys, Navajo Lands and other Indian reservations.

Some of these subcultures have lost their uniqueness and culture and have become assimilated over time. One of these unique subcultures was east of Downtown Atlanta: it was a very distinct and isolated Scots-Irish Appalachian neighborhood. The folks of Atlanta named it "Cabbagetown" because the Appalachians made a soup from cabbage, typically on Fridays, which could be smelled for some distance. In 1881, the Fulton Bag and Cotton Mill was founded by a German Jewish immigrant named Jacob Elsas. He needed a reliable labor supply so he began recruiting the Scots-Irish from the Appalachian Mountains. He provided these workers with a job and company housing for their families called "shotgun houses" that were built for them in the Appalachian style. They were small houses with a long hall running down one side from the front door to the back door with all the rooms connected by the hall. They were called shotgun houses because it was said that you could fire a shot gun down the hall without hitting anything by opening the front and back doors. This design was actually a very efficient style for cooling in days before air conditioning. The Appalachian residents of Cabbagetown also had their own country store which emulated an Appalachian country store, which Elsas also built. It was a very tight-knit community.

In 1977, the mill closed and the Scots-Irish Appalachians slowly moved away. Today it is an artists' community as poor artists began buying the small cheap homes in the 1980s; the mill was turned into condos. In 2008, much of the neighborhood was destroyed by a tornado.

Southern culture isn't just about White plantations and "Gone with the Wind." Like Cabbagetown there are many Southern subcultures combining various Native American, White European and African-American heritages. In South Carolina they have the annual Gullah Festival at the end of May, celebrating the Gullah language, culture and the long history of the African-Americans in the South Carolina "Low Country." While the festival is a rather new, it celebrates some long celebrated and very old African-American cultural traditions.

From the Louisiana Bayous to Okefenokee Swamp of Southern Georgia, to the Everglades in southern Florida, Southern Swamp Culture is unique. For many Whites who were excluded from Southern plantation society, mixed-race people, Native Americans, and runaway slaves, Swamp country was a retreat that offered separation and protection from mainstream White Southern society. This culture is nicely summed up in Anthony Wilson's book, *Shadow and Shelter, the Swamp in Southern Culture.*

California was for many years politically more liberal than the rest of the United States, and more so in Northern California. As far as food, it has deep Spanish and Asian influences; and in general it is a culture that welcomes change and fads. It is highly influenced by the movie and television industries that it hosts. California is a major wine producer, and its cuisine is sometimes described as "California fusion," a mix of Asian, Mexican, and other American foods. San Francisco and Berkeley and \New York City's Greenwich Village were the homes of the Beat Generation that greatly influenced American music, art and literature; they were also the birthplace of the Hippie and 1960s counterculture movement.

American English also shows regional features, with Southern drawls, Western twangs, New England and Boston accents. Every region and sub-region has its peculiarities and slang. In 2013 Joshua Katz from North Carolina State University made maps based on the research of Bert Vaux and Scott Golder documenting some of these language differences. Some of the results were as follows: A soft drink is called "soda" in the Northeast, California, St. Louis and Milwaukee. It is called "pop" in the Midwest and the Pacific North West, and until the last decade or two, in Boston. And it is called "coke," regardless of the brand, in Texas and the South.

Fresh water crustaceans are called "crawfish" in the South, "crayfish" in New England, Michigan, Wisconsin, Minnesota, and North Dakota, and "crawdads" in the lower Midwest and most of the West.

Gym shoes are called "tennis shoes" everywhere but in the Northeast and South Florida, where they are called "sneakers." This South Florida–New York connection makes more sense if you know that South Florida has a heavy population of former New Yorkers, particularly retirees, most of whom are New York Jews, and thus they have a much different culture from local White Floridians who may refer to themselves as "Florida Crackers." The term "Cracker" is also sometimes a derogatory term used by African-Americans for Southern Whites.

In most of the United States, "the City" means New York City, except for Illinois where it means Chicago, Northern California where it means San Francisco, and in Minnesota where it is called "the Cities" and refers to the Twin Cities of Minneapolis and St. Paul.

Chapter 11. The 1950s

> The reason we have such a high standard of living is because advertising has created an American frame of mind that makes people want more things, better things, and newer things.
>
> — Robert Sarnoff, President of NBC

> History is on our side. We will bury you!
>
> — Nikita Khrushchev

> The fifties—they seem to have taken place on a sunny afternoon that asked nothing of you except a drifting belief in the moment and its power to satisfy.
>
> —Elizabeth Hardwick, literary critic and novelist

The 1950s were the zenith of this nation's military and economic power. It was a unique time that too many Americans think of as the norm. In the wake of World War II, the United States was the only major nation whose industry wasn't substantially destroyed. And because of this, competition for American products was non-existent. This golden period lasted from the war's end in 1945 until approximately 1963 and the death of President John F. Kennedy. In this period the fascination with consumer goods took off. After the poverty of the Great Depression and then the deprivations and rationing of goods that accompanied the war effort, a massive appetite for consumer goods developed and, for those who could afford them, new houses and cars. Because of this pent up demand, there were massive shortages of housing, cars and other goods in the post-war world. While it took time for Europe to get to its feet again, most White Americans who wanted to work could, and American jobs paid good wages, with health care and pension benefits. The G.I. Bill gave US veterans an opportunity to go to college or trade school, and millions of working class men took advantage of this chance to better themselves and their families and to move up into the American middle class. Despite the American myth of mobility, this was the only time in American history where any substantial upward class mobility took place.

The housing shortage was resolved with large amounts of new inexpensive mass-produced housing built in the newly created suburbs around the great cities. New cars were produced to fill the new garages and driveways. New refrigerators, stoves, washing machines, and televisions were produced by the millions. New "convenience" foods were developed like TV dinners and other prepared, frozen and packaged foods, along with things like margarine, and sugar substitutes, and the chemical food additive industry was born. The development of new pesticides and herbicides that could kill anything, and unfortunately did, added to the growing food supply. "Better living through chemistry," was the motto of the day.

Many Americans were so well off that frivolity and fads could now be afforded and things like school pictures, tennis shoes, transistor radios, hula hoops, and cowboy hats and raccoon caps could be bought by (or for) millions of children. Ice cream was delivered to children by "Good Humor Men" and other ice cream trucks. Teenagers could afford hot rods, drive-in movies and restaurants, records and record players, class rings, black leather and letterman jackets. Teenage girls could afford makeup, pedal pushers, oxfords, penny loafers, and poodle skirts. Previously reserved for the rich, in-ground swimming pools became affordable additions to middle class homes, while above-ground pools were available to the working class; tennis and golf became middle class games. The many stay at home moms could have things like electric mixers and blenders, electric roasters and frying pans and automatic can openers, coffee percolators, and freezers. Some moms even had a second car to chauffeur children and shop for food and other errands.

It was different for minorities, but even many African-Americans, Native Americans, Latinos, and Asian-Americans had it somewhat better than before. African-Americans on the whole still lived segregated second class lives, many in poverty. Latinos and Asian-Americans were discriminated against as well. And Native Americans were still primarily confined by the US government in ghettos called Indian reservations.

Women may have received new household gadgets, but they did not have economic parity with men, and most of American society still considered women more or less as property. Occupations were divided between male and female, with the well-paying occupations being male. Even in the same professions, doing the same work, women were paid much less, and this was justified by saying they didn't have a family to support—even when they did.

The 1950s was also a time of mass hysteria. Xenophobia came over the nation like an epidemic as Americans feared anything foreign, and particularly the subversive "communists-atheists." Americans believed the Soviets and communists were coming to take away their new goodies, their freedoms, and their religion. Somehow, people like Senator Joseph McCarthy, FBI Director J. Edgar Hoover, and the CIA kept 1950s America in fear of anyone who seemed different, and managed to hold onto their leadership positions for quite some time. The radio drama *I was a Communist for the FBI* and the television show *I led Three Lives* played on these fears and spread paranoia nationwide. New right-wing groups like the John Birch Society flourished as America panicked.

Public and private schools showed propaganda films to children depicting communism as a hell on earth. American children were forced to perform silly drills to duck and cover under their desks in the event of nuclear war, as if this could protect them from a nuclear blast. The government encouraged anyone who could afford it to build a nuclear fallout shelter in their backyards so their family might survive a thermonuclear war.

The 1950s and the flight to the suburbs also contributed to the eventual destruction of America's great cities; some, like Detroit, may never recover. The inner city schools suffered the worst as their tax bases shrunk, monies were less, their students were poorer and they needed more services, and their facility and class room costs kept rising. As the schools declined it caused even more people to flee the cities.

The large central city's revenues also declined and their aging infrastructures and services began to strain their financial viability. All of this was the consequence of cheap housing being built in the suburbs. It was if the cities were being sucked dry by their suburban parasites. Other unfortunate consequences would appear as well. These suburbs required massive building of duplicative infrastructure that was already available in the cities. It is a duplication that America still struggles to maintain and replace.

Another innovation of the 1950s was the national interstate highway system. Championed by Dwight Eisenhower and originally built as a civil defense tool to move armies and enable the evacuation of cities in the event of nuclear attacks or other catastrophes, it was modeled after the German autobahns. This system soon became the backbone of the American transportation and economic systems. Unfortunately it also destroyed the American passenger railroad system and much of American mass transit, as people preferred to drive by themselves in cars. Where much of the developed world has built bullet trains and other good public transportation, the US has fallen behind because of our car culture and its demanding road system.

During this time many large cities gave up their street cars and commuter rail in favor of petroleum powered buses. At the same time middle class people began leaving mass transit en masse for the privacy of their own cars leaving mass transit and the new bus systems to the working class and the poor. As a consequence less money went into the expansion, care and maintenance of these systems furthering their decline.

The faster Interstate system also caused or enabled America to build more suburbs even further out from the cities, worsening what has now become a large national crumbling infrastructure problem, including roads and bridges, and basic utility systems like sewer, water, electric, and natural gas.

In many ways the 1950s was the best and the worst of American decades.

The Decline of the Cities

One of the more interesting parts of American culture is that of the American city, more particularly, the decline of the large cities, the urban centers. In most of the world, the wealth and the wealthy are concentrated in the large urban centers and poverty is at the extreme edge of the cities. In America, perhaps starting in the 1920s with commuter rail and street car suburbs, the wealth began leaving the cities for the suburbs. This of course was greatly hastened during the 1950s and the availability of the automobile and a new highway system.

American urban planners debated whether this phenomenon was something unique to American culture, and more particularly American car culture? While this debate continues, a new settlement pattern has appeared and America is now seeing wealth beginning to return and concentrate in the urban centers. For example in the large Twin Cities Metro area of Minneapolis and St. Paul, which is a new immigrant center, this phenomenon of wealth returning to the urban center is pushing poor new immigrants like the Somali, the Hmong, the Latino, and the Russian-speaking populations into third and fourth ring traditionally-White suburbs as the rapidly gentrifying central cities now have housing prices unaffordable to these groups. Many of the existing poor are also finding life in the central cities too expensive and are also leaving for the suburbs.

About five years ago, I was asked to be on a committee, the New Immigrant Task Force for the St. Paul Public Schools. The city and schools in their recent past had seen much of the new immigrant migration coming to Minnesota living in the city of St. Paul and attending school there. They wanted our committee made up of new immigrant leaders and other so-called experts like myself to tell them how to prepare for the expected new wave of immigrants that were coming to Minnesota. Our advice was that the St. Paul Schools didn't need a lot of preparation since we all agreed the new immigrants would mostly go to the suburban schools. This has proven to be true.

American large cities and urban centers, as it turns out, are not different than large urban centers in the rest of the world. It now appears that they were just younger and there appears to be a natural aging process that cities go through where they build, spread and decline, and then contract and rebuild in the center. This gentrification and return to the urban center will cause other problems as American suburbs age, decline, and as they will also grow more poor. It may prove to be impossible to maintain the infrastructures of these far flung developments. To make matters worse, the types of housing in these suburbs does not match the new demands of the new housing market. The "under forty" population has different housing preferences than their parents. Where their parents largely preferred a large, three- or four-bedroom single family dwelling with a two- or three-car garage, their children have smaller families and generally prefer smaller houses, and many are perfectly happy with multi-family low-maintenance housing such as condos or apartments. Moreover, they seem to prefer to be in or near to the central cities and away from the suburbs where many of them grew up. They are also marrying later in life than their parents did, and a growing number of this generation end up not having children at all. This also reduces the kind and amount of housing needed or desired.

The question then becomes who will buy the big houses that will soon be vacated by the aging and incredibly numerous generation of Baby Boomers? The answer is no one. Many of these homes will not have new owners. Even if the next generation preferred such houses, they are fewer in number and there will not be enough of them to buy most of these soon-to-be-vacant Baby Boomer homes. Yet America goes on building more and more housing for fewer people to occupy. It is supply and demand. Unfortunately, in America, we build until it is painfully obvious there is no more demand.

Chapter 12. Bohemians, Beatniks, Hippies, and the 1960s Counter-Culture

> The hippies wanted peace and love. We wanted Ferraris, blondes and switchblades.
>
> —Alice Cooper

> As a kid I quite fancied the romantic, Bohemian idea of being an artist. I expect I thought I could escape from the difficulties of math and spelling. Maybe I thought I would avoid the judgment of the establishment.
>
> —Peter Wright

> My advice to people today is as follows: If you take the game of life seriously, if you take your nervous system seriously, if you take your sense organs seriously, if you take the energy process seriously, you must turn on, tune in, and drop out.
>
> —Dr. Timothy Leary

> This business of burning human beings with napalm, of filling our nation's homes with orphans and widows, of injecting poisonous drugs of hate into veins of peoples normally humane, of sending men home from dark and bloody battlefields physically handicapped and psychologically deranged, cannot be reconciled with wisdom, justice and love. A nation that continues year after year to spend more money on military defense than on programs of social uplift is approaching spiritual death.
>
> — Martin Luther King, Jr.

There were always American intellectual bohemians who had a different cultural outlook than the norm, but they became a highly visible force during two times in the twentieth century, the first in the 1920s, and then again in the 1960s. The 1920s was a reaction to Prohibition, while 1960s counterculture was a reaction to the stifling conformist and anti-communist culture of the 1950s. The 1960s counterculture actually began in the 1950s with the Beat generation writers. Many give credit to the writing of Jack Kerouac. Although his novel *On the Road*, published in 1957, is the most cited and is a very important influence, I believe *Dharma Bums* published in 1958 was more influential in inspiring the counterculture and the Hippies of the 1960s. Kerouac's *Dharma Bums* was inspired by the poet Gary Snyder, who introduced Kerouac to Eastern philosophy, Buddhism, meditation, and nature studies, and was major influence in his writings. In fact one of the major characters in *Dharma Bums*, *Japhy Ryder*, was based upon Gary Snyder. Snyder was a man of high intellect who won a Pulitzer Prize for his poetry and also translated literature to English from ancient Chinese and modern Japanese. And he was very bohemian.

Dharma Bums showed alternatives to and questioned Western philosophy, materialism, sexual mores, societal authority and conventionalism. This questioning became the founding principle of the 1960s counterculture. Later counterculture figures like Ken Kesey and Timothy Leary were also inspired by *Dharma Bums*.

The 1960s counterculture had some lasting impacts, both positive and negative. On the positive side, in my view, the counterculture generation brought a revival of folk music and the entrance of Rock and Roll. Rhythm and Blues, which had been considered "negro music" until then, also became mainstream and music festivals and rock concerts became part of mainstream American culture.

Although innovative artists like Alexander Calder, Helen Frankenthaler, Jackson Pollock, and Willem de Kooning were already noted in the 1950s for their genius, such modern art was adopted by mainstream America in the 1960s, and new pop artists like Andy Warhol enhanced this modern style.

In addition to the influence of Beat literature, a sampling of the books that became popular during the counterculture movement included: *The Silent Spring, The Feminine Mystique, Catch 22, One Flew Over the Cuckoo's Nest, The Electric Kool-Aid Acid Test,* and *Zen and the Art of Motorcycle Maintenance.* There were also interesting publications like *Zap Comix* featuring the controversial work of the satirical cartoonist Robert Crumb, along with The *Whole Earth Catalog,* and the book *Grow It!,* aimed at helping the communes and those going "back to the land" to be self-sufficient. The commonality of these books was that they were mostly anti-authoritarian and anti-establishment and that they were primarily written for a young audience, those in their teens and twenties. While most of them were important works in their own way, they were initially popular because of their unconventionality. They were a slap in the face of conventionalism.

A sampling of anti-authoritarian countercultural movies would include three anti-military movies: *Dr. Strangelove*, the movie *Catch 22*, and the movie *M*A*S*H*. It also includes anti-authoritarian movies like *Cool Hand Luke*, *Easy Rider*, and *Wild in the Streets*. Then there were movies exploring sex, like Woody Allen's *What's New Pussycat?*, *The Last Tango in Paris*, *The Graduate*, and *Midnight Cowboy* which was the first movie to feature gay sex. *Harold & Maude* which challenged ideas about age, sex, and suicide, and *Bob and Carol and Ted and Alice* looked at wife-swapping. And while breaking other stereotypes, the first "mainstream" pornographic movies, *I am Curious Yellow* and *Deep Throat* also premiered.

The Myth of the Me Generation

There are myths about each generation. The generation of World War II was memorialized by Tom Brokaw as "The Greatest Generation" for winning the war. However Franklin Roosevelt, Harry Truman, George Marshall, Dwight Eisenhower, Douglas MacArthur, and George Patton, of the generation before them, were much more responsible for the victory than their young, brave soldiers, marines, and sailors. Likewise, Lyndon Johnson, Richard Nixon, Melvin Laird, Robert McNamara, William Westmoreland, and Creighton Abrams, all of the World War II generation, were more responsible for the tragedy of Vietnam than the young, brave soldiers, marines and sailors of the Baby Boom generation who were drafted as teenagers and fought that war.

The Baby Boomers have been given the title of "The Me generation" for their supposed self-obsession and selfishness. It was a false claim. For hundreds of thousands, it meant being drafted at eighteen or nineteen and sent overseas, where many would be killed and maimed in a war that no one wanted. It meant coming home to people who spat upon them for their sacrifice. There were no parades and no idol worshiping public like those that greeted "The Greatest Generation." The average age of the combat troops in Vietnam was nineteen. None of this is very selfish or "Me Generation."

And their service wasn't fair. There is a scene in the television show *China Beach*, a show about the Vietnam War, where a middle-aged sergeant laments: "I served with lawyers and teachers in World War II, and again in Korea, but Vietnam is different: it's all poor Black kids and big dumb White farm boys." Vietnam was a class war.

The working class kids, White, Black, Latino, Native American and Asian, were forced to serve. Even mildly retarded working class kids, as depicted in the movie *Forest Gump*, who were called "McNamara's 100,000," were forced to serve. Meanwhile middle and upper class kids like George W. Bush, Dick Cheney, Donald Rumsfeld and Paul Wolfowitz received exemptions and didn't have to serve in Vietnam. Those four became known as the Chicken Hawks for their failure to serve their country, followed by their pushing of pro-war policies. Bush was also in the National Guard, which was a refuge for middle and upper class kids; in those days, reserve units were rarely called to fight. College students like Bill Clinton didn't have to serve. The young women also didn't have to serve and many working class boys lost girlfriends to middle class and upper class boys who didn't have to go. The working class boys in the service derisively called the middle and upper class boys "Jody," as in "You had better watch out, or Jody will steal your girl." At the same time, many young women lost boyfriends, fiancés, and young husbands in the war.

The "Me Generation" label was applied by conservatives to denigrate the anti-war, pro civil rights, women's rights, gay rights, and the environmental movements that were being fueled by mostly middle class college students. They saw this as a generation that was only interested in sex, drugs, and rock and roll, apparently missing their passions for making the world a better place, while ignoring the boys they sent to war. They also believed this generation of war victims was somehow "pampered."

Rock & Roll

The roots of Rock & Roll and Rock Music come from the African-American genres of blues, jump blues, jazz, and gospel music and combined them with other genres from country and western to swing music. It began evolving in the post War 1940s and the early 1950s. One of the first White groups credited with bringing this new music to mainstream America was Bill Haley and His Comets. But Black artists were already performing this music before him, such as Ike Turner and The Kings of Rhythm, Chuck Berry, Fats Domino, Bo Diddley and Little Richard. After them came the White Rockabilly artists like: Jerry Lee Lewis, Carl Perkins, Buddy Holley, Gene Pitney, Roy Orbison, and the most notable, the performer they called "The King," Elvis Presley.

The most popular music identified with the 1950s was probably Doo Wop. These performers got their inspiration from earlier crooner groups like the Mills Brothers, and the Ink Spots. Doo Wop produced artists like the Coasters, The Platters, The Fleetwoods, The Mystics, Dion and The Belmonts, The Dell Vikings and The Impalas.

Rock & Roll was at first the music of the young lost generation of teenagers who had were born during World War II, and was then later adopted by their pre-teen younger siblings, the first Baby Boomers. Most adults thought the music was depraved and lustful, and many White parents disliked it as "negro music." There were many attempts to ban the music, but Rock & Roll became the backbone of a new teen culture that would eventually lead this generation into the counterculture.

The music began to decline in the late 1950s and early 1960s when a series of tragedies, scandals, and other events seemed to signal the end. Buddy Holly, the Big Bopper, and Richie Valens were killed in a plane crash. Little Richard retired to become a minister. Elvis was drafted onto the Army. Chuck Berry was arrested and convicted of having sex with a fourteen-year-old Native American girl. Jerry Lee Lewis was reviled for marrying his thirteen-year-old cousin. And the radio disc jockey who supposedly named the music "Rock & Roll," Alan Freed, was one of many in the music industry who were arrested in the Payola Scandal involving record companies bribing radio stations and disc jockeys to push and play their artists.

During this dark time Rock & Roll returned to its African-American roots. In 1959 Barry Gordy began Motown Records in Detroit, Michigan. And his music was to become known as The Motown Sound. His first group was called the Matadors, who later became famous as Smokey Robinson and the Miracles. Motown produced an impressive list of artists including the Marvellettes, the Temptations, the Supremes, Martha and the Vandellas, the Four Tops, the Jackson Five, Little Stevie Wonder, and Marvin Gaye.

In 1961, the California Sound gave birth to Surf Music. It came from California teen beach culture in Orange County and spread throughout Southern California. It was influenced by guitarist Duane Eddy and an early Rock group, the Ventures. Dick Dale and the Belltones were the originators soon followed by the Beach Boys, the Surfaris and Jan & Dean. The first songs were about surfing, beach culture and teen romance, but a sub-genre soon emerged called Hot Rod Rock which was about cars and girls and began with groups like the Rip Chords and their hit "Hey Little Cobra." The Beach Boys also produced some Hot Rod Rock with "Don't Worry Baby" and "Little Deuce Coop." Surf Music and Hot Rod Rock was soon emulated across the United States with groups like The Trashmen from Minneapolis, Minnesota, and the Rivieras from South Bend, Indiana.

Rock & Roll became as popular in Britain in the mid-1950s as it was in America. Soon young British musicians were emulating American rock groups and artists, playing their music and singing their songs. Eventually some of these British artists began writing and performing their own Rock music and groups like the Beatles, the Dave Clark Five, Herman's Hermits, and edgier groups that were more influenced by Rhythm and Blues like The Animals, The Rolling Stones, The Moody Blues, The Kinks, The Who, and Small Faces came to prominence. The British Invasion, as it was called, dominated Rock & Roll in the mid 1960s as the British groups began releasing their records and touring the United States.

Psychedelic Rock began in the middle and late 1960s as the counterculture came to full bloom. It was the music of Hippies, drugs and eastern mysticism. The artists that came from this genre were: The Byrds, The Grateful Dead, Big Brother and the Holding Company, Jefferson Airplane, Jimi Hendrix, The Doors, Iron Butterfly, and British groups like Cream, Pink Floyd, The Yardbirds. This shift even caused the Beatles to move away from "Bubble Gum" music with songs like *I Want to Hold Your Hand* for the more counterculture tunes of *Lucy in the Sky with Diamonds* and *Nowhere Man*, as they too began to flirt with eastern mysticism and the counterculture movement.

The impact of Rock music on US culture was the equivalent of a social tsunami. It hit during the tumultuous Civil Rights era, when the country was still fighting segregation and the obstruction of rights of African-Americans. Young Americans of all races adopted the new music which helped bring about a rapid change in attitudes about race. Some of the many White teens who idolized African-American performers of Rock, Jazz and Blues became the first significant group of Whites to become involved in the civil rights movement. And that also led to other movements, like Women's rights, Latino and Native rights, gay rights, and the environmental movement. It would also lead to the anti-war movement that would dominate the era.

Drugs

The counterculture came with some significant negatives. The acceptance and promotion of drug culture caused horrific damage in America. And while the counterculture receives the largest share of blame for this damage, American drug culture didn't start with the counterculture movement.

There have always been drugs and drug abusers in America, but it didn't become epidemic until the government, more precisely the Central Intelligence Agency and the US military, became involved with drug experimentation in the 1950s and 1960s. It also didn't help that America had forgotten the lessons of prohibition, and rather than concentrate on education and treatment, they prohibited drugs and criminalized addicts. They created a war on drugs, which America has been steadily losing. America now has the highest percent of incarcerated people, mostly due to drugs.

America's drug problem was started by the CIA. Nazi Germany began experimenting with drugs and mind control in their concentration camps in World War II. The American military and the OSS (the fore-runner to the CIA) took notice and began to investigate their use. The OSS brought these experiments and some of the Nazi doctors to the United States and also conducted some experiments in Canada to avoid breaking US laws. LSD was one of these drugs. The CIA was very interested in LSD for mind control purposes.

In 1953, the drug and mind control experiments were expanded under President Eisenhower when the CIA convinced him that the Russians and the Chinese were conducting mind control experiments on US prisoners during the Korean War. The CIA mind control experiments were called by many code names, but the entire operation ultimately became known under an umbrella as Operation MK-ULTRA. As part of this operation, LSD and many other drugs were widely tested on inmates of mental health facilities, CIA agents, military personnel (some volunteers and some not) and average unsuspecting American citizens. In one outrageous experiment in San Francisco, the CIA conducted Operation Midnight Climax, where they operated several brothels where the prostitutes would drug unsuspecting customers with LSD so the CIA could study their reactions. The bedrooms were all equipped with one-way mirrors and all subjects were filmed for later study. The victims were frequently forced and blackmailed into new drug tests by the CIA.

In many other experiments people were given LSD without their knowledge, and then they were interrogated under bright lights with doctors in the background taking notes. The subjects were told that their "hallucinogenic trips" would be extended indefinitely if they refused to reveal their personal secrets. The people being interrogated this way were CIA employees, and US military personnel along with many patients in mental hospitals. Ted Kaczynski, the Unabomber, was one of these patients according to Alston Chase in his article "Harvard and the Making of a Unabomber" for *Atlantic Magazine* in June of 2000. Another of these subjects was Ken Kesey the author of *One Flew Over the Cuckoo's Nest*, according to Christopher Lehmann-Haupt who wrote the obituary of Kesey in the *New York Times* in 2001. Candy Jones, a model and radio talk show hostess, also claims she was a victim of these drug experiments as chronicled in a book by Donald Bain, *The Control of Candy Jones*.

The US Army and the CIA conducted many drug experiments. The first were volunteers, but as there was a shortage of volunteers, the Army began to force drug users and people who had broken other army regulations by convicting them and giving them stiff prison sentences for their violations, and then offering immunity if they volunteered for the drug testing. Criminals were another group used for testing and the Boston Mobster and murderer James "Whitey" Bulger was one of these, according to Anthony Bruno at True tv.com.

The drugs the CIA and the Army experimented with included: LSD, barbiturates, amphetamines, morphine, mescaline, heroin, and marijuana, and they also used hypnosis to see if mind control could be achieved. The goal was to perfect a "Manchurian Candidate," a person who could be subconsciously programmed to perform such dangerous tasks as espionage and assassination.

In 1973, at the height of the Watergate scandal, CIA Director Richard Helms feared discovery of the project and ordered all the documents on MK-ULTRA destroyed, and the project almost disappeared. However, some documents had been improperly stored and were later discovered during a congressional investigation. Although some of these abuses were discovered at this time, the major part of the operation will likely never be revealed. A Congressional committee, chaired by Senator Frank Church investigated in 1974 and concluded that the experiments had happened and that "prior consent was obviously not obtained from many of the subjects." On the Senate floor in 1977, Senator Ted Kennedy said the Deputy Director of the CIA revealed in testimony that over thirty universities and institutions were involved in an "extensive testing and experimentation" CIA program which included covert drug tests on unwitting citizens.

The US General Accounting Office issued a report on September 28,

1984, which stated that, "between 1940 and 1974, DOD and other national security agencies studied thousands of human subjects in (drug) tests and experiments."

In his book *The Politics of Heroin in Southeast Asia*, Alfred McCoy states the CIA and the US military were also involved in drugs and drug running in Vietnam. After losing mainland China, a group of approximately twelve thousand Kuomintang soldiers escaped to Southeast Asia in what became known as "the Golden Triangle" and continued launching guerrilla attacks into southern China. During the 1950s and 1960s, the CIA supported and supplied this army, even secretly supplying reinforcements at times. The Kuomintang grew opium and the drug trade was their main source of revenue to finance their operations. It eventually became their primary business. The French crime organization, the Unione Corse, operated the drug trade in Vietnam and operated what was called "Air Opium" flying the opium to the Southeast Asian markets for the Kuomintang and other opium tribes, like the Hmong and Meo.

General Ed Lansdale, the CIA chief in Vietnam and his old friend Lt. Col. Lucien Conein, the CIA agent who had helped engineer President Diem's election and then overthrow for the CIA in 1963, came to an agreement with the Unione Corse. As a former OSS liaison officer with the French Resistance during World War II Conein had some experiences and connections in common with many of Saigon's Corsican gangsters. He convinced Lansdale that they could be a good source of financing for covert activities like the secret war in Laos. The Unione Corse also hated the Vietnamese communists and were willing to partner.

Soon the CIA and the Unione Corse were operating in cooperation in the drug trade. Air America, a private air company operated by the CIA, became the drug transportation system after the French Air Opium was shut down, according to Alexander Cockburn and Jeffrey St. Clair in their book, Whiteout: The CIA, Drugs and the Press. The Hmong armies were also backed by the CIA and were supported by the drug trade. The CIA also created a Meo mercenary army whose support also came from the manufacturing of heroin for sale in South Vietnam including to American GIs. At this time the US State Department as a policy also provided unconditional support for corrupt governments in the area that were openly engaged in the drug traffic as long as they were pro-American.

According to Cockburn and St. Clair, the American Mafia was also looking for financial opportunities and saw Vietnam as fertile ground. They began sending younger members of their crime families to Saigon. The most important of these Mafioso was Frank Carmen Furci, a young Mafioso from Tampa, Florida, who was a soldier in the crime family of Santo Trafficante, the Mafia boss of Tampa. Furci arrived in Vietnam in 1965 with solid financial backing and soon became a key figure in the systematic graft and corruption that began to plague US military clubs in Vietnam as hundreds of thousands of GIs poured into the war zone. A lengthy US Senate investigation later exposed the network of graft, bribes, and kickbacks that Furci and his fellow Mafia profiteers employed to cheat military clubs and their GI customers out of millions of dollars. The Mafia also got into the drug trade with the Unione Corse and began buying from them to sell to American soldiers and Marines and also began to export to the United States. One of their alleged methods was to smuggle the drugs to the US in the body bags of dead soldiers, according to Mike Levine, a former DEA agent who claims to have witnessed this. Levine was also a radio talk show host in New York and has become a journalist and has written on this subject. An Air Force Chief Master Sergeant, Bob Kirkconnell, also claimed to have witnessed this as part of a heroin investigation in Vietnam in 1972. Levine and Kirkconnell had a radio interview on New York's WBAI on June 21, 2004, titled "The Vietnam Body Bag Case," talking about their experiences.

In late 1960s, new heroin laboratories sprang up in the Golden Triangle area where Burma, Thailand, and Laos converge, and suddenly unprecedented quantities of heroin started flooding the troops in Vietnam and began to be smuggled into the United States by the Mafia. Fueled by these seemingly limitless supplies of heroin, America's total number of addicts skyrocketed.

Heroin and many other drugs were a large part of what was going on in Vietnam and were part of US soldiers', sailors' and marines' experience in Vietnam, and drug addiction became an epidemic. Many young veterans came home with addictions, and many more young men were recreational users.

Vietnam wasn't the end of CIA involvement in the drug trade. In 1996 investigative journalist Gary Webb wrote a series of articles called "Dark Alliance" exposing the CIA in their assistance to Latin American gangs in drug trafficking in cocaine to support various CIA black operations in Latin America, such as support for the Nicaraguan Contras.

Webb also alleged that this influx of Nicaraguan-supplied cocaine sparked, and significantly fueled, the widespread crack cocaine epidemic that swept through many US cities during the 1980s. According to Webb, the CIA was aware of the cocaine transactions and the large drug shipments into the US by Contra personnel. Webb charged that the Reagan Administration shielded inner-city drug dealers from prosecution in order to raise money for the Contras, especially after Congress passed the Boland Amendment, which prohibited the Reagan Administration funding the Contras.

Although the government tried to discredit Gary Webb and he died mysteriously with two gunshots to the head, a CIA internal investigation by Inspector General Frederick Hitz later vindicated Webb and stated that despite the campaign against Webb, his reporting was the truth. The government eventually admitted to even more than Gary Webb had reported. The CIA inspector general released a second volume to this report, wherein his investigative team admitted that CIA assets had traded in cocaine and crack, and that the CIA had pressured Department of Justice agencies (such as the DEA and FBI) to drop or suspend their own drug-related investigations of such assets. These drug sales were used to fund CIA operations in Latin America.

One of the areas hardest hit by this cocaine epidemic was Los Angeles, which prompted Congresswoman Maxine Waters to tell the *Los Angeles Times* in 1997: "It doesn't matter whether the CIA delivered the kilo of cocaine themselves or turned their back on it to let somebody else do it. They're guilty just the same."

At this same time the Regan Administration and the CIA were also guilty of illegally selling weapons to Iran to support the Contra. Several investigations were made, including by the Congress and a three-person, Reagan-appointed Tower Commission. In the aftermath fourteen administration officials were indicted, including Secretary of Defense Casper Weinberger. Eleven convictions resulted, but some were vacated on appeal. The rest of those indicted or convicted were all pardoned in the final days of the presidency of George H.W. Bush who had been vice-president at the time of the affair and was privy to these dealings as the former CIA Director.

While the young people of the counterculture bear some responsibility for the disastrous effects of drugs on the American culture and society they may be much less guilty and responsible than their government.

Feminism and the Sexual Revolution

Just as there were two Bohemian counter cultural movements in twentieth century America, the 1920s and the 1960s, there were also two sexual revolutions that occurred with them in the 1920s and 1960s. Both sexual revolutions had to do with birth control and changing sexual mores. In World War I the condom was a new form of birth control and American soldiers were given condoms by the Army to prevent disease. Young American men found the young French women to be far less puritanical than American women and this, with the war induced heightened sense of life and death, caused the young soldiers to be more active than they may have been in other circumstances. In addition to the American soldiers, a large number of young American women went to Europe during the war as Red Cross workers, nurses and other volunteers. They too became involved in this sexual revolution and when the young men and women returned home, they brought these new liberal sexual attitudes with them. America's first sexual revolution would last through the "Roaring Twenties" and crash with the stock market in 1929 at the start of the Great Depression.

The 1960s sexual revolution also occurred with the availability of even more reliable birth control. At the same time this occurred, the Women's Movement was beginning to attract ever greater numbers of young women who suddenly proudly claimed their sexuality and began to admit that they were as interested in sex as their male partners. Books like *Sex and the Single Woman*, *The Feminine Mystique*, and Erica Jong's novel *Fear of Flying* reinforced women's new attitudes about sex, permanently changing American sexual conventions.

There were some excesses like the Summer of Love and the "free love movement" that had been started or inspired by the Beat generation writers who readily broke American sexual taboos with public nudity, sharing lovers, and dabbling in homosexuality. Mainstream America was shocked, which caused great amusement among the Beats and later the Hippies and counterculture revolutionaries. The excesses did lead to sexual abuses when drugs, alcohol and peer pressure were involved. There was also an epidemic of sexually transmitted diseases, none more horrible than the AIDS epidemic. The AIDS virus popped up in America in 1969. It spread rapidly, at first in the Gay community, but became a nationwide epidemic affecting everyone by the 1980s. This put a damper on the sexual revolution.

At this time the Catholic Church was being told by its demographers that the Church had reached its peak and that the Catholic religion would start losing population. The Church had every reason to worry. In America many Catholics were converting to the Protestant churches or becoming atheists. Europeans were increasingly less religious, and Catholic families were having fewer children. And while the rising populations of Catholics in the Third World were still contributing to Catholic growth, the demographers said that this too would likely end. They said birth control was a big part of the problem.

In 1969 after five years of consideration, on July, 29, 1969, the Pope rejected birth control in an encyclical entitled *Human Vitae,* which is Latin for human life. The encyclical was about banning birth control, but abortion was also banned. This was interesting because abortion had been promoted for many years as birth control for large poor Catholic families who couldn't support their many children. In the late nineteenth century, the Church decided it would not promote abortions but would leave it as a family choice. In 1969, the encyclical made it a sin and set in motion one of the most politically divisive movements in American history.

At the time the encyclical was written, seventy percent of American Catholics approved of birth control. At the urging of many Catholic women, 172 American priests signed a letter of protest to Cardinal O'Boyle. He responded for the Church by delivering a sermon demanding obedience at St. Matthew's Cathedral in Washington, DC. Over two hundred Catholic women walked out during his sermon. Ironically the Catholic Church began losing members faster because of this decision.

Historically in America Catholics had been Democrats and liberals, but soon they began to side with the Evangelical Republican Christian-conservatives because of this issue. And soon many priests were openly campaigning for conservative Christian political candidates. It dramatically changed the balance of American politics in a short period of time and pushed the country further to the right. The American left had been destroyed in the anti-communist 1950s and the abortion issue along with the perceived excesses of the anti-war and anti-establishment counterculture also fed the dramatic decline of the liberals and moderates in American politics.

However the abortion issue also began to slowly solidify the Women's movement, and women began slowly gravitating toward the center and left and Democratic politics, as women's reproductive and other rights have been trampled by the Republicans and the Christian right, causing what many women view as "a war on women." The overwhelming numbers of women voting Democratic in the 2008 and 2012 presidential elections came as a result of this.

Feminism and the women's movement is not just a gender issue, although gender issues have been great emotional triggers for both sides. The women's movement of the 1920s was about the right to vote. Today it is also about women in the workplace, including the military, about pay equity and gender equality.

Chapter 13. Radio & Television

Radio Days

> I was always fishing for something on the radio. Just like trains and bells, it was part of the soundtrack of my life. I moved the dial up and down and Roy Orbison's voice came blasting out of the small speakers.
>
> —Bob Dylan

> ...Some nights I'd sneak out and listen to the radio in my Dad's old Chevy — children need solitude — they don't teach that in school...
>
> —John Geddes

> I was raised to think the best thing in the world is not to read. The best thing is television and radio and ball games and a home I can't afford.
>
> —Ray Bradbury

There is controversy as to when was and what is the first American radio station. The first commercially licensed broadcast station was KDKA in Pittsburgh, which began operating in 1920, but their engineer had been operating a non-licensed station there since 1915. Some claim that the University of Wisconsin-Madison had the first station it began broadcasting as the first licensed experimental station, 9XM, which originally broadcast in Morse code in 1914, then broadcast the first music in 1917 and the first speech in 1919. The station continues to broadcast today as WHA. Also claiming to be the first is WBL, now WWJ in Detroit, which claimed that it was broadcasting two months before KDKA even though their license was granted after. And Charles David Herrold who built the first radio broadcasting station in 1909 for what would later become KCBS in San Francisco has also claimed to be the first. WEAF in New York became the first to air a commercial in 1923 and it was from this that product-sponsored programming was born.

AT&T had a monopoly on radio and in the late 1920s and federal government pushed the creation of what was to become the NBC and CBS radio networks to break up this monopoly. Walter Cronkite and Edward R. Murrow became the first electronic journalists as radio soon became the most important source for American news. The radio news was especially important during the war years. Most Americans first learned of the attack on Pearl Harbor from the radio (or from their neighbors who heard it on the radio). During the war the radio was a constant source of news, reassurance, and it was a significant factor in keeping civilian morale at a high level. Roosevelt's Fireside Chats on the radio became a staple in almost every household.

The first radio shows were music sprinkled with some comedy as radio became an extension of Vaudeville. In the 1930s radio began creating its own shows including dramas, mysteries and comedy. Some were very realistic. In October of 1938, Orson Welles aired a show called *War of the Worlds* adapted from the story by H.G. Wells on the CBS network. The program ran commercial free to promote realism, and many listeners panicked thinking the world was actually being invaded by Martians.

Another famous radio broadcast was the Hindenburg disaster. A reporter from Chicago's WLS, Herbert Morrison, and a Chicago radio engineer, Charlie Nielsen, went to New Jersey to cover the arrival of a zeppelin called the Hindenburg on May 6, 1937. His report on WLS and radio stations worldwide was as historic for the broadcast as much as it was for the terrible disaster it covered.

In 1921 the first religious service was broadcast. Also in 1921 the first sports coverage occurred with the broadcast of the Dempsey-Carpenter fight to an estimated 300,000 listeners; that year also saw the broadcast of the first Baseball World Series. The first presidential nationwide address took place with President Wilson addressing the nation on radio also in 1921. The Democratic and Republican Conventions first aired in 1922. In 1924 a show called *The National Barn Dance* began playing country music and in the following year of 1925 the radio broadcast of *The Grand Ol'Opry* started. Humorist Will Rogers began his famous radio show that year, along with Father Coughlin, the nation's forerunner to the televangelist and radio talk show host.

In the 1930s–1950s, comedy shows like *Burns and Allen, Jack Benny, I Love Lucy, Our Miss Brooks* and *My Little Margie* would air and later find their way to television. Following the same path from radio to television were variety shows like: *The Ed Sullivan Show, Dinah Shore* and *The Red Skelton Show.* The game shows would also start on the radio and then move to television with shows like: *Truth or Consequences,* and *What's My Line.* There were also the dramas like: *Boston Blackie,* and *The Shadow,* and the westerns like: *Rin-tin-tin, Death Valley Days, the Lone Ranger, Red Ryder, and the Roy Roger's Show.* The melodramatic soap opera was invented for radio and moved to television with the popular show, *The Guiding Light,* which also found years of success in television after years of success on the radio.

After World War II with the advent of television, radio began to decline dramatically. However in the late 1950s because of the transistor and car radios, and Rock & Roll music which appealed to teenagers, radio had resurgence, and although television replaced it as the primary medium, it survived to find its own niche in music, news and what has become known as "talk radio."

Television

> The most corrosive piece of technology that I've ever seen is called television — but then, again, television, at its best, is magnificent.
>
> —Steve Jobs

> Thanks to television, for the first time the young are seeing history made before it is censored by their elders.
>
> —Margaret Mead

> Television is a medium of entertainment which permits millions of people to listen to the same joke at the same time, and yet remain lonesome.
>
> —T.S. Elliott

Perhaps one of the most innovative creations of American culture is television. In the middle of the twentieth century television became the backbone of American culture. Enshrined in most living rooms it became the window in which most Americans began to look at and understand their lives, their culture and the world. The dramas helped them understand human nature. The comedies forced them to look and laugh at themselves. The educational shows brought culture and music, the children's shows baby sat, entertained and educated their children. Television news brought them to the scene as if they were there. Suddenly events across town or on the other side the world didn't seem so distant and made people realize that these events were closer to them than they used to think. It gave them empathy for different and distant people and places.

Television was one of those innovations where many inventors can claim credit, but two of these stand out, Philo Farnsworth and Vladimir Zworykin.

Both Americans, these two independently developed the technology, although Farnsworth was awarded the patents. Regular television broadcasts began in America in 1928, in a Washington, DC, suburb but they were crude and experimental. The National Broadcasting Company, NBC, began regular broadcasting in 1938 in New York, coinciding with the World's Fair. In 1939 they expanded to Los Angeles, broadcasting about 58 hours per month. There was no real audience, with only 2,000 television sets available, and the television stations could only reliably broadcast up to forty miles. The first advertising came in 1941 and was in the form of a test pattern which advertised Bulova watches. Television broadcasting was largely suspended during World War II. Wartime production priorities shut down the electrical manufacture of commercial televisions, and the nation's forty million existing radios seemed adequate to the country's needs.

After the war NBC and the DuMont Television Network began regular network programming in 1947, with the American Broadcast Company, ABC, and the Columbia Broadcast Company, CBS, starting in 1948. In the late 1940s television stations began broadcasting in major cities across the United States. By 1951 stations could be found in every major city from New York to Los Angeles. The audience expanded rapidly as the price of televisions started to decline because mass production made television sets more affordable. In 1947 about 44,000 televisions were made and sold, although most of these were in New York City. By 1954 well over half of American households owned a television set, and by 1962 over 90% of American homes had a television.

American mass culture is a result of television. Regional differences began to give way to the larger American culture with the advent of television. And television changed the culture. Perhaps the Civil Rights movement of the 1950s and 1960s is the best example of this change.

Southern discrimination and segregation was still in full bloom a hundred years after the Civil War. Southern culture had changed very little in this regard. Television changed that. Prior to television there were too few outside of the South to see or complain when dogs were set on a group of marchers, or African-American children were violently attacked for attempting to go to a White school, or when people were denied the right to eat at a lunch counter, or a Black woman was jailed for refusing to give up her seat on a bus to a White man, or when little girls were killed as Whites blew up a Black church. Television changed this. All of a sudden what happened in the South, even the rural South, was on television for everyone to see and know.

Television was an empathetic window to the world. It was as Margaret Mead said, "Thanks to television, for the first time the young are seeing history made before it is censored by their elders." Adults saw, too. It was hard to not to recognize gross injustices when they were played out in your living room every night on your television news. It was hard not care when you could see these cruelties as clearly as if it were next door. There started to be a broad-based public outcry. Even many Southerners and segregationists were offended by the images that kept coming out of their televisions.

Television had its impact on other American traditions. Until television most Americans did not question their country or its leaders in times of war. That changed with television. Vietnam was fought in front of Americans in their living rooms. They saw Buddhist monks immolating themselves in protest and naked children running from burning Napalm. They saw a Viet Cong man executed by the police with a pistol put to his head and with his blood spurting over American living rooms as he died. They also saw the thousands of young Americans, most in their teens, dying in front of them in a war that was never satisfactorily explained on television or elsewhere. These were the images that Americans saw of Vietnam and they were aghast and revolted by them.

In future conflicts the US Government would limit the press, particularly television, because of their experience in Vietnam. In the Persian Gulf War and the wars in Iraq and Afghanistan, the television news networks were severely limited in their access and appeared to be advocates and apologists of the war as they tried to curry favor with the military and the government for greater access and pictures to send to American televisions. Much of the success of CNN came as a result of their coverage of the Gulf War. The media became so supportive of the government and the military that by the time of the war in Iraq, the government's official reason for going to war, that "Iraq had weapons of mass destruction," was never really investigated by the media. Nor was it extensively covered by the media when it was found to be a blatant lie. The networks covered a supposedly triumphant President Bush as he pompously strode across an aircraft carrier dressed in a flight jacket under a banner proclaiming "Mission Accomplished" at what turned out to be the beginning of a long war and not the end of a short, triumphant war.

Television also has had other negative cultural impacts. In 1961, Newton Minow, the Chairman of the Federal Communication Commission, said that television was a "vast wasteland." It became known as "the boob tube." The American intellectual community was dismayed as Americans watched soap operas, Westerns, and what they considered to be "low-brow" comedies. They argued that television would discourage reading, shorten attention spans and turn Americans into super consumers, all of which was true. And one of television's unfortunate consequences didn't become apparent until later when American obesity became an epidemic as American diets changed toward prepared foods and to fast food in which television advertising played a significant factor. Obesity also became a greater problem as Americans became more sedentary, with increased time sitting in front of their televisions. In fact many Americans now eat their lunches and dinners in front of their television, which started with a little frozen tray of prepared food called "the TV dinner."

The Sitcom

> If sitcoms were easy to write, there'd be a lot of good
> ones. And there aren't.

—Alexei Sayle

The American television situation comedy, the sitcom, is one of the most derided and maybe the most prominent American cultural features of the twentieth century. It has been damned as being written and produced for common people with a sophistication that is accused of being at about an eighth grade level. The sitcom is the most enduring and most popular form of television. The sitcom was a cozy invention of radio. They used the same familiar characters from week to week, which became like friends to their audiences, to present comedy for the general American appetite. The first television sitcoms that came from radio were *Jack Benny, Burns and Allen, I Married Joan, Our Miss Brooks, The Life of Riley,* and *Topper.* The number one favorite show of the 1950s, *I Love Lucy,* also came from radio. They all successfully made the transition to television. Television soon developed comedy that would become known as the "Hi honey, I'm home" popular family sitcoms with *Ozzie and Harriet, Father Knows Best, Leave It to Beaver,* and *The Donna Reed Show.* These shows were complete with mom, dad, and kids to show the idealized version of the American dream in comedy form. Twists on the family sitcom were soon added with *The Dick Van Dyke Show,* where much of the show revolved around Dick's job as a television writer, and *The Andy Griffith Show,* with Andy's job as a small town sheriff. Other family sitcoms included *My Three Sons* about a widowed father and *Bachelor Father* about an uncle who was raising his niece. Then we had *The Brady Bunch,* a mixed family of a father with three sons marrying a mother with three daughters, and *The Partridge Family* who performed as a musical act.

All in the Family put a sharp edge on the family sitcom by taking on what was at the time very controversial issues like racial prejudice, women's rights and gay and lesbian issues. *Married with Children* poked fun at the American family, and today's currently popular sitcom, *Modern Family* continues this tradition.

Like *All in the Family,* many American sitcoms sometimes have a serious side. *M*A*S*H* raised serious questions about war and American militarism. *The Mary Tyler Moore Show* was the first to show a single working woman as an acceptable and even desirable situation. Later *Seinfeld* made single seem normal. The sitcoms *Ellen* and *Will & Grace* brought gay and lesbian issues out of the closet into American living rooms.

One of the most controversial but popular television and radio shows was *Amos & Andy.* It was a comedy about a dysfunctional African-American community. The show was written and acted out by two White men, Freeman Gosden and Charles Correll, who re-enforced bigoted White stereotypes about Blacks as lazy, simple, and uneducated people. They spoke in an exaggerated "negro accent" complete with malapropisms and half-baked ideas portraying their characters as lovable but less than Whites. This was a long-running popular radio show from 1928 to 1955; it was on television from 1951 to 1953 and was aired in regular re-runs on television until 1966 when it was pulled off the air. Originally Gosden and Correll performed in blackface (radio shows were performed before large live audiences in order to add live laughter; there were no fake laugh tracks in those years) and when the show went to television the two men wanted to hire black actors to lip-sync their recorded words, but when this proved to be too difficult they trained the Black actors to speak in their exaggerated dialect. The show was controversial from its beginning with protests from both the African-American and the religious community.

Some sitcoms were more fantasy than social commentary, with shows like *I Dream of Jeanie, Bewitched, Mr. Ed, The Beverly Hillbillies, My Favorite Martian, The Munsters* and *The Addams Family*. And some made comedy of some serious not very funny situations like war in *Hogan's Heroes* and *McHale's Navy*. Some sitcoms are just funny for their witty creative writing like *The Mary Tyler Moore Show, The Bob Newhart Show, Newhart, Taxi, Cheers* and *Fraser*. *The Mary Tyler Moore Show* is the most award winning television sitcom, followed by Cheers.

All sitcoms are reflections of their times, however the best example of this may be the unique sitcom *The Monkees* which was written and produced as a prime time sitcom for the nation's 1960s young rock and roll rebellious teenagers.

Animated sitcoms started with the prime time cartoon *The Flintstones*, which was a blatant knockoff of the popular sitcom *The Honeymooners* in a prehistoric cartoon setting. Because of its popularity it was soon followed with another prime time animated show about the future with the *Jetsons*. *The Simpsons* continued the prime time animated sitcom, and shows like *Bevis and Butthead, Family Guy* and *South Park* continued the tradition but with a more outlandish and a sometimes controversial edge.

Although sitcoms are disdained as bubble gum for the brain and dismissed as low-brow entertainment, along with rock and roll music they are likely the art forms that will define the last half of the twentieth century and early twenty-first century American culture. They are a very accurate reflection of the people and times of when they were made. The sitcoms appear to be enduring as many of the originals are still being watched today about sixty-five years after they first aired, not including those that aired on radio long before their television debuts. It is interesting to keep in mind that the plays of Shakespeare were also written in their time for the common masses and not the intellectuals.

Children's Shows

> From television, the child will have learned how to pick
> a lock, prevent wetness all day long, get laundry twice as

white, and kill people with a variety of sophisticated arma-
ments.

—John F. Kennedy

Starting with radio in the 1930s and moving to television with the Baby
Boomers, radio and then television became the primary cultural medium for
the young. The children's shows were their first introduction. It started on
radio with national shows like *Little Orphan Annie*, and *Jack Armstrong the All
American Boy*. Soon stations started developing their own children's shows
which added to local subculture. In 1921 at WIP in Philadelphia the first
children's regional show debuted as *Uncle Wip*, named after the station's call
letters, which started a trend in naming children's shows and characters
after stations to advertise them by their call letters. Even then advertisers
and marketers realized the huge importance of the children's show. If you
could get the children interested, you would eventually get their parents to
buy.

In 1926 Chicago station WMAQ began airing *Topsy Turvy Time* where the
host read children's books. Also in 1926 one of the most famous of the local
radio children's shows made its debut, *Uncle Don*, which became so beloved in
New York City that the show went national on the Mutual Radio network.
It remained a fixture in New York for over thirty years and its theme song
was sung by at least several million children.

When television began some of the very first programming were
the children's shows. In 1939 at the New York World's fair television
demonstration, puppeteer Burr Tillstrom created a puppet show for the
Fair television that would later come to commercial television and would
be known as *Kukla, Fran and Ollie*. It first aired commercially in Los Angeles.
All of the early television networks, CBS, NBC, ABC, and Du Mont had
children's shows. In 1948 to 1950 most of these children's television shows
had a Western theme as the stars of the "horse operas" realized it was a good
way to market their Western and cowboy movies to children. Hoot Gibson,
Gene Autry, Roy Rogers and other stars of the cowboy genre all hosted
children's shows.

Children's art, the cartoon show, soon followed. The first cartoon
created exclusively for television was *Crusader Rabbit*. While *Crusader Rabbit*
was a children's show, many of its sophisticated comedic lines were aimed
at their parents. The show was created by Jay Ward who would later create
Rocky and Bullwinkle, which also appealed to as many adults as it did children
for its adult humor. The Minnesota Vikings Hall of Fame Quarterback
Fran Tarkington later admitted that he usually watched *Rocky and Bullwinkle*
on Sunday mornings as part of his pre-game ritual before heading to
Metropolitan Stadium in Bloomington, Minnesota, to play football for the
Vikings.

Another children's puppet television show that was watched by as many
adults as children was *Time for Beany*, which was sometimes called *"Beany and*

Cecil" by the children who followed it. It aired in 1949 and was created by Bob Clampett and included the writing and voice of the comedian-writer Stan Freiberg, and voice actor Daws Butler who would later do the voices of many Hanna-Barbera cartoon characters like Yogi Bear and Huckleberry Hound. While *Time for Beany* was a children's show it contained some very good satire and humor about American politics for the adult audience. It first aired as a local show on KTLA in Los Angeles.

Another pioneer children's television show was *Howdy Doody* which began in December of 1947 and ran on NBC until 1960. It was the first of many NBC television shows to be produced at the Rockefeller Center in studio 3A. It was also the first show produced in color and was used by its owner, RCA, to market the first color television sets. (Get the kids interested, and their parents will buy.) One of the popular characters of the show, Clarabell the Clown, was played by actor Bob Keeshan who was fired in 1952 in a salary dispute. Keeshan then took his talents to CBS where he would later create and star in his own television show in 1955 called *Captain Kangaroo* which would air until 1984. It was the longest running children's television show at that time. It was later surpassed by *Romper Room* which aired from 1953 and ran until 1981, and then was overhauled and continued as *Romper Room and Friends* until 1991. Both shows have since been eclipsed in duration by *Sesame Street*.

Sesame Street began airing in 1969 and is still broadcast internationally. In 1996 a survey found that 95% of all American preschool children had started watching the show before they were three years old. In 2008 a survey determined that over 77 million American children had watched the show on a regular basis. It has also been broadcast in over 140 countries, and has won eight Grammys and a record 143 Emmys.

In addition to the national shows, local children's television shows added to local American subcultures. Some of the more notable were *Sheriff John* on KTTV Los Angeles. The show aired from 1952 until 1970 and again in 1979. It won an Emmy in 1952. The show was developed by and played by John Rovick, a World War II hero who served as a bomber gunner and radio operator with the Army Air Corps and had 50 combat missions to his credit during the war.

Bozo the Clown was created as a character for children's records as a 'read-along" book series owned by Capitol Records. In 1948 Capitol franchised Bozo the Clown to local television stations to air their own local shows. The first television Bozo broadcast was *Bozo's Circus* at KTTV Los Angeles in 1949. WHDH in Boston aired their *Bozo's Circus* from 1959 to 1970. One of the most popular of the *Bozo the Clown* franchises was in Chicago. The show first aired in 1961 and eventually became one of the first cable television children's shows on WGN. Willard Scott played Bozo the Clown on local television in Washington DC. His show was sponsored by McDonalds which created their own clown inspired by Bozo, called Ronald McDonald. He was also was first played by Willard Scott and later by Ray Rayner who had been the

Bozo in Chicago. Rayner was a prisoner of war in World War II at Stalag Luft III and was also a creative consultant for the movie *The Great Escape*.

Another notable local show, *Axel and His Dog*, which was later changed to *Axel's Tree House*, went on the air for the first time on August 5, 1954 on WCCO in the Twin Cities of Minnesota. Axel was played by Clellan Card a well known radio personality who created the children's show after the accidental deaths of his two children. The show featured Axel in his tree house with his animal puppet friends. Don Stolz, the owner of a local community theater played *Towser* the dog on the show, and local singer and entertainer Mary Davies played *Carmen the Nurse*. In October 1954, the show became one of the first local television programs ever to be broadcast in color. The show aired *Little Rascal* shorts and was responsible with a handful of other children's shows, especially *Clubhouse Gang* in Atlanta for creating a resurgence of the once popular *Our Gang* children's movies. It was alleged that *Dusty's Tree House* which began airing on KNXT in Los Angeles, and was one of the first cable children's shows on Nickelodeon, was inspired by *Axel's Tree House*.

One of the most popular shows in the South was *Woody Willow* which aired on WSN Atlanta in 1948 and ran until 1956 when the creators moved to Ohio. It was a puppet show with a live host similar to *Howdy Doody*. Another popular Atlanta show was on WSB called *Clubhouse Gang* and featured an extensive collection of *Little Rascals* movie shorts.

Milton Supman first began his show *Lunch with Soupy* in 1953 which aired on WXYZ in Detroit. The show was first named *12 O'Clock Comics*. Later it was known as just the *Soupy Sales Show*. In 1959 the show became so popular it went national on the ABC network. Milton Supman allegedly got his nick name from his older brothers who called him "Soup bone," which was then shortened to "Soupy." He took the name *Sales* after the Vaudeville comedian Chic Sale. Sales was also a jazz aficionado who had started his career as a jazz DJ on the radio, and he also had a night time television jazz show in Detroit called *Soups On* and featured such jazz greats as guests like Miles Davis, Stan Getz, Billie Holiday and Charlie Parker. It has been rated as one of the best jazz television shows of all time and is prominently mentioned in most jazz histories.

Lunch with Soupy moved to Los Angeles in 1960 but lasted for only two more years and was cancelled. It was rumored that Sales told blue jokes on his children's show (which he always denied). However, one of his routines was "Why is it that when I see F you see K?" which many little boys loved to mimic "F you see K."

Sales briefly went on air replacing the late night *Steve Allen Show*. In 1964 he moved to New York where the *Soupy Sales Show* continued with his original children's show gags but featured music artists like the *Supremes*, the *Shangri-Las* and the *Temptations*, and other guests like Frank Sinatra, Sammy Davis Jr. and Judy Garland. This show attracted his former audience of children who were now in their teen years.

Soupy Sales was a regular panelist on the game show *What's My Line* from 1968 to 1975. He was on various other game shows until 1991.

Almost everyone in America under the age of seventy was introduced to American culture by children's television. It could be argued that children's television shows had one of the largest influences on twentieth century American culture.

The Theatre

> I regard the theatre as the greatest of all art forms, the most
> immediate way in which a human being can share with another
> the sense of what it is to be a human being.
>
> —Oscar Wilde

Native Americans and Spanish colonists performed theatrical events in America long before the English colonies. The first American theater in the English colonies was built in Williamsburg in 1716. In January 1736, the original Dock Street Theatre was opened in Charles Town, South Carolina. The Walnut Street Theatre was founded in 1809 at 825 Walnut Street in Philadelphia, Pennsylvania. It is the oldest continuously operating theatre in the English-speaking world and the oldest in the United States.

In the early years of American theater, acting troupes came from mostly from Europe to perform. The Lewis Hallam Troupe was the first complete company of actors from Europe and came to perform in 1752. They brought a repertoire of plays popular in London at the time, especially Shakespeare, which became the standard fare in early American theater. The early theatre troupes would travel from town to town, as only a very large city could afford consecutive multiple performances of a production. In most cities there was one performance, but even the largest cites were mostly limited to two or three performances. Frequently performances were given in odd public places like saloons and on riverboats. In addition to Shakespeare or other English plays, there was the occasional American melodrama like *Uncle Tom's Cabin*.

Plays and actors became a rarity in the nineteenth century. Many Americans began to view theatre as hedonistic or sometimes "uppity." Minstrel and variety shows then became the most popular entertainment and began to be performed along with burlesque shows. The minstrel show was an American entertainment consisting of fast-paced comic skits, very short dramatic plays, variety acts of jugglers, magic, along with a lot of dancing and music. The music and songs, along with dancing, was usually performed by white people in "blackface" who made fun of African-Americans as lazy, stupid, superstitious, but also musically gifted. The minstrel shows started in the 1830s and by the 1840s became White America's most popular entertainment. By the turn of the twentieth century, the minstrel show was still enjoyed but began to be stigmatized as racist, and it lost much of its former popularity. It was replaced for the most part by Vaudeville. Performances in blackface continued through Vaudeville and beyond, but these were usually minor acts, unlike the minstrel show where it was the primary focus. Minstrel shows survived as professional entertainment until about 1910, but long after this community and amateur groups still performed minstrel shows until the 1960s Civil Rights Era.

American burlesque shows were originally an offshoot of Victorian burlesque satire variety shows. This English genre had been successfully staged in New York from the 1840s, and it was popularized by a visiting British burlesque troupe called Lydia Thompson and the British Blondes, who began performing in the US in 1868. The first American burlesque shows incorporated elements and the structure of the popular minstrel shows. They consisted of three parts: first, songs and ribald and risqué comic sketches by comedians; second, assorted talent acts, such as acrobats, magicians and solo singers; and third, musical and chorus numbers, which eventually evolved into the striptease in the late nineteenth and early twentieth century. They sometimes included satire and jokes in the English style about current politics, music or a play. Burlesque eventually became chiefly associated in American culture with off-color jokes, female nudity and scantily clad chorus lines.

Vaudeville was common in the late nineteenth and early twentieth century, and is notable for heavily influencing early American film, radio, and television productions in the United States. Vaudeville was born from an earlier American practice of having singers and novelty acts perform between acts in a play and during the intermission. Most vaudeville theaters were built between about 1900 and 1920, and some have managed to survive today. Many of these went through periods of alternate use, most often as movie theaters and community and amateur playhouses. However most Vaudeville theatres were permanently converted to other uses as the movies became dominant.

American drama and musical plays continued during this time, but they were attended primarily by the upper middle class and the wealthy. Much of this was confined to the New York Theater which we have come to know as "Broadway."

Theatre in New York moved from downtown gradually to Midtown beginning around 1850, as they sought less expensive real estate prices to build theatres. Theatres did not arrive in the Times Square area until the early twentieth century, and the Broadway theatres did not consolidate there until a large number of theatres were built around the square in the 1920s and 1930s. Broadway's first "long-run" was a fifty performance musical hit called *The Elves* in 1857. But the New York performance runs and theatre continued to lag far behind those long running plays in London. However in 1860 Laura Keene's musical *Seven Sisters* shattered previous New York records with a run of 253 performances, and even compared very well to many of the successful plays of London. Keene's work became enormously popular. It was at a performance of Keene's *Our American Cousin* at Ford's Theatre in Washington, D.C. where President Lincoln was assassinated.

The advent of motion pictures mounted a severe challenge to live theatre. At first, films were silent and presented only limited competition because they were a curiosity, but by the end of the 1920s, films like The Jazz Singer were presented with synchronized sound, and critics wondered if the cinema would replace live theatre altogether.

American theatre survived and oddly the movies may have helped to save it. In order to compete with the fast-growing popularity of movies, theater was forced to find "more common" and popular shows, which then also attracted many lower middle class and working class people to the theatre. Today Broadway productions still entertain millions of theatre goers as productions have become more elaborate and expensive. Some have also argued that they have become more coarse. Broadway and American theatre has survived and thrives and has ceased to be entertainment for just the upper classes. It is now enjoyed by Americans of every income and class.

Hollywood and the Movies

> A film is, or should be, more like music than fiction. It should be a progression of moods and feelings. The theme, what's behind the emotion, the meaning, all that comes later.
>
> —Stanley Kubrick

The first real motion picture was in 1878. It featured a horse called Sallie Gardner and was made in Palo Alto, California, using 24 stereoscopic cameras. It was a preview of bigger things to come. The movie camera was an invention of the 1880s and was thought of at first as nothing more than a curiosity and carnival novelty. The movie camera was an invention of W.K.L. Dickson who worked for Thomas Edison. The Edison Company soon developed the projector using 35 millimeter film, which became the standard. The first motion picture shown in a theatre was at the 1893 Chicago World's Fair (called the Columbian Exposition). At the same fair

Edison also introduced the new motion picture camera.

It was always intended that movies would have sound, but initially there were too many technical difficulties in synchronizing images with sound. However, there was still sufficient interest in motion pictures to launch the "silent era of film," and some significant movies were made. Silent films were frequently accompanied by organists or other live musicians, and sometimes sound effects, and occasionally commentary or lines spoken by a showman or the projectionist to enhance the viewers' experience. In 1899 animation was created and also became a staple in motion pictures. By 1907 there were an estimated 4,000 nickelodeon theatres in the United States showing these movies.

The film industry was initially dominated by France and Italy, and artistically American film was second rate, with the disruption of the movie industry by World War I, the US became the center of the movie world. By the 1920s, the US reached what is still the era of greatest-ever output. Hollywood was producing an average of 800 feature films annually, which was a whopping 82% of global production according to Louis Giannetti and Scott Eyman in their the book, *Flashback*.

There were a number of experimental movies with some coordinated sound in the early years. In late 1927 Warner Brothers released *The Jazz Singer* which was mostly silent but contained what is generally regarded as the first synchronized dialogue and singing in a feature film. The change to sound then came remarkably fast. By the end of 1929, Hollywood films were almost all-talkies. There were several types of competing sound systems and quality, which did not become standardized until the 1930s. It also changed the movies. Many major silent filmmakers and actors were unable to adjust and found their careers severely curtailed or even ended. Voice was now as important to film actors as their visual looks and presence and some silent actor's voices did not project well in the new "talkies."

In the 1930s the motion picture industry exploded with innovation and creation forever changing American culture. The movie musical was born and the creative Busby Berkeley put his signature on what film could do with musical production and dance numbers. Disney, who had been making cartoon shorts for the movies, created the first full-length animated motion picture with *Snow White and the Seven Dwarves*. The horror and monster movie genre began with films like *Frankenstein, Dracula,* and *King Kong*. The Comedies of the Marx Brothers, Laurel and Hardy, and Mae West took up where Charlie Chaplin had left off in the Silent Era. The gangster movie with stars like James Cagney and Humphrey Bogart reflected what was happening in America. And the end of this decade saw two all time classic American movies produced, *The Wizard of Oz* and *Gone with the Wind*.

The 1940s saw a wave of patriotism and propaganda through the war years. Perhaps the best of these films was *Casablanca* which romanticized war sentiments. Some of the war time movies were pure propaganda and some war films were very racist. There was a proclivity of grade B films showing

Japanese pilots laughing as they sadistically gunned down American boys on the ground. Even comedies like the *Bowery Boys* had war themes. But there were also some classic films produced like *Citizen Kane* and *The Maltese Falcon*. There were also a number of new Disney animated films like *Pinocchio, Dumbo* and *Bambi*. The Academy Award winning film *The Best Years of Our Lives* captured the Americans return from war and their struggle to reclaim civilian life. The classic, *It's a Wonderful Life* was made in 1946.

The end of World War II also brought the Cold War which had an enormous impact on movies. The Cold War culture was a stifling and had a negative impact on movie culture as Senator Joseph McCarthy and the House Un-American Activities Committee investigated Hollywood in the 1950s. Actors like Charlie Chaplin, along with writers and directors, lost their jobs in the wave of mass hysteria. This atmosphere of repression hit the motion picture industry hard, and with much of their former audience now watching television, many thought the best days of the movies were over. Hollywood turned to B grade horror movies like *I was a Teenage Werewolf, The Blob*, and *The Invasion of the Body Snatchers* which were being made for the Saturday matinee and drive-in movie audiences of mostly teens and children. Westerns were another popular genre and these productions continued in this era. Both the television and movie versions of *Davy Crockett* and *the Alamo* started a fad that saw waves of little boys dressed in coonskin hats with toy rifles and rubber Bowie knives. The cowboy was king in the 1950s and people who had never ridden a horse were going to rodeos. "All hat and no horse" became an American expression for the large number of want-to-be cowboys.

Other films were also made for the new teenage market. Hot rod movies mirrored America's love of the automobile in the 1950s. Some of these were horrible like *Jalopy* in 1953 with Leo Gorcey and Huntz Hall reprising their roles as the *Bowery Boys*. Other significant titles in this genre were *Hot Rod* in 1950, and in 1954 *The Fast and the Furious* which was advertised as "hot rods, hot babes and crooks!"

The best of the American classic teenage film was *Rebel without a Cause* in 1955. This film began the careers of several American icons including James Dean, Dennis Hopper, and Sal Mineo, and advanced the career of the child actress Natalie Wood, and also starred Jim Backus of Gilligan's Island and Mr. Magoo fame.

As the movie industry continued to decline and theatres continued to close, Hollywood answered its decline with the large epic films which were advertised as having "a cast of thousands." These included pictures like: *The Ten Commandments, Spartacus, Ben- Hur, The Vikings* and *El Cid*. These big pictures successfully encouraged audiences to see them on the "big screen" versus staying home to watch their "small screens."

By the 1960s many of the old movie theatres were now closed and gone in favor of the new multi-plexes which could show multiple movies at the same time and maximize profits for their owner's with longer runs.

Hollywood returned to making blockbusters and everyone wanted to see the next big film, movies that could sustain long runs in the new multiplexes. In the 1960s this rebirth included films like: *The Graduate*, and a 1930s gangster film with a 1960s tone *Bonnie & Clyde*, and pictures like *2001: A Space Odyssey*, *Rosemary's Baby*, *Easy Rider*, *Midnight Cowboy*, and *Dr. Strangelove*.

In the 1960s Hollywood found it could be much edgier than the highly censored G rated television. The first mainstream pornographic films of *I am Curious Yellow*, and *Deep Throat* were also shown in mainstream movie theatres with their X ratings to allow no one under the age of eighteen to enter during their showing.

American films continue to be an entertaining mirror of not only what American culture is, but what Americans think or what Americans want their culture to be. And although the ability to watch movies at home on a variety of electronic devices erodes movie theatre audiences, the desire and fun of seeing a film in a large theater with an audience is still a pleasure many Americans continue to seek.

Chapter 15. Literacy, Education and Literature

> You teach a child to read, and he or her [sic] will be able to pass a literacy test.
>
> —George W. Bush

> This will never be a civilized country until we expend more money for books than we do for chewing gum.
>
> —Elbert Hubbard

> Not all readers are leaders, but all leaders are readers.
>
> —Harry S. Truman

The US Department of Education's Institute of Education Sciences conducted large scale assessment of American adult education levels in 1992, and again in 2003, called the National Assessment of Adult Literacy (NAAL). There was no significant difference in the results of these two assessments. The studies measured three categories: reading, writing and basic math skills. The sample was designed to accurately represent the US population as a whole. The conclusion from 2003 was that roughly 15% could function at the highest levels in all three categories, but that 40% of Americans were at either basic or below basic levels of proficiency in all three categories.

The study showed that almost a quarter of Americans could not understand basic written information or follow written directions. According to this study, the literacy rate for the United States would be about 65% to 75%, depending of the definition of "literacy." This result is dramatically lower than the officially proclaimed literacy rate in the US Census, 86%.

Jonathan Kozal, in his book *Illiterate America*, suggests that these deceptively high census numbers for US literacy may be due to poor methodology. The Census Bureau bases its literacy rate on personal interviews of a relatively small portion of the population and on written responses to Census Bureau mailings. They also consider that individuals are literate if they simply state in the interview that they can read and write. The Census also makes the very broad assumption that anyone with a fifth grade education had at least an 80% chance of being literate, which has not proven to be very accurate.

The US has always touted its high literacy rates compared to the rest of the world. Colonial America claimed to have better literacy rates than England; however not everyone in the Colonies was counted. If they had counted everyone, the American literacy rate was actually much lower than in England. The website *Colonial Quills, Literacy in Colonial America* states that the literacy rate in New England was about 60% in 1650–1670. It was much less in the South. For example, in Virginia it was between 54% and 60% in the late 18th century. In the New York and Pennsylvania colonies, it was higher because of the Dutch and German immigrants who set up public schools for religious training. In the South during this time education was considered a family responsibility and was given very little public support. This allowed for some wealthy Southerners like Thomas Jefferson to receive a very good education, but the children of Jefferson's White employees and other working class Southerners would likely have remained illiterate. It was of course illegal to teach Blacks to read in the Colonial South.

As stated, these early US literacy figures did not take into account everyone. Indians and African-Americans and even most indentured servants were not included. Women were also not included. There were varying levels of literacy among New England women in the eighteenth century, estimated at between 45% and 67% during 1731–1800, and much less in the South.

The Boston Latin School is the oldest public school in the United States, founded in 1635. It is still operating as a public school. However, it charged fees in its early days and admitted only male students and hired only male teachers. After 144 years of operation the school did begin operating a separate Girls' Latin School, starting in 1877. The school's first co-educational class was not until 1972.

Most Americans believe that America operated a quality universal public school system from the beginning, but this is far from the reality. The colonists tried at first to educate by the traditional English methods of family, church, and apprenticeship, with the rudiments of literacy and arithmetic taught inside the family. This assumed that the parents or older siblings had those skills and had the ability to teach their children or siblings. Unfortunately many families lacked those skills and their children remained illiterate.

In the 1640s, the New England colonies required towns to set up schools, and many did so, but not all. In 1642 the Massachusetts Colony made elementary school education compulsory and other New England colonies followed, but education was still far from universal. Similar statutes were adopted in other colonies in the 1640s and 1650s but these laws were very loosely enforced as child apprentices and child labor to support the family was deemed more important. The schools were also all male, with few or no schools for girls. However, some colonial women could read, as Bible reading was taught to some women. Most could not write, even to sign their names, and they were allowed to legally sign with an "X" when a signature was required. At this time most reading was primarily taught to give students a sufficient skill in reading and understanding the *Bible* and most early school instruction was religious.

The US school system remained largely private and unorganized until the 1840s. At this time public schools were always under local control, with no federal funding, and very little state funding. The 1840 US Census shows that of the 3.68 million children between the ages of five and fifteen, only about 55% attended schools.

Teaching was not perceived as an occupation for educated people. Many people became teachers without any particular skill or advanced education or training. In 1837, the secretary of education in Massachusetts, Horace Mann, began to create a statewide system of professional teachers based on the German Prussian model of "common schools," which held the belief that everyone was entitled to the same content and quality in education. Mann's early efforts focused primarily on elementary education and on educating and training those teachers. The common-school movement quickly gained strength in the New England and the Midwest in the 1840s and 1850s.

In the 1840s Mann also introduced the German concept of assigning children by age to grades. Prior to this, children with ages from six to fourteen were placed together in the same class room. Mann won widespread approval for building quality public schools. Most New England and Midwestern states adopted the system he established in Massachusetts, and his program for "normal schools" and to train professional teachers. These teacher trainings have become today's teacher's colleges and departments of education at major universities.

It wasn't until the year 1870 that all the states provided free elementary schools. However there were still many rural areas, particularly in the South and West, which still had no schools, and where there were schools the quality was very poor. Schooling for women in most areas did not become commonplace until the mid to late nineteenth century.

In the South, education was particularly divided by class and income. The planter class hired tutors for their children or sent them to private schools. During the colonial years, many in the planter class sent their sons to England for schooling. Most middle and working class parents in the South either home schooled their children or relied on local ministers to teach basic Bible reading. Illiteracy was high in the South and has largely remained so. Much of the rural South lacked public schools until the twentieth century, and the Southern schools were segregated until the late 1960s. After segregation many Whites began to send their children to private schools, and funding to Southern public schools suffered. More recently, the school voucher program and charter schools were set up to allow Whites and the middle class to send their children to government-subsidized private schools while the poor and minorities suffer with ever-deteriorating public schools.

School segregation was not just a Southern problem. Prior to the 1954 Supreme Court ruling *Brown v. The Board of Education*, segregated public schools were found in 17 states of the South and but also in the border states of West Virginia, Kentucky, Missouri, Maryland, and Delaware, where public school segregation was also required. In another four states, Kansas, Wyoming, Arizona, and New Mexico, segregated schools were optional and were decided by local school boards. School segregation was totally forbidden in 16 states, and 11 states had no legislation on the issue at all, which also allowed local school districts to decide.

The South continued with its system of quality private schools and poor public schools dividing the South by race and class. Many Southerners derided the North's free public schools as inferior to their private schools, but since most Southern children could not afford these "quality" private schools Southern education was poor and illiteracy rates were very high.

According to Patricia A. Graham in her book *Community and Class in Education 1865 to 1918*, by 1900, there were only 34 states that had compulsory schooling laws, with 30 states requiring compulsory school attendance until age 14 or above. As a result, by 1910, only 72 percent of US children attended school. The majority of these were in the North, and even there half the nation's children still attended a one-room school. However by 1918 every state in the nation had laws requiring children to complete elementary school.

In the late nineteenth century the large majority of Protestants allowed most states to pass constitutional amendments called Blaine Amendments. The amendments were originally intended to stipulate the separation of church and state, but they soon were turned into anti-Catholic measures as they were used to forbid any type of public support for parochial schools, most of which were Catholic. Meanwhile the Blaine Amendments allowed Protestant education to continue to be promoted and taught in public schools. Protestant religious instruction was still common in public schools well into the 1960s.

The Blaine Amendments were not about a separation of church and state, but were primarily an anti-Catholic movement in response to the heavy immigration of Catholics from Ireland and Germany after the 1840s.

Prior to 1910 most American high schools were preparatory academies for college, and mostly for middle and upper class children. Most working class children ended their educations by the age of fourteen or younger. However, by 1910 the US education system began to be transformed into the core elements of the modern school system. High school education was now increasingly necessary, bringing the number of students from 200,000 in 1890 to 1,000,000 by 1910, and to almost 2,000,000 by 1920. Only seven percent of American youths aged 14 to 17 were enrolled in high school in 1890, but this rose to thirty-two percent in 1920 according to Robert Church in his book *Education in the United States*. The new high school graduates found jobs in the rapidly growing white-collar sector. After 1910, vocational education was added as a mechanism to train the technicians and skilled workers needed by the rapidly expanding industrial sector. Cities large and small across the country raced to build new schools to meet these professional and industrial demands.

The comparative quality of education among rich and poor districts is still often the subject of dispute. At least on the surface, middle class African-American and middle class Latino children have mostly the same educational opportunities as Whites. However the working class and poor minorities, including almost all Native Americans, and some poor Whites, especially in the South and in Northern rural areas, do not enjoy the same quality of education. With school systems funded by property taxes there are wide disparities in funding between wealthy suburbs or districts, and the poor inner-city areas or poor small towns and rural areas. De facto segregation and classism are prevalent in residential neighborhoods and many rural schools have remained poor and isolated based upon on income, race, ethnicity and class. Indian reservations are but one glaring example of this.

The American public school system also regularly discriminates against children with physical and mental disabilities. It was such a prevalent problem that in 1975 Congress passed Public Law 94-142, Education for All Handicapped Children Act (EHA). One of the most comprehensive laws in the history of education in the United States, this Act created legislation making free, appropriate education available to all students with a physical or mental disability. The act allows parents to design an "Individual Education Program" (IEP) with the school to meet their child's needs. It also allows administrative and/or court remedies for parents who believe the school is not sufficiently meeting their child's needs.

The current American concept of the public school is not that old. American's support of public schools is also waning, as private schools and parochial schools once again are calling for school vouchers and various charter schools are competing for public funds. It appears that all these alternative institutions are eroding precious resources needed to continue a universal public education that serves a fundamental function of crossing social and cultural boundaries to create a more unified citizenry. This destruction of universal education serves racial, class, religious and political biases.

American Colleges & Universities

> My mother said I must always be intolerant of ignorance
> but understanding of illiteracy. That some people, unable to

go to school, were more educated and intelligent than college professors.

—Maya Angelou

American culture has been enormously influenced by American colleges and universities. And these influences were primarily Christian and capitalist. Most colleges and universities have very deep religious roots. Most of the early American colleges were created as religious training institutions for the ministry and were operated by mostly the Protestant clergy.

Harvard was America's first college and was founded by a deathbed request of Reverend John Harvard, a Puritan minister who left money and a significant library to start a college for ministers. John Harvard was originally from Stratford on Avon and his father, Thomas Rogers, was said to have been an associate of William Shakespeare.

Harvard's offer to found a college was so well received that the colonial legislature helped finance it and named the college after him. After its founding in 1636, most of the operating funds came from the colony, but early on the college also began to build an endowment. Harvard's mission was to educate young men for the ministry, but as "god's chosen" many alumni also went into law, medicine, government, or important business positions.

The College of William and Mary was founded by the Virginia colonial government in 1693, with 20,000 acres of land for an endowment, and a penny tax on every pound of tobacco, together with an annual colonial appropriation. It was designed to educate Virginia's elite planter class. This too was a religious institution and James Blair, the leading Anglican minister in the colony, was its president for fifty years. The college received broad support of the Virginia gentry, most of whom were Anglicans. It trained many of the lawyers, politicians, and the leading planters. Students headed for the ministry were given free tuition paid by the colony.

Yale College was founded in 1701 in Connecticut. The conservative Puritan ministers of Connecticut had grown dissatisfied with what they considered to be the more liberal theology of Harvard, and they wanted their own school to train more conservative ministers.

Presbyterians in 1747 set up the College of New Jersey in the town of Princeton. Later it was renamed Princeton University. Rhode Island College was begun by the Baptists in 1764, and in 1804 it was renamed Brown University. In New York City, the Anglicans set up King's College in 1746. It was closed down during the Revolutionary War. After the war, it was re-opened as Columbia College and later became Columbia University. The Dutch Reformed Church in 1766 started Queens College in New Jersey, which later became Rutgers University. These so-called "Ivy League" schools became the model for both American public and private colleges and universities. One of the first non-religious public colleges was The Academy of Pennsylvania. It was created in 1749 by Benjamin Franklin and would later become the University of Pennsylvania.

In twenty-first century America a higher education is now required to have a good income and to have a satisfactory life, although it does not guarantee one. According to the 2000 US Census the average annual income over the forty years of a person's working life, with differing levels of education, is as follows: A person with less than a high school education will earn an average of less than $20,000 per year. A person with a high school education will earn an average of $24,000 per year. A person with two years of college or completes trade school will average $30,000 per year. A person who has a four-year college degree will average $42,000 per year. A person with a graduate degree will average $50,000 per year, and a law or medical degree will average $88,000 per year. Education attainment has shown to be the primary factor in determining US incomes. As the world increasingly becomes a more global economy, education will be the determining factor in personal prosperity or poverty.

The Rise and Fall of American Education

An investment in knowledge pays the best interest.

—Benjamin Franklin

On June 16, 2013 in *The New York Times*, Rebecca Strauss from the Council on Foreign Relations in an opinion piece entitled "Schooling Ourselves in an Unequal America" wrote: "America's average standing in global education rankings has tumbled not because everyone is falling, but because of the country's deep, still-widening achievement gap between socioeconomic groups."

The American education system is relatively new in historical terms. The United States did not really achieve real education for the average person until the twentieth century. A high school education did not become the norm until the 1950s and 1960s and as desegregation was enforced. Indeed less than a third of 14 to 18 year old American children attended high school in 1920, and only seven percent in 1890. Yes there were some literate Americans who did not have a high school education, but not that many.

Likewise a college education, once only for the upper and some middle class Americans, only became universally available in the 1950s, 1960s, and 1970s, mostly because of the G.I. Bill and the well financed and inexpensive public universities and colleges. Today college educations have become affordable for only a few. The GI Bill is not as universal as in previous eras. Tuition and other costs have risen sharply, and student loans are more expensive and are being cut back. An average undergraduate of a public institution can expect to graduate with debts of over $40,000.

The brief window of universal American public education appears to be closing. America's public school system, and universal education and literacy which Americans touted as one of the characteristics justifying their notion of American Exceptionalism, is failing. It is failing, as Strauss said, "because of the country's deep, still-widening achievement gap between socioeconomic groups." It is failing because a college education is increasingly unaffordable and unavailable. The radio host and newspaper columnist David Sirota asked recently, "Are we really expected to believe that it's just a coincidence that the public education and poverty crises are happening at the same time? ...That everything other than poverty is what's causing problems in failing public schools?"

I would also ask the question: Is it any surprise that poverty rates would rise in a nation that is failing to provide everyone with a basic education and where college is largely affordable only to the upper class? In comparing us to other industrialized nations, it appears that America is much less than exceptional. In terms of education, American exceptionalism is not the reality.

American Literature

> All modern American literature comes from one book by Mark Twain called Huckleberry Finn.
>
> —Ernest Hemingway

The first piece of American literature was written in 1637 by Thomas Morton, an American colonist who became a political celebrity with the publication of his three-volume *New English Canaan*. The books mocked the religious Puritan settlers and declared that the Native Americans were actually better people than the English and the Puritans. He was popular in Europe, but unpopular in the colonies.

Morton headed the Merrymount settlement in Massachusetts. Under Morton's leadership a utopian project was started, in which all the colonists were declared "free men" and given the freedom of integrating with the local Algonquin culture, including promoting inter-marriage. Morton began to convert the Native population to his liberal form of Christianity by providing them with trade goods and free salt for food preservation. These practices soon got him into trouble with his Puritan neighbors who strongly condemned his colony as hedonistic. They were also very jealous because his settlement with the help of the Native Americans was by far the most prosperous.

The Plymouth Militia under Myles Standish took the settlement by force and received little resistance by the passive people of Merrymount. He arrested Morton on a trumped up charge of "supplying guns to the Indians." Morton was put in stocks in Plymouth until he was given a mock trial. He was then was sentenced to be marooned on a deserted island off the coast, where the Puritans thought he would soon starve to death. The Native Americans secretly fed him until he was rescued by an English ship and

Morton went to England to write his books.

Ann Bradstreet was the first poet and first female writer in the British North American colonies to be published. Her first volume of poetry was *The Tenth Muse Lately Sprung Up in America*, published in 1650.

Most of the other early American literary works were religious pamphlets and essays, and journals and histories of the settlements and colonies. An early classic was *Travels through North and South Carolina, Georgia, East and West*, written by naturalist William Bartram in the 1780s. It described in great detail the Southern landscape, the lives of colonists and the Native American peoples along with the topography, flora and fauna that he encountered. The book was translated into a half dozen languages and was widely read in Western Europe as well as America.

Another American naturalist author that is worth noting is John James Audubon, a French-American. His book *Birds of America* is still considered one of the greatest examples of book art. His influence on ornithology and natural history was far reaching. Nearly all later ornithological works were inspired by his artistry and high standards. Charles Darwin quoted Audubon three times in his work, *On the Origin of the Species*, and again in later works. Audubon personally discovered 25 new species and 12 new subspecies of birds.

After the War of 1812 America began to discover its own identity and there was an increasing desire to produce uniquely American literature and authors. New literary figures emerged such as Washington Irving, William Cullen Bryant, James Fenimore Cooper, and one of the most different American writers, Edgar Allan Poe. These were all of English heritage, but Irving is often considered the first writer to develop a unique American style. He was America's first largely acclaimed and internationally best-selling author. Irving advocated for writing as a legitimate profession, and argued for stronger laws to protect American writers from copyright infringement. He was also was an inspiration for other American writers such as Nathaniel Hawthorne, Herman Melville and the poet Henry Wadsworth Longfellow. He was even an inspiration to several noted British writers like Charles Dickens.

Hawthorne went on to write full-length romances and novels that explore such themes as guilt, pride, and emotional repression in his native Puritan New England. His best book, *The Scarlet Letter*, is a dark drama of a woman cast out of her community for committing adultery. His work has held up over time as *The Scarlet Letter* was made into a movie starring Demi Moore not that long ago. He was the first writer in English Puritan America to write significantly about sexual relations. (A personal note: During my final draft of this book I discovered that Hawthorne is a distant relative of mine.)

The next significant group of writers were the Transcendentalists, most notably Ralph Waldo Emerson and Henry David Thoreau both of English heritage. Thoreau was a resolute nonconformist and urged resistance to the mundane dictates of organized society. His radical writings express a deep-rooted passion for individualism in the American character. His philosophy would be revived in the 1960s counterculture and later by left-leaning libertarians.

One of the most prolific American writers was Samuel Clemons, better known as Mark Twain. Twain grew up in Missouri and was the son of two Southerners of English heritage. Twain began his career writing humorous verse, but evolved into a chronicler of the American culture, its hypocrisies and the darker side of mankind, particularly Southern culture. In his book *Huckleberry Finn*, he combined humor, along with a realistic narrative and social criticism. Twain was a master at colloquial dialects and helped to create and popularize a distinctive American literature built on American themes and language. His books have been banned at times for this language. Twain's humor far outlasted him inspiring future writers, humorists and comedians like Will Rogers and Groucho Marx.

According to Connie Ann Kirk in her book *Mark Twain: A Biography*, a complete bibliography of Twain's writings is impossible to compile. Apparently a very large number of pieces written by Twain were often in obscure newspapers and he frequently used different pen names. A large portion of his speeches and lectures have been lost, however the collection of Twain's works is an ongoing process as researchers discover his works in obscure places and researchers have rediscovered more published material by Twain as recently as 1995.

The early twentieth century saw an intense group of American writers like English-Americans Ezra Pound, William Faulkner, Ernest Hemingway and Irish-American F. Scott Fitzgerald. The great Depression produced another crop of passionate writers, but none better or more prolific than John Steinbeck who was of German and Irish descent. His novels *The Grapes of Wrath, Of mice and Men, Tortilla Flat, Cannery Row, East of Eden,* and one of the best books about the 1950s, *The Winter of Our Discontent,* still rank at the top of American literature.

American playwrights also came into their own in the twentieth century with writers like Irish-American Eugene O'Neill, Tennessee Williams of English and French descent, Jewish-Americans Arthur Miller and Neil Simon, African-American August Wilson, and Edward Albee who is of unknown ethnicity because he was adopted at birth.

World War II produced an interesting group of books and new writers with German-American Kurt Vonnegut's *Slaughterhouse Five,* Jewish-Americans Joseph Heller's *Catch 22,* along with Norman Mailer's *Naked and the Dead.* These books would later help give rise to the American peace, anti-war and countercultural movements. The Counterculture was most influenced by the Beat writers. Works like Jewish-American Allen Ginsberg's poem *Howl,* the English-American William S. Burroughs' *Naked Lunch,* and three works of Jack Kerouac (of French-Canadian ancestry) — *On the Road, The Subterraneans,* and perhaps the most influential, *The Dharma Bums* — were arguably the primary inspiration for the counterculture, Beatnik and Hippie movements.

CHAPTER 16. BLUES AND JAZZ

Gospel and the blues are really, if you break it down, almost the same thing. It's just a question of whether you're talkin' about a woman or God.

—Craig Werner

She's no lady. Her songs are all unbelievably unhappy or lewd. It's called Blues. She sings about sore feet, sexual relations, baked goods, killing your lover, being broke, men called Daddy, women who dress like men, working, praying for rain, jail and trains, whiskey and morphine. She tells stories between verses and everyone in the place shouts out how true it all is.

—Ann-Marie MacDonald

Jazz is known all over the world as an American musical art form and that's it. No America, no jazz. I've seen people try to connect it to other countries, for instance to Africa, but it doesn't have a damn thing to do with Africa.

—Art Blakey

One chord is fine. Two chords are pushing it. Three chords and you're into jazz.

—Lou Reed

The Blues

Willie Dixon said, "The Blues are the roots, everything else is the fruits." The Blues are probably the most influential music in American culture. Jazz and Rock

& Roll were inspired by the Blues. The phrase "the blues" comes from an early American idea of the attack on the mind from "the blue devils," meaning melancholy, depression and sadness. "The blues" was a common phrase since colonial America, and was also frequently used to describe the life of Black slaves. The origin of the term of was most likely derived from African mysticism. It involved blue indigo dye, which was used by many West African cultures in death and mourning ceremonies where all the mourner's garments would have been dyed blue to indicate suffering. Blue indigo was also one of the first crops grown by African slaves in America also adding to its cultural significance in the African-American community.

According to Francis Davis in his book *The History of Blues: The Roots, The Music, The People*, the use of the phrase "the Blues" in African-American music is very old. However the first copyrighted use of the "Blues" was in a composition in 1912, with Hart Wand's *Dallas Blues*. One of the best descriptions of the Blues comes from Edward Comentale in his book *Sweet Air: Modernism, Regionalism and American Popular Song*. He wrote: "The blues takes many forms... It is variously a feeling, a mood, a nameless threat, a person, a lover, a boss man, a mob, and, of course, the Devil himself. It is often experienced as both cause and effect, action and reaction, and it can be used as both hex and counter hex, poison and antidote, pain and relief. Most importantly, the blues is both the cause of the song, and the song itself."

Sex was a major theme in the Blues. Sex was often portrayed humorously as in Big Joe Turner's song *Rebecca* with his lyrics: "Rebecca, get your big legs off of me. It may be sending you baby, but it's worrying the hell out of me." And in Roy Orbison singing "She's got groovy lips she's got shapely hips, but I gotta woman as mean as she can be." Even the term "Rock & Roll" was first used as a Blues term for sex.

Tragedy, misery and disaster were the backbone of the Blues. Cheating lovers, rejection, death, poverty, the exhaustion of back-breaking work, storms, floods, and fires have all been used to inspire Blues songs. The Blues is a cyclical musical form with a repeating progression of chords and also uses the African-American call and response in its lyrics.

In 1920 Americans quickly bought more than a million copies of "Crazy Blues" by Mamie Smith, the first Black female to record a blues vocal. This unexpected success forced White and mainstream record labels to see the potential profit of "negro and Blues records." Outstanding performers such as Ma Rainy and Bessie Smith began to introduce the blues to an even wider audience of African-Americans and eventually to Whites through their recordings.

As the African-American community and Southern and rural Whites began moving away from the South to find work in the quickly industrializing North, Blues music evolved to reflect urban circumstances. Thousands of farm workers migrated north to cities like Chicago and Detroit during both World Wars, many began to view traditional Blues as an unwanted reminder of their slave and Jim Crow days of field work and they wanted to hear Blues music that reflected their new urban lives. Transplanted blues artists such as Muddy Waters, who had lived and worked on a Mississippi plantation before coming to Chicago in 1943, began to change their music. He and other Blues artists swapped their acoustic guitars for electric guitars and filled out the Blues sound with a backup of drums, harmonica, and brass. This gave rise to an electrified Blues sound with a stirring beat that would be a new signature American sound and provide the foundations for both Jazz and Rock & Roll.

In the late 1940s and early 1950s, the electrified blues reached its peak, but then it began to decline as White and African-American listeners turned to Rock & Roll and soul music. In the early 1960s, however, as English bands like the Animals and The Rolling Stones began to perform covers of traditional Blues songs and many Americans became once again interested in the Blues.

Jazz

Jazz came of age with America in the twentieth century. It is purely American music with roots that originated, within the African-American communities of the South. As Art Blakey, one of the originators of the Bebop movement, said, "No America, no jazz." Its roots lie in the adoption by African-Americans of European harmony and form, and taking those European elements and combining them into their long existing African-based music. Its African musical roots are evident in its use of the Blue note which is sung or played at a slightly lower pitch than that of the major scale for expressive purposes, along with improvisation, polyrhythm and syncopation.

Jazz has developed regional and local musical styles influenced by the local sub-cultures. Some of these include: New Orleans Jazz dating from the early 1910s. Dixieland Jazz which developed in Chicago and spread to New York. Big Band or Swing Jazz came from the large orchestras with crooners like Frank Sinatra. Kansas City Jazz was developed by artists like Charlie Parker who transitioned from Swing to Bebop. Many other forms have been created since World War II. Some jazz purists have disdained these newer forms as "commercial." These forms of jazz that some feel are commercially oriented or influenced by popular music have been criticized since emergence of bebop and there is an on-going tension in America between jazz as a commercial music and an art form.

Chapter 17. American Gun Culture

> A well regulated Militia, being necessary to the security of a free State, the right of the people to keep and bear Arms, shall not be infringed.
>
> — The Second Amendment to the US Constitution

> Militia: 1. A body of citizens enrolled for military service, and called out periodically for drill, but serving full time only in emergencies.
>
> —Webster's New Universal Unabridged Dictionary

"A well regulated militia" is the most misunderstood phrase in American culture. The dictionary clearly defines "militia" as military unit of citizen soldiers who are called up during emergencies. They are what we now call the National Guard or the military reserves. However, this phrase of the Second Amendment is now being used to justify the right of virtually everyone, with no exception, to own a gun.

The legal history of gun rights are interesting. In 1875 the Supreme Court ruled in *the United States v. Cruikshank* that the right to bear arms is not guaranteed by the Constitution. In 1939 the Supreme Court ruled again in the *United States v. Miller* that the Second Amendment was for "the preservation or efficiency of a well regulated militia." However in 2008 the Supreme Court in the *District of Columbia v. Heller* by a partisan vote of five to four decided that it "protects an individual right to possess a firearm unconnected with service in a militia, and to use that arm for traditionally lawful purposes, such as self-defense within the home." But the Court also ruled that "the right is not unlimited. It is not a right to keep and carry any weapon whatsoever in any manner whatsoever and for whatever purpose." Justice Stevens in his dissent of the opinion wrote: "When each word in the text is given full effect, the Amendment is most naturally read to secure to the people a right to use and possess arms in conjunction with service in a well-regulated militia. So far as appears, no more than that was contemplated by its drafters or is encompassed within its terms."

And in 2010 the Supreme Court again in a very politically divided decision ruled in *McDonald v. Chicago* that the Second Amendment also limits state and local governments to regulate guns to the same extent that they claim it limits the federal government.

The definition of the right to own and use guns keeps changing, depending upon which way the political pendulum swings in the court. For those who debate what the founding fathers meant by "militia," Alexander Hamilton made it clear in the Federalist a year before the Constitutional Convention was held. He wrote: "It is, therefore, with the most evident propriety, that the plan of the convention proposes to empower the Union to provide for organizing, arming, and disciplining the militia, and for governing such part of them as may be employed in the service of the United States." His writing clearly does not convey these rights to individuals.

American gun culture has two roots. The first was the hunter/sportsman group and the second was the frontier self-protection group. The hunter/sportsman group are those sports enthusiasts who participate in sports such as hunting, skeet shooting and marksmanship. The second group are the people who believe they must have guns for their personal protection, perhaps even against their government. This fear and need for protection originally developed on the American frontier in areas where the Army or the police were not present and guns were necessary to protect against marauders, murderers, thieves and to fight Native Americans for the land. This frontier self-reliant gun mentality was romanticized in Western movies and television shows, particularly in the 1950s westerns and it has now achieved cult-like status with the paranoid right-wing who want to stockpile weapons to fight "government tyranny" should they wish to do so at some future date.

This is a dangerous cultural ethos which has enabled mass murders by people like Ted Kaczynski, the Oklahoma Bombers, many school shooters, and many others who have decided that the time to fight the government is now. This wild west frontier mentality is the most problematic as it insists on the absolute protection of all individual rights to handguns and automatic and military style weapons. They oppose government regulation or gun registration of any kind and these rights have very little to do with hunting or sports. It is the personal protection group, with their paranoia and their weapons, that are responsible for the majority of mass murders, gun crimes, and even accidental gun deaths in the United States. They encourage the notion that an individual has both a right and a duty to challenge their government or society with violence if they perceive anything wrong.

The National Rifle Association

The NRA was founded in New York in 1871. It was organized to provide gun safety, police training, and to improve marksmanship of the National Guards and Reservists. Its first President was Civil War General Ambrose Burnside who was concerned that most of his troops during the Civil War had very poor marksmanship.

Contrary to their current positions, the NRA in the past strongly supported and lobbied for gun control on individuals and promoted gun safety measures. The NRA supported the 1934 National Fire Arms Act, and they also supported the Gun Control Act of 1968 to license guns and impose taxes on the private ownership of automatic weapons. Until 1992 the NRA governed shooting sports in the United States, but has gradually phased out of much of these efforts in favor of the more lucrative efforts of lobbying and advocacy for the gun and ammunition industry. In short, it has been made into a political weapon.

As of 2013 the NRA has a membership of about five million with an annual budget of $231 million. Congress has rated the NRA as the most powerful lobby. During the 2008 presidential campaign, the NRA spent $10 million in opposition to the election of Barack Obama. In six out of seven surveys conducted by Gallup since 1993, the majority of Americans reported holding a favorable opinion of the National Rifle Association. A Gallup survey conducted in December 2012 found that fifty-four percent of Americans held a favorable opinion of the NRA, with Republicans responding significantly more positively about the organization than Democrats. A Reuters-Ipsos poll conducted in April 2012 found that eighty-two percent of Republicans and fifty-five percent of Democrats see the NRA "in a positive light." And politicians fear the power of the NRA because of their financial ability and willingness to generously finance campaigns against any politician they dislike.

Despite their public popularity the organization has come under criticism recently for its hard rightwing viewpoints and its opposition to any kind of gun regulation in favor of gun manufacturers and ammunition companies. Much of what the organization vehemently opposes today they have supported in the past, such as registration, limits on automatic weapons and high capacity magazines, and the registration of automatic weapons and assault rifles.

The NRA has been increasingly hostile and unwilling to discuss any kind of gun control since Wayne LaPierre became its Chief Operating Officer. In 1995 LaPierre began playing to the paranoid rightwing quasi-military groups and wrote a fundraising letter describing federal Bureau of Alcohol, Tobacco and Firearm agents as "jack-booted government thugs "who wear Nazi bucket helmets and black storm trooper uniforms." Former President George H.W. Bush was so outraged by the letter that he resigned his lifetime membership in the NRA. In 2000 LaPierre said that President Bill Clinton "tolerated a certain amount of violence and killing to strengthen the case for gun control and to score points for his party."

In December of 2012 in the wake of the Sandy Hook Elementary School shootings where twenty children and six adults were murdered, LaPierre blamed the gun violence on gun-free zones, violent films and video games, the media, weak databases and poor control of those with mental illness and lax security. He called for armed police officers in all American schools in an effort to protect children from gun violence. It is recognized by most as a nonsense proposal even if it was affordable, which it is not.

After the 2012 Sandy Hook shooting LaPierre and the NRA produced an online video they created blaming poor local policing and response time, and a lack of school security and teacher and staff training. The video blamed everyone and everything but guns. At LaPierre's direction the NRA began a massive postcard mailing and a robo-calling effort in Connecticut to prevent the legislature from enacting stronger gun safety regulations. These postcards and robo-calls were sent to many of the families of the Sandy Hook victims and the suffering Newtown residents. One resident, Christopher Wenis, said he received numerous robo-calls despite calling the NRA twice to request to be placed on the "Do Not Call" list. These NRA videos ran in New Jersey where Republican Governor Chris Christie called it "reprehensible" and said that it "demeans" the NRA.

In the wake of Sandy Hook President Obama tried to get Congress to enact gun legislation. When President Obama asked for support on gun legislation banning assault weapons and high capacity magazines, he received support from the Philadelphia Police Commissioner Charles Ramsey, the president of the National Police Chiefs Association. Ramsey said that the deaths of twenty students and six teachers and staff members at Sandy Hook Elementary School in Newtown had settled the issue. He said, "If the slaughter of 20 babies does not capture and hold your attention, then I give up, because I don't know what else will."

Unfortunately the Congress, fearing LaPierre and the NRA and their political reprisals, never seriously considered the bill.

According to LaPierre, "The only thing that stops a bad guy with a gun is a good guy with a gun." LaPierre has also said: "Hurricanes, tornadoes, riots, terrorists, gangs, lone criminals, these are perils we are sure to face, not just maybe. It's not paranoia to buy a gun. It's survival. It's responsible behavior, and it's time we encourage law-abiding Americans to do just that." LaPierre is the Elmer Gantry of guns playing upon American paranoia and the America's outdated Wild West and frontier gun culture. LaPierre is a gun salesman of the worst kind.

If Wayne LaPierre represented the nuclear industry, would Americans then all have a nuclear weapon in their basements as a deterrent to their neighbors? If anyone can own military weapons like assault rifles and machine guns, will they next expect to own rocket launchers, anti-aircraft weapons, attack helicopters and tanks? Are these also a part of a right to bear arms?

Obviously American gun culture has run amok. It has nothing to do with a misreading of the Second Amendment or personal liberties. It is about right-wing paranoia and the gun and ammunition industries playing upon these fears and paranoia. It is about a history and culture of gun violence. It is a warped philosophy that believes that if we reach a point where an individual or a group decides to dislike their school or government then they have the ability and freedom to start killing and asserting their will on others.

Today we allow children to be mass murdered in schools, police officers to be killed by people with better weaponry, snipers to kill motorists along freeways, assassins to commit mass killings in movie theatres, schools, medical clinics, public sporting events, and other public places. And a majority of Americans think this is all necessary to protect their gun freedoms and to protect them from a potentially bad government. Unfortunately American politicians and judges who know better are too cowardly to change this disastrous course.

Chapter 18. American Military Culture

> In the councils of government, we must guard against the acquisition of unwarranted influence, whether sought or unsought, by the military-industrial complex. The potential for the disastrous rise of misplaced power exists and will persist.
>
> —Dwight D. Eisenhower

> History demonstrates that previous military drawdowns invited aggression by our enemies. After World War I, America drew down forces until the US Army had fewer than 100,000 men in uniform. That weakness invited Nazi aggression in Europe and the imperial Japanese attack at Pearl Harbor.
>
> —Frank Gaffney, founder and president of the Center for Security Policy

The military culture is a significant part of mainstream American culture. Americans, like the above quoted Frank Gaffney, believe that bigger is better when it involves the US military and we have largely ignored Eisenhower's warning. The Pentagon's 2010 Base Structure Report lists 4,999 total base sites in the US, American territories, and overseas. According to the Report, the US military maintained 662 foreign sites in 38 countries around the world. America still maintains permanent bases in Italy, Japan and Germany from World War II, and in Korea from the Korean War.

According to the National Defense Authorization Act for 2013 the US spends about $554.2 billion annually to fund its military forces. This does not include the CIA or "black ops" budgets which are classified. There are 1,429,995 active duty military personnel in the United States Armed Forces and 850,880 Reserves.

There are also 108,833 civilian contractors working for the military. This does not include a federally funded private army of private security contractors (PSCs). These include Blackwater (now Academi), who works for the Department of Defense in the USCENTCOM area of operations, according to a Secretary of Defense report on PSCs in 2011. The report said that in Iraq and Afghanistan there were over 137,400 PSCs working for the military in 2011.

According to the US Department of Veteran Affairs, the Office of the Actuary, there were approximately 23 million military veterans in the United States in 2010.

President Eisenhower in his 1961 speech on the Military Industrial complex said about American military culture that "the total influence economic, political, even spiritual, is felt in every city, every State house, every office of the Federal government."

American military culture has always been an important element in American culture but it has been a very major influence in the twentieth and twenty-first centuries.

It is also very male dominated. Lt. Colonel Karen O. Dunivan in her paper *Military Culture a Paradigm Shift* referred to the traditional US military as an "exclusionary combat, masculine-warrior paradigm or belief system." And although the culture is changing, it is definitely a male-dominated warrior culture and still stands in opposition to America's changing gender equality. This is evidenced by the continuing harassment and sexual abuse of women in the military and a still prevalent opposition to gay and lesbians serving in the military. Dunivan's paper shows the difference between what she labels as "old thinking vs. new thinking." She uses two recent cases to illustrate the divergence between the paradigm and the desired new model of women in combat and gays in the military.

False Idol Worship

America has a supposed reverence for its 23 million veterans. This is disproven by our failure to provide these veterans with the services they need and deserve. The large number of homeless veterans and veterans with unaddressed health issues haunts America today. The Veteran Administration wait lists are long and it can take years to process a claim. Currently veterans wait up to two years for their claims to be resolved and needed medical services provided. For many years, the military and the US government and the American taxpayer denied veteran's claims of post-traumatic stress disorders, as well as service-related chemical dependency. They have consistently denied veteran claims about Agent Orange and other hazardous exposures which have caused cancer and destroyed the central nervous systems of veterans and caused birth defects like spina bifida in their children. Veterans face long waits for care. They are forced to re-apply multiple times or are denied care outright. As the number of veterans has grown with the wars in Iraq and Afghanistan, the system failures are more and more evident.

America is a jingoistic country that ties yellow ribbons around trees and posts loving tributes to veterans and service members on Facebook. It thanks veterans for their service and applauds veterans at public events. Americans proudly shout the Pledge of Allegiance when requested, and will stand and sing the Star Spangled Banner at sporting events. They will quickly rally to war at the slightest provocation by their government. But Americans refuse to pay higher taxes to care for the disabled veterans. Americans love their fighting men and women overseas, but leave them begging on the streets upon their return.

The Chicken Hawks and Lies Leading to Unnecessary Wars

American jingoism and the military industrial complex was at its worst in the lead up to the Vietnam War where a fake battle in the Gulf of Tonkin was an excuse for America to begin a useless war. Americans also tend to repeat their historical mistakes.

The Iraq War, where America was again the aggressor, was again a war where the President and his cronies lied to the American people to make war. Bush, Vice President Cheney and Secretary of Defense Rumsfeld and Under Secretary Wolfowitz said that it was about defending the world against terrorists who were developing weapons of mass destruction. These men have been dubbed "the Chicken Hawks" as explained above. Although Bush was briefly in the Air Reserves, most of his service time was spent assisting in a Republican senatorial campaign in Alabama. The wealthy and connected placed their children in the Military Reserves during the Vietnam War because the reserves were rarely called up during that conflict. By contrast, a draft (conscription) took millions of working class men to war. When men in Washington are willing to send other men to war for questionable causes, but were themselves unwilling to serve in the active military when it was their turn, we as a proud and patriotic nation have some questions to ask ourselves.

Vice President Dick Cheney said on August 26, 2002, "Simply stated, there is no doubt that Saddam Hussein now has weapons of mass destruction." President George W. Bush said on September 12, 2002, "Right now, Iraq is expanding and improving facilities that were used for the production of biological weapons." And on March 18, 2003, "Intelligence gathered by this and other governments leaves no doubt that the Iraq regime continues to possess and conceal some of the most lethal weapons ever devised." Secretary of Defense Donald Rumsfeld said on March 30, 2003, "We know where they are. They are in the area around Tikrit and Baghdad."

They also persuaded the Generals to repeat their lies: General Colin Powell said on February 5, 2003, "We know that Saddam Hussein is determined to keep his weapons of mass destruction, is determined to make more." And General Tommy Franks said on March 22, 2003, "There is no doubt that the regime of Saddam Hussein possesses weapons of mass destruction. As this operation continues, those weapons will be identified, found, along with the people who have produced them and who guard them."

No weapons of mass destruction were ever found because there were none. The Administration also knew there were none. A glimpse into why the administration lied was given in a statement by Deputy Secretary of Defense Paul Wolfowitz on May 28, 2003. He said, "For bureaucratic reasons, we settled on one issue, weapons of mass destruction [as justification for invading Iraq] because it was the one reason everyone could agree on [as sufficient to go to war]."

The Bush Administration also falsely claimed that Iraq was trying to buy uranium in Africa to make a nuclear bomb. When former Ambassador Joseph C. Wilson stated his opinion in various interviews and in his 2004 memoir *The Politics of Truth* that Iraq was *not* purchasing uranium, members of President George W. Bush's administration revealed that Wilson's wife Valerie Plame was a covert CIA agent. This destroyed her career and Wilson's diplomatic career. It was the Administration's revenge for Wilson's statements and his op-ed titled *What I Didn't Find in Africa*, published in *New York Times* on July 6, 2003. The article was the first to publicly expose the Bush Administration lies.

Because "outing" a CIA agent is a felony, someone had to go to jail. Scooter Libby, a senior aide to Vice President Cheney, was convicted of this and of perjury and was sentenced to prison. But his two-and-a-half-year prison sentence was commuted by George W. Bush, and later Virginia Gov. Republican Bob McDonnell very quietly restored his voting rights to allow him to participate in Republican politics again.

The Bush Administration's war in Iraq was not about weapons of mass destruction or military threats. Many now believe it was about oil reserves and what the Bush Administration would call "Nation Building," a blatant attempt to create a pro-American Christian-capitalist type of government in Iraq. President George W. Bush has since dedicated his presidential library to this concept of Nation Building.

Most Americans believed the Bush Administration's lies about weapons of mass destruction and cited it as their reason for supporting the war. Most US polls showed that immediately before and after the 2003 invasion of Iraq, a substantial majority supported the war, but by December 2004 when no weapons of mass destruction were found and it was apparent that the administration lied, the polls began to then consistently show that a majority of Americans thought the Iraq invasion was a very bad mistake.

Homeland Security

Those who sacrifice liberty for *security* deserve neither.

—Benjamin Franklin

In the wake of September 11, 2001, the Department of Homeland Security was created. It was the biggest reorganization of the federal government since the Cold War. It had an authorized budget for Fiscal Year 2012 of $46.9 billion. It has eight so-called "child agencies" that were reorganized under its leadership including the Coast Guard, the US Customs and Border Security, the US Secret Service, the Federal Emergency Management Administration, US Customs and Custom Enforcement, US Citizenship and Immigration Services, the National Protection and Programs Directorate, and the Transportation Security Administration.

The Transportation Security Administration (TSA) was a new agency and was also created after 9/11 to provide airport security. In June of 2013 an editorial by radio talk show host and newspaper columnist Glenn Mollette entitled: *We Must Overhaul the Role of the TSA*, was published in various newspapers. Mollette wrote that the TSA budget is now over $7.6 billion and the average paycheck for the 3,900 administrative employees at the Washington, D.C. office is $103,852.

According to the TSA website they have 65,000 employees and much of TSA's workforce is Transportation Security Officers (TSOs). About 50,000 TSOs screen 1.8 million passengers everyday at more than 450 airports across the country. A June 2008 study by the US Travel Association shows a deep frustration among air travelers because of the TSA and their intrusive security measures that caused them to avoid an estimated 41 million trips over the past 12 months at a cost of more than $26 billion to the US economy. The effect of these avoided trips cost airlines more than $9 billion. Hotels lost nearly $6 billion and restaurants more than $3 billion. Federal, state and local governments lost more than $4 billion in tax revenue because of reduced spending by travelers who travel less because of the difficulties brought about by the TSA. Congressman Mike Rogers, an Alabama Republican, and chairman of the House Homeland Security Transportation Security Subcommittee, said at a June 12, 2012 hearing: "The American people are just really disgusted and outraged with the department, (TSA) which they see as bloated and inefficient."

In addition to discouraging air travel and dampening the American economy, the TSA is a costly intrusion on American freedoms. The TSA also plays upon American's xenophobia encouraging a fear of others. Despite TSA's army of personnel and large budget it is also debatable whether the TSA actually makes Americans safer or just makes them feel safer. It doesn't matter most Americans are xenophobic and paranoid and will believe they need the TSA even if they are really an unnecessary harassment and are losing their liberties in the process.

CHAPTER 19. AMERICAN OIL CULTURE

"Black gold," "Texas Tea," whatever it was called it was cheap energy in the form of oil that made the American economy the world's largest. Cheap abundant energy was the reason for American success and may be the reason for its downfall as the United States has began to run out of cheap oil, and as the effects of global warming and climate change become more apparent.

Petroleum became a major industry following the oil discovery at Oil Creek Pennsylvania in 1859. The principal product of oil in the 19th century was kerosene, which quickly replaced whale oil for illuminating purposes in the United States (thereby saving the whales from sure extinction).

John D. Rockefeller formed the Standard Oil Company of Ohio in 1870. In the early 1870s, oil exploration in Pennsylvania's Oil Creek region grew rapidly, and Rockefeller also expanded the exploration of oil to other states and nations during the next decade. By 1879, his Standard Oil controlled 90 percent of US refining capacity, as well as the majority of rail lines between urban centers in the northeastern US and most oil exploration equipment leasing companies at most sites of oil speculation throughout the country and the world. Due to Rockefeller's efforts and developments, petroleum became the primary energy source not only in the US, but for markets around the world. Rockefeller and Standard Oil recognized the potential market and he worked to dominate everything that controlled the flow of oil, its refinement and its sale and delivery to markets. Rockefeller's system of refineries and oil drilling leasing companies had grown immensely by the close of the nineteenth century. This monopoly and the shear the size of his holdings allowed him to demand and get lower rates and kickbacks from independent rail companies and shipping lines that transported his products.

He ruthlessly drove any competitors out of business and made Standard

Oil into a mega-monopoly. Standard Oil's reach extended throughout the world, making it a prominent symbol of the "Gilded Age," when businesses were allowed to grow unregulated, charging whatever prices they wanted, paying whatever wages they wanted and benefiting only a few wealthy owners. It made a lie of the American free market. Rockefeller also presided over a very large army of industrial spies and lobbyists who stole secrets and bribed governments and officials all over the world. This army of spies and industrial thieves would be drafted intact and become the Office of Strategic Services in World War II and continue afterward as the Central Intelligence Agency.

Ida Tarbell's *The History of the Standard Oil Company*, published in 1904, caused a national furor over the company's unfair trading practices and ruthless bribery and domination of governments around the world. President Teddy Roosevelt used the information in Tarbell's book to enforce anti-trust laws, eventually resulting in Standard Oil's dissolution in 1911. Rockefeller's monopoly had become so large, that when broken into subsidiaries, the pieces would themselves become giant oil companies which included: Mobil, Exxon, Chevron, Amoco, Conoco, and Atlantic among others.

American oil companies dominated the world market treating other nation's oil supplies as colonies. Rockefeller had organized an army of spies, security people, and influence peddlers to control the oil supplies of the US and other nations. It was so vast that after Pearl Harbor when Roosevelt and the military realized that they desperately needed an intelligence and security organization they were forced to borrow Rockefeller's spies and they formally became the OSS the forerunner to the American CIA. During World War II Rockefeller Center in New York was known as "the House of Spies," according to Daniel Okrent in his book *Great Fortune, The Epic of Rockefeller Center*.

One of Rockefeller's business partners, Allan Dulles would become the first Director of the CIA. His brother, another Rockefeller crony, John Foster Dulles would become Eisenhower's Secretary of State. Another business partner, Prescott Bush, would become a Senator and his son another oil man, George Herbert Walker Bush, became CIA Director and president, and his grandson George W. Bush would also become president.

On September 14, 1960, a new organization, the Organization of the Petroleum Exporting Countries (OPEC) was formed to eliminate US domination and to curtail US companies from making most of the money by extracting the oil resources of other countries for little or no benefit to the nations with the oil. OPEC had definitive objectives, to protect their oil from US dominance and to defend the price of oil. OPEC also began to insist that US and other Western oil companies consult with them before exploring and developing their oil. They also committed themselves to solidarity, and aspired to reach a day when the giant oil companies and the Western nations would come to them to negotiate fair prices for their oil.

Rockefeller and the United States propped up a number of royal families and dictators in the Middle East to control the supply of oil. The House of Saud in Saudi Arabia in particular. This manipulation of the oil resources and politics in the Middle East is one reason for such high tension and dislike for Americans and the West in the region. It is at least as divisive as the American support of Israel which is usually the only reason given in the American press for Middle East tensions between America and Islamic Nations.

For much of the nineteenth and twentieth centuries the US was the largest oil producing country in the world, and despite Middle East oil it is still the third largest. According to the latest International Energy Agency report published in November 2012, the US is projected to become the largest global oil producer by at least 2020. It will overtake Saudi Arabia, and together with improvements in transportation energy use, the US will become a net oil exporter by 2030. Currently the US is a net importer of twenty percent of its energy needs. (Some recent numbers have shown America to be currently oil independent.) Some of this is due to environmentally controversial technology like fracking which uses a hydraulic process to free oil and gas from rock, but much of this is also due to the waning oil supplies in the rest of the world.

Another fossil fuel, natural gas, was also a by-product of the American oil culture. The US natural gas industry started in 1821 at Fredonia, New York, when William Hart dug a well to a depth of 27 feet into shale rock discovering natural gas. He then drilled 43 feet further, and piped the natural gas to a nearby inn where it was burned in gas lamps for illumination. Soon many gas wells were drilled in the area, and the gas-lit streets of Fredonia became a large tourist attraction.

During most of the 19th century, natural gas was used almost exclusively as a source of light, but in 1885, Robert Bunsen's invention of what is now known as the Bunsen burner opened vast new opportunities to use natural gas. Once effective natural gas pipelines were built in the 20th century, the use of natural gas quickly expanded to home heating and cooking. It became the fuel for appliances such as water heaters and ovens, and for manufacturing and processing plants, and in boilers to generate electricity. It is estimated that America currently has enough natural gas reserves for about a hundred year's supply of American energy.

As the oil company's search for new supplies wanes, American consumers have slowly begun to consider alternative methods of powering automobiles and their other energy needs. America has started a serious search for new and alternative energy sources, as most industry analysts now agree that the American oil culture will end by 2050. According to the latest International Energy Agency report, published in November 2012, we have consumed 800 billion barrels and there are supposedly 850 billion barrels of reserves left. There is some serious disputes about these reserves as some think they are very highly overstated for political and other reasons. There are also some estimates that up to 150 billion barrels of oil remain undiscovered which may also be very optimistic, but even if these optimistic figures are true there is still an end in sight, and with increased usage around the world that end is about 2050. Hopefully this end is not too late to prevent more catastrophic climate change.

American Car Culture

> Someone should write an erudite essay on the moral, physical, and esthetic effect of the Model T Ford on the American nation. Two generations of Americans knew more about the Ford coil than the clitoris, about the planetary system of gears than the solar system of stars. With the Model T, part of the concept of private property disappeared. Pliers ceased to be privately owned and a tire pump belonged to the last man who had picked it up. Most of the babies of the period were conceived in Model T Fords and not a few were born in them. The theory of the Anglo Saxon home became so warped that it never quite recovered.
>
> —John Steinbeck

Americans love their cars. They live much of their lives in them, they eat in them, they watch movies and listen to radio and music in them, and make love in them. Even though it is the smell of potentially harmful chemicals, "new car smell" is one of America's favorite odors. If you ask Americans what defines their freedom, a good number of them would describe the freedom of the open road. It is the ability to get in a car and to go anywhere at any time, or to pickup everything and move to a new life. America is so crazy about mobility and automobiles that a good number choose to live their lives in things called recreational vehicles which are homes you can drive down the road. They get poor gas mileage and considering their cost, gas and maintenance they make little sense in that a person or two could spend their lives on the road in motels for less money.

The peak of American car culture was in the 1950s when cars were king and gasoline was cheap. In the 1950s cars were big and fast. To many Americans, cars are like fatty fast foods, bad for you but totally irresistible. In the 1950s American life increasingly revolved around the automobile. Americans created suburbs far from work. They put heat and air conditioning in their cars. They created car washes to bathe them and service stations to care for them. They bought insurance for them, and polished them. They created drive-in movies and theatres, and drive-up windows for restaurants, banks, pharmacies, and even groceries and liquor. They created drive-in church services, and strip malls, and drive-through coffee shops. They created car radios, car phones and a variety of other electronic devices for exclusive use in the car. They built garages attached to their houses originally for one car, then two and then three cars. They overpaid for them to show off for neighbors and friends. They customize them as "low riders" and "hot rods" and restore older models to their original conditions. They race them and show off their driving skills. They personalize them with vanity license plates, and with things on their windows and hanging from their rear-view mirrors. Some have plastic statues of Jesus and Mary on their dashboards and St. Christopher Medals on their visors, and even rubber cactus on their radio antennae. They have symbols to let other drivers know they are Catholics, Knights of Columbus, atheists, Rotarians, belong to the Shrine, or are veterans, police officers, or firefighters. They let others know their politics and opinions or their tastes in humor with bumper stickers.

Americans are fiercely loyal to their cars. Many buy the same make of cars repeatedly and become known as a "Ford," "Chevy" or "Buick" family. And they mourn for the models of yester year and collect, restore and preserve them. The American automobile is a symbol of freedom, and it is more about freedom, style and culture than it is about transportation.

Chapter 20. Class & Culture

> The concept of dignity, worth or honor, as applied to either
> persons or conduct, is of first-rate development of classes and
> class distinction.
>
> —Thorstein Veblen: *The Theory of the Leisure Class*

Class is America's forbidden thought and many Americans deny the existence of class and class bias. But each time Americans meet each other they subconsciously rate the other on the basis of class. Is the person better than me or less than me? Should I dismiss them or impress this person?

Class and culture is a deep topic, too deep to cover in just a chapter. I wrote the book *The Making of the Slave Class* in 2010 which tackles this subject in great detail. However a brief summary of class in this book is appropriate in the overall understanding American culture.

America is not a middle class country, as most Americans commonly say and think. It is a working class country and has always been so. The Europeans called America a "nation of farmers" understanding that it is a working class country. The class system is divided by cultural traits and income. And while these are generalizations, there are very surprisingly few exceptions to them. America is divided into three classes: working class, middle class and the leisure class. The working class and middle class can be divided into two subcategories. The underclass and blue collar households make up the working class, and the middle class can be divided into lower and upper. The leisure class is less than one percent of the American people, and for our purposes that's too small to be further subdivided. Its members share the same culture.

According to the Census the American population can be divided as follows: The underclass has 73 million people or about 29.3% of all Americans, these are households that are poor and have a median household income of less than $24,000 per year. There are 69 million blue collar workers or 27.4% who live in households with medium incomes less than $50,000. This means that almost 57% of all Americans are working class by this definition. The lower middle class has 73 million people and is 29.3% of the population. These are families that live in households making more than $50,000 but less than $80,000. The upper middle class is only 32 million people or 13% of the population and make incomes between $80,000 and $1 million. And although this is a large variation in income, culturally they behave remarkably the same at both ends of the income spectrum. The leisure class makes well over $1 million per year and is 2.6 million people or less than 1% of the entire US population.

In America, class is important, contrary to all claims. In *The Making of the Slave Class* I argued that America is much more classist than it is racist. Americans also inflate their class to seem more important. It is the primary reason why they buy houses, cars and clothes they can't afford.

Blue collar workers will insist they are middle class and the upper middle class will insist they are leisure or upper class. Contrary to what most Americans think, there is very little upward mobility. In 2005 *The New York Times* published a series of articles entitled *Class Matters* which showed that there is virtually no upward mobility in America. A person born into a class will with very few exceptions will stay in that class. The only exception to this was briefly in the 1950s, and 1960s and early 1970s when the G.I. Bill allowed millions of mostly American working class male veterans to go to trade school or college and as a consequence these working class men and their families moved from the working class into the lower middle class. It is why there are 73 million in the lower middle class today. Unfortunately many of the children of these men are now falling back into the working class as their educational opportunities and incomes are much less than their fathers. It would be interesting to study how much the lower middle class has shrunk since the 2008 economic crisis.

Class is as much about culture as it is about income. And it is an important to note that contrary to what most Americans think, class is different than not better than. Upper class is not better than middle class, and middle class is not better than working class, despite a large American bias on this subject. They are different because they have different cultural traits.

For example the primary cultural priority of the working class is people. The primary cultural priority of the middle class are possessions, and the primary priority of the leisure class is rare and one of a kind items. You could argue that in this case the working class have better values and therefore are better than the two others. However each class has its positive and negative traits. The classes are different than, not better than.

Class Traits

Despite most American's claim that we are a classless society, if I say: lunch pails, used cars, work uniforms, truck stops, greasy spoon cafes, fast food, garage sales, pool halls, honky-tonks, hand-me down used clothes, trailer parks and Wal-Mart, almost everyone knows I am speaking about the working class. If I say mini-van, golf, soccer moms, the PTA, public colleges, chain restaurants, fad clothing, suburban single family housing, IRAs and Roths, most know I am speaking about the middle class. If I say au pairs, one of a kind designer dresses, tailored clothing, yachts, polo, Rolls Royce, Cayman Islands, Swiss bank accounts, and homes abroad, everyone knows this is the leisure class.

Each of the three classes has a culture and has different cultural traits; some of these traits are positive and some negative. For example each class views food differently. In the leisure class food is about presentation. In the middle class food is about quality. Is it fresh? Is it organic? Etc. But with the working class food is about portions and getting enough. For many working class, particularly the under class, getting enough food is sometimes problematic. If you come from an American family that asks if you would like seconds or thirds, you are likely working class.

Woody Allen, who grew up in a poor working class family area of New York called the Garment District used to tell a joke about his family. Woody had an Aunt and Uncle who would save up for a year to go to a nice restaurant on their wedding anniversary. When they returned each year the extended family would gather around to hear their tale about what it was like to eat in such a place. Woody said that one year the family gathered around to hear their tale but on this particular year his aunt just shook her head in disappointment and said, "It was awful. The food was so bad it was totally inedible." And Woody's Uncle added, "It was totally horrible and inedible, and the portions were also way too small."

It is amusing to think why someone would care if the portions were too small with horrible and inedible food, but the joke illustrates the working class trait for large portions and getting enough food.

Each class has a different time priority. The leisure class has an outlook about time that is multi-generational, as in preserving the family fortune from generation to generation. The middle class it is about their future, as in saving money for something special, or going to college now and studying to get a better job later, etc. The working class is about now and the present. Those that have jobs in the American working class live pay check to pay check, and frequently have economic, medical and family crises that require immediate attention. Their time priority is immediate as most of their situations demand it to be. This time priority of now is also why many working class people have difficulty in sacrificing now for something better later, even when it is sometimes possible. And this trait coupled with predestination is also a burden that keeps many working class people in poverty.

The most damaging class traits of the working class is predestation, the concept that you are poor because you were meant to be poor. It is part of the European Christian concept of "The Divine Right of Kings." It was brought to America by the Puritans and still haunts Americans. "I am king because god made me a king. You are poor because god made you poor, and who are we to question god."

The working class is taught by their religion and culture to serve their "betters and their masters faithfully." They believe that what they have is what they deserve. It is why a large number of the working class will support conservative economics that are contrary to their economic wellbeing. They will support lower taxes for the rich, because they believe the rich deserve their wealth.

Predestation is a self-fulfilling prophecy. Many working class people don't believe they could get a college education, or buy a house, or own a business, or succeed, so they don't try. One of the first barriers to overcome in any anti-poverty program is to convince the poor working class that an alternative is possible and that they actually do deserve better. Predestation is also reaffirmed every time a working class person strives for better and fails, as those around them will quickly say that "it wasn't meant to be." And a person that tries and succeeds at something is accused of being "uppity" and not knowing "their place." Uppity referring to an attempt at raising one's class, and "place" being your place in the class system.

Many years ago I heard a conversation in an African-American neighborhood in St. Paul. A former resident of this working class neighborhood had moved away and done well for himself, and he returned to his old neighborhood in a new car. After he left, a man who had known him from the neighborhood said to the amusement of others, "I don't know why he thinks he has it so good going to work in a $30,000 car, when I go to work in a $250,000 bus every day." His old neighbors thought that he was "uppity." It meant that he was no longer one of them.

This highlights another reason why there is such little upward mobility in the American class system. I call it Anomie. The dictionary defines anomie as: a state or condition of individuals or society characterized by a breakdown or absence of social norms and values, as in the case of uprooted people. And in very real terms people who rise in class will most often find that they are uprooted and rootless people. Frequently they are no longer considered part of the class they left and not fully accepted or considered part of the new class they aspire to be.

Although all three classes see education as valuable, each class sees education differently. In the working class, higher education is seen as mostly for people who are very smart or very wealthy. In the middle class education is seen as a way to get a job, a career, or a profession. In the leisure class education is seen as a place to make useful connections.

Money is another area where there are very different views according to class. The working class sees money as something that is spent on one of the many immediate needs or on something you immediately want. As money is frequently in short supply the concept of saving is foreign to many in the working class. In the middle class money is a tool to be used wisely to provide for the things you need and want, and for saving for the future. In the leisure class money is to be preserved. The leisure class which makes more than $1 million per year wants to preserve their wealth by finding ways to avoid taxes, and to pass on their fortunes to future generations of their children and to endow foundations that will enhance their family's standing and reputation.

Fiscal literacy, which is thought by many Americans to be "common sense," is not. It is learned behavior. Mostly this behavior is taught in middle class households. American schools do not teach financial literacy, and since most working class families have a shortage of money, it is not likely that they can (or know how to) save and invest; so they will not be able to teach this to their children. Money is a tool and like all tools you have to be taught how to use it properly. The lack of fiscal literacy in working class households is another factor in ensuring that they will never rise in class or develop wealth.

Gender roles differ with the classes. The leisure class is determined by family status. For example when Governor Arnold Schwarzenegger was married to Maria Shriver he was considered a member of "the Kennedy family." Although he is a Schwarzenegger and his wife was a Shriver, her mother was a Kennedy and that was the most important family with the most status even though he was a film star and a governor of the largest state.

The middle class is patriarchal, although this is changing somewhat, for the most part Dad is in charge in the home, he is king of his castle. A pop cultural example of this is the late 1950s and 1960s television show *Leave It to Beaver* where June would say, "Ward, I am worried about the Beave." And Ward, with sweater and pipe, would solve whatever problem the child had.

Working class households are matriarchal. Dad is supposed to earn a living and "bring home the bacon." And since many working class men, especially in the under class, do not provide a very good living, they are expendable, which may be one reason why there are so many female headed households in the working class. Mom is in charge of the household and the children. And Dad, especially if he is not too good at providing a living is sometimes an unwanted appendage. Another pop culture example of this is from the 1970s and 1980s television show *Alice*, the story about a divorced woman with a child whose car breaks down on the way to California, and she takes a job as a waitress in a diner.

Class, race and ethnicity are particularly volatile in America. Most Americans have little time for someone they see as lower class than they are, but have much greater disdain for a person of a different race or ethnicity who is also a lower class than them.

America is however more classist than racist. This isn't to say that we are in a post-racial society. American racism as a very serious and on-going problem, but America is more classist than racist. As a diversity trainer I have used a test with audiences to prove my point. I start by telling my participants that this test is private and they need not share their results with anyone. Then I ask that they imagine that they just obtained the job of their dreams. Because of this they could buy the house of their dreams, and to celebrate these two events they would have a dinner party and invite their boss and his or her significant other and their neighbors. Then I tell them that the neighbors turn out to be Cliff and Clare Huxtable from the 1990s television *The Cosby Show*. And I ask them would they feel comfortable? Most Americans even many racists would feel comfortable. Cliff is a doctor and Claire is an attorney and they would likely bring a bottle of wine and that you, the Huxtables and your boss would likely have a pleasant evening. But then I ask, but what if you invite the neighbors and instead of the Huxtables, Fred Sanford and his unemployed friend Grady from the *Sanford and Son* television show come to your house for dinner. Are you still as comfortable? Many people will laugh at this point and some will admit they are not. And I ask are you uncomfortable because you are worried for your safety, or theft, or what? The truth is that most Americans would worry that Fred and Grady would embarrass them in front of their boss. That the boss would see them as "ghetto dwellers," "dirt balls," "trailer trash" "White, Black, or Brown Trash," or as "lower class" or one of a thousand put downs Americans use to "put people in their place." America is a very classist country and has definitive class cultures designed to perpetuate the class system and to keep most Americans one paycheck away from poverty. The American class cultural system regulates who you will know, what you will do, how much money you will make, and how much education you will have. It may also determine what your politics will be.

Republicans and the Christian Right, the Politics of Xenophobia

President Obama got into trouble by explaining why many White working class Americans prefer right-wing politics, when he said that because of their circumstances "they cling to their guns and religion." He apologized for his remarks saying they were insensitive, but he shouldn't have because he was also correct. Because of their fundamentalist religion, their gun culture, and their belief in predestination and the Divine Right of Kings, the politics of many White working class people, particularly White males, is far to the right. They are also xenophobic as this group fears others like women, African-Americans, Latinos and Native-Americans and Asian-Americans, and believe these groups are, or will be taking jobs and opportunities that should be theirs.

The Republican Party and right-wing Christian Evangelicals play to this xenophobia. They continue to argue for a Christian male dominated society at the expense of women. Spokesmen like Rush Limbaugh have severely polarized the issue with quotes like, "I prefer to call the most obnoxious feminists what they really are: feminazis.

And while a few Republicans and a few Christian Evangelicals will state that Rush Limbaugh doesn't represent the thinking of all of the right, no one from the right or the Republican Party dares to challenge him for fear of retaliation from the White male majority. Rush Limbaugh is the spokesperson for the conservative Christian right, and with his radio show attracting millions of American listeners, mostly working class White males, Limbaugh has become the Father Coughlin of the twenty-first century. Republican politics and the Christian-right are promoting the politics of hate and exclusion by playing on the xenophobic fears of primarily working class White males.

It is also apparent that most other Americans increasingly understand this. Voter turnout by gender, race and ethnicity in the 2012 Presidential election for Obama and the Democrats was as follows: 93% of African-Americans, 73% of Asians, 71% of Latinos, 55% of all women, and 76% of the GLBT vote. The only demographic groups where the Republicans did very well were with White males and Evangelicals.

Perhaps the American political pendulum is starting to swing back from the conservative far right. The younger generation also shows less bias and is more open to change and 72% of voters under 30 also voted for Obama and the Democrats. And as the nation is becoming a majority minority with all the Democratic demographic groups growing and the Republican groups shrinking, and with a sizable majority of young voters favoring the Democrats, the Conservative Christian right and the Republicans have much to worry about. They have tied their future to a declining demographic. This is why they currently support legislation like voter ID and limited poll hours to suppress voting for some of these groups.

CHAPTER 21. IMMIGRATION, MIGRATION AND MOBILITY

With the exception of Native-Americans, America is a nation of immigrants. It is good business for America as we are the only first tier country with a population that is growing instead of shrinking according to James Smith. Smith is a senior economist at Santa Monica-based Rand Corporation and the lead author of the US National Research Council's study: *The New Americans: Economic, Demographic, and Fiscal Effects of Immigration.* Smith states that immigrants contribute as much as $10 billion to the American economy each year.

Despite these advantages many Americans in recent years are complaining that Latino immigration is over-running the country. This fear has manifested into a political movement toward "immigration reform." Much of this is White xenophobia which has been greatly agitated by the Republican Party and their right-wing sub-group, the Tea Party.

According to the Southern Poverty Law Center website, *Teaching Tolerance,* of the approximately 31 million foreign-born people living in the United States in 2009, about 20 million were either citizens or legal residents. Of those 11 million who did not have authorization to be in the US almost half entered the country legally and then let their papers expire. The numbers of illegal immigrants are not as large as they are generally perceived.

Although many Americans are critical of immigration most Americans have very little understanding about the Immigration system. They complain that their ancestors came legally without understanding how the system worked. For over a hundred 100 years, the United States had an open immigration system that allowed any able-bodied immigrant to enter and become a citizen, which is why there were no illegal immigrants. But under current policy, many American's immigrant ancestors who arrived between 1790 and well into the twentieth century would not be allowed to enter today. Today gaining permission to live

Tapestry: The History and Consequences of America's Complex Culture

and work in the United States is limited to just three groups: This includes people who are highly trained in a skill that is in short supply in America. It also includes some who are escaping political persecution. And it includes people who are joining immediate family already legally here.

Americans also complain that the new immigrants refuse to speak English insisting their immigrant ancestors had to do so. This is another misconception. *The Teaching Tolerance* website points out that although German immigration peaked in the 1870s almost fifty years later during World War I there were still 700 German language newspapers. Indeed in Waconia, Minnesota, where I went to high school in the 1960s there were many older people who still spoke German who were second and third generation Americans. While today's immigrants may speak Spanish or another language at home, two thirds of those older than five years of age speak English "well" or "very well" according to research by the independent, nonpartisan Migration Policy Institute, and the demand for English language training (ESL instruction) in the United States far outstrips available classes.

The critics of immigration also say that illegal immigrants bring crime and violence. This is not the reality. Nationally, since 1994, the violent crime rate has declined 34 percent and the property crime rate has fallen 26 percent, even as the number of undocumented immigrants has doubled during this same time. According to the conservative Americas Majority Foundation, crime rates during 1999 to 2006 were the lowest in California and other states that had the highest immigration growth rates.

Another myth is that undocumented immigrants are a financial drain of the economy. This too is untrue. A non-partisan report in 2007 from the Congressional Budget Office concluded that while some illegal immigrants impose a net cost to state and local governments, particularly the State of California, "that no agreement exists as to the size of, or even the best way of measuring, the cost on a national level." The US National Research Council's study also found that illegal immigrants, especially those from Latin America, can cause a net loss in terms of taxes paid versus social services received. However this immigration also provides a larger overall gain to the domestic economy due to an increase in pay for higher-skilled workers, lower prices for goods and services produced by immigrant labor, and more efficiency and lower wages for many businesses. The study also notes that although immigrant workers compete with American workers for some low-skilled jobs, most immigrants specialize in activities that otherwise would not exist or take jobs that most Americans would not work.

In 2009, a study by the conservative free market Cato Institute, found that legalization of low-skilled illegal resident workers in America would result in a net increase in the US Gross Domestic Product of $180 billion over ten years. Immigration, legal or not, is good business. Much of the food industry work including harvesting and field work, food processing, fast food and other restaurant work is from illegal workers.

And contrary to what many Americans believe much or most of the illegal workforce is very temporary with many Mexican workers returning home according to a 2012 Pew Hispanic Center Report. Their study analyzed data from both the US and Mexico. Jeffery Passel, the lead author of the report said, "There was a suspicion that people were going back and the results of the Mexican census confirms it. They point to a fairly larger number of people going back to Mexico." It is important to note that 58% of the estimated 11.2 million illegal immigrants are Mexican. This doesn't mean the other illegal immigrants aren't returning home, it just means that they have not been studied.

All illegal immigrants are not Latinos. While Latinos make up 80% of illegal immigration to the United States, with the largest share being Mexican, 11% of illegal immigrants are from Canada and Europe, 9% are Asians, and there are smaller amounts of others. Also contrary to what most American's think, the majority pay taxes, about $11.2 billion in taxes in 2010 according to the *Institute for Taxation.* However according to Center for Immigration Studies America does pay $4.2 billion for their uninsured health care, but even with this expense it is still a net gain of $7 billion. Meanwhile the cost of detaining and deporting one illegal immigrant is an incredible $25,482.

Illegal immigration is clearly an economic and financial issue. However it is an economic issue that largely benefits the United States. America and these undocumented immigrants could both profit more from some kind of immigration reform, if that reform is unbiased and doesn't come in the form of a Cold War type of Berlin Wall built between Mexico and the United States. It would be more beneficial to the United States if a pathway to legal status was found for those who have remained in the shadows too long.

American Mobility and Internal Migrations

Americans are mobile. It is part of the American culture. Americans have no problem moving across town, across the state, or across the country if they believe they will find a better life. There have been four major migrations within America that have affected the culture. The first was the great movement from east to west as Americans settled the "frontier." This is many times referred to as Manifest Destiny. It started as the first English-Americans set up their Puritan colonies and felt that it was god's will that they settle and own everything west of them. These were initially rural settlements, small farms and small towns supporting the farmers. It was why the Europeans called America "a nation of farmers." Up until the 1880s a large majority of Americans lived a rural life. While there were large cities of note like New York, Boston, Philadelphia on the east coast and a few in the Midwest like Chicago, these large cities were largely disdained by most Americans whose rural culture saw the cities as "dens of inequity" and places for "scoundrels" and "city slickers."

In the 1880s and 1890s as America began to industrialize, a second movement began which saw Americans move from rural to urban. It also included a large migration from the South to the North. African-Americans who had been primarily a Southern population began to move north for a better life where they could be employed in the factories, the railroads, and other big industries in northern cities. During this time the railroads like the Illinois Central carried hundreds of thousands of African-Americans from places like rural Mississippi, Louisiana, and Tennessee north to the big cities like Chicago, Detroit, Milwaukee and Minneapolis.

This migration saw large migrations of both rural Whites and African-Americans move to the big cities. By the 1920s there were more Americans living in cities than in rural areas. America became an urban nation, but it wasn't easy. The country song *Detroit City* written by Danny Dill and Mel Tillis was about this struggle. Their lyrics state: "Last night I spent the night in Detroit city and I dreamed about the cotton fields back home." And it has a repetitive refrain of "I want to go home. I want to go home. Oh how I want to go home."

This movement from rural to urban would see American rural areas and small towns shrivel and die. What was once the primary American way of life is still dying or in some places already completely gone. Andy of Mayberry became the Andrew of 125th street. The family farm died and was replaced by the giant corporate farms. Small livestock farms were replaced by the huge feedlots. Poultry is now produced in large odorous metal sheds containing tens of thousands of animals who spend their entire short life in one very small cage covered in their own feces. Grain that was produced on farms of a couple of hundred acres fertilized with manure is now produced on farms of thousands of acres fertilized by chemicals. Food became factory made, and is no longer farm produced. Small town elevators, creameries, and other local agricultural business were replaced by giants like Cargill, Archer Daniel Midlands and Monsanto. Food went from natural to processed, complete with chemical additives of questionable value and contains poisons like herbicides, pesticides, and hormones.

The third migration, suburbanization, began in the 1920s with street cars, but became a national wave in the 1950s and 1960s with cars and freeways. Americans left the city in favor of a house in the suburbs. They were called "garden cities" recalling a more rural pastoral life. It was of course a mirage as the suburbs while pleasant were not the country. American's new cars and roads allowed them to live in the far suburbs and still drive to their jobs in the cities. This movement began the slow death of America's once great cities. It was also the beginning of America's infrastructure problems as schools, hospitals, sewer, storm sewer, water, electrical, natural gas, and phone systems, and bridges and road systems were duplicated for the population leaving the cities where they already had these things. They were now being built for them in farm fields that were fast becoming housing subdivisions and strip malls.

The fourth migration was an amenity migration which began in the 1950s but gained real momentum in the 1980s. Americans began to move from the "rust belt" to the "sun belt." Much of this reversed the south to north migration that occurred with urbanization. This movement saw the populations of states like California, Arizona, Texas and Florida boom. There was also an amenity migration occurring in many other states as families moved to mountains, lakes and rivers and other pleasant places where perhaps they once vacationed. The amenity migration also saw the first exurban developments where urban and suburban people began to move out to what they perceived as rural areas further from the metro areas. They brought with them their large suburban style homes, coffee shops, malls, fast food, and other urban amenities to what they believed was "the country." This too has strained American infrastructure problems. And as already mentioned this pattern has started to reverse itself with Americans beginning to return to the cities at the expense of the suburbs.

Interestingly enough some of this amenity migration has reversed itself as Americans are rediscovering the benefits of some, but not all, of the rust-belt and the inner-cities. Cold Minnesota for example has recently seen more people moving to Minnesota from sunny California and Florida, than the other way around. Some families or their children who have moved to the sun-belt and lived for many years are now reversing their moves for cultural reasons, and want to "go back home." And then there are the Snow birds that live the winter in warmer places and return home when the weather is more pleasant.

The advent of the computer, the cell phone and other electronic devices are making it possible for Americans to be even more mobile than they have been in the past as these devices free people to work from any fixed location on the planet. Telecommuting is a real thing. Jala International and the *American Demographics* magazine stated that there were about twenty million telecommuters in 2000, and they expect at least fifty million by 2025. American mobility culture is about to become unlimited.

Chapter 22. American Cyber Culture

> The new electronic independence re-creates the world in the image of a global village.
>
> — Marshall McLuhan

> You could go crazy thinking of how unprivate our lives really are—the omnipresent security cameras, the tracking data on our very smart phones, the porous state of our Internet selves, the trail of electronic crumbs we leave every day.
>
> —Susan Orlean, *The New Yorker*

> It is my well-researched opinion that the Mark of the Beast, as related in scripture, is absolutely literal. Soon, all people on earth will be coerced into accepting a Mark in their right hand or forehead. I am convinced that it will be an injectable passive RFID transponder with a computer chip — a literal injection with a literal electronic biochip mark. . . I believe that such an implanted identification mark literally will become Satan's Mark of the Beast.
>
> —Terry Cook, *The Mark of the New World Order*

According to Lev Manovich, a professor of media theory at City University of New York, the definition of Cyber Culture is: "the culture arising from the use of computer networks for communicating, entertaining or conducting business. It is also the study of various forms of social phenomena associated with the Internet and other new forms of the network communication, such as online communities, online multi-player gaming, social gaming, social media, augmented reality, and texting, and includes issues related to identity, privacy, and network formation."

For many older Americans this new electronic culture is daunting, but for their children and especially their grandchildren it is the way of the world. Many couples no longer meet at school, or at dances, in bars, or even at work. They are increasingly meeting "on-line." Social networking is replacing American concepts of community, friendship and even dating. Americans network on *Facebook* with friends and professionally on *LinkedIn.* They tweet and twitter and share details of their lives with people thousands of miles away, many times with people they have never met in person. People fall in love while never actually meeting face to face. And all this is having a profound impact on American culture.

Ken Anderson is a research ethnographer at Intel. Ethnography is the branch of anthropology that involves trying to understand how people live their lives. He says that their studies are finding actual differences in the brains of those who grew up wired. He states that tests are showing that the neurons in the brains of younger people who have used electronics from an early age fire much differently than in those of older less electronic generations. He believes there seems to be something profound and evolutionary that is changing the human brain. And he cautioned, "I don't know what that means; I don't think anybody knows." Dan Siewiorek, the director of the Human-Computer Interaction Institute at Carnegie Mellon University said "We're in a big social experiment. Where it ends up, I don't know."

One of the more interesting possibilities of an American future to come is the linking of biological humans with electronics with the biochip. Typically, a biochip's surface area is never larger than a fingernail. And where a computer chip can perform millions of mathematical operations in one second, a biochip today can perform thousands of biological reactions, such as decoding genes in a few seconds. Biochips helped to dramatically accelerate the identification of the estimated 80,000 genes in human DNA, in an ongoing world-wide research collaboration known as the Human Genome Project.

In addition to genetic applications, the biochip is currently being used in toxicological, protein, and biochemical research. Biochips can also be used to rapidly detect chemical agents used in biological warfare so that defensive measures can be taken.

One of the current uses of biochips is the VeriChip, a potentially a billion-dollar business. The firm's parent company, Applied Digital Solutions, won FDA approval in 2004 as the world's first human implantable microchip. It is a radio-frequency identification (RFID) transponder the size of a grain of rice, the VeriChip contains a 16-digit personal ID number that can be scanned like a bar code, providing health-care workers access to your medical records online. It is like carrying your complete medical history with you at all times. And this is the device that has American Evangelicals calling it "Satan's Mark of the Beast." I have quoted Terry Cook, from his book, *The Mark of the New World Order,* at the beginning of this chapter as an example.

Evangelicals and conservatives are always afraid and paranoid about things that are new, especially from the scientific community, but Evangelicals aside, the biochip has the potential for great good and great harm and certainly great change. We are just scratching the surface of the possibilities of biologically linking us to our computers and electronic devices. For example: It is quite possible, even probable that a future biochip could be planted in the brain to allow the brain to function like a computer that can perform millions of mathematical operations in less than a second, or allow people to instantly translate one or more foreign languages. But with these great changes come great questions. Will this change greatly speed up the human evolutionary process? Is this good or bad? There are also ethical question to which Americans and others may need answers to very soon. Will biochips be used to physically track people or monitor their thoughts? Will the biochip replace forms of identification allowing others to instantly know you and your information? Will it be used to invade your privacy or control your actions?

Another issue with our online electronic world is that where Americans have more information presented to them, perhaps it is too much for one person to process. Because of this people naturally tend to focus on just one information source. For example, most people doing an internet search will stop at the first one or two entries in their internet search engine. Television and other visual media also tend to use most of the same sources. It becomes the same story told through the same lens. It doesn't provide for a complete picture. For example most people saw the same few pictures of the 9/11 attacks. They also tend to accept the common first internet source as fact rather than verifying this source or researching issues. It has become a media issue recently as more than a few television news shows and newscasters have been caught disseminating false information they obtained from internet sources without properly verifying the information. Many of us tend to do this in our daily lives assuming what we learn from these few sources is true. Humorous and satirical stories on the internet like those from the satirical newspaper *The Onion* are sometimes seen by readers as actual truth. In one such mistake the press of North Korea actually believed and briefly disseminated a story from the *Onion* that Kim Jong-il is more popular in America than President Obama!

The Iraq War showed how the media tends to function as one lens. Since the US Military controlled the media's access, just a few censored pictures, opinions and stories of journalists who were "embedded" with the troops were electronically submitted around the world. However because this same story was presented by many multi-media sources, it gives the false impression that everyone is getting a very comprehensive picture of the war. And because these few highly managed pictures, opinions and stories were delivered by many media sources and formats as "the facts" we believe by their sheer numbers that they must be true. If FOX, CNN and MSNBC are all reporting the same story we assume it must be true even if they all received their information from one unreliable source. CNN reporters who were embedded with US troops during the Iraq War were highly criticized afterwards for what appeared to be their wave-the-flag enthusiasm and jingoism in the build up to, and the start of, the war in Iraq. And later their medical reporter, Dr. Sanjay Gupta, who was embedded and performed surgery with military medical personnel on the battle front, seemed more as a justification of the war, and an advertisement for CNN, than the humanitarian effort they hoped it would portray.

The US government and the American military learned from media exposure in Vietnam that realistic and uncensored views of the brutalities of war would quickly raise the anti-war opinions of the masses. "Embedding" makes it easier to hide bad things such as the total lack of weapons of mass destruction, the reason given for fighting the war. It also hid how badly the war was actually going, and the atrocities that were committed. On television the Iraq War initially looked like a fast victory because it was a controlled story. Everyone remembers the television pictures of President Bush in a flight jacket on an aircraft carrier under the banner of "Mission Accomplished" which proved only to be the start of a long war.

Cyber culture could be a vehicle for the government, the corporations or other powers to control the opinions and will of the American people, and with the Iraq War in mind it already has. Television and Madison Avenue showed how powerful this electronic media could be by creating or shaping American desires for their commercial products. And in the age of cyber culture this new media could be many times more effective in influencing and controlling the minds of the American population.

It has been recently learned that our government has been allowed to spy, read our mail and telegrams, and listen to our phone calls since World War II. In the modern electronic era the government has continued with those methods of spying and added internet searches, emails, text messages and cell phone calls, Facebook, Twitter, Linked-In, etc. The majority of this spying is not done by permission of the courts or Congress and is done without court warrants as most Americans naively believe. It is wholesale random spying and surveillance on virtually every American. Big brother is constantly watching you on cameras, and listening to your phone calls, sometimes bugging your home or business, and reading your letters, telegrams and emails, your twitters and Facebook posts and looking at what you search for on the internet. All these illegal acts are done to supposedly to prevent terrorism and to keep America "safe." Cyber culture has its consequences as well as its advantages.

Chapter 23. The American Cult of Personality

> The cool thing about being famous is traveling. I have always wanted to travel across seas, like to Canada and stuff.
>
> —Britney Spears

> Yeah, I like to be the maker of the art. And I like and want the money. But I don't really dig being famous.
>
> Liz Phair

> Cult: 1. Extreme religious veneration. 2. A great devotion to a person, idea, movement or work.

Americans love famous and infamous people. They love anyone who can sing, dance, act, play a sport, play a musical instrument, or even a person who has no talent but is on television. They love Koreans that can dance like a horse and promiscuous girls with bad behavior on reality shows. They venerate athletes, movie stars, singers, musicians, comedians, talking heads on news shows, and radio talk show hosts. They adore mayors and politicians and other elected officials and most others who they think may have power. They envy anyone who is rich, has a back stage pass, a private box, or who walks a red carpet. Americans think these people are important and they think by knowing them, or being like them, or with them, then they too will be important and their lives will have meaning.

Americans look to celebrities for advice on politics, life and death issues, war and peace, and any other subject, even when it is apparent that the celebrity clearly has no better idea about this than they do. They copy their dress, repeat their comments and jokes, and want to be them. Most Americans want to be famous just to be famous and not to be the best at or to be famous for some kind of greatness. Americans love people for their wealth and fame not their greatness, which is why people like Snooky, Paris Hilton and Kim Kardashian, and Donald Trump can be famous with very little talent or values. America loves Wolf Blitzer and Candy Crowley because they can read a teleprompter on television. They love Anderson Cooper, and Suzanne Malveaux because they look very good reading a teleprompter on television. Marginal talents like Ron Reagan Jr. and Abby Huntsman can become "television political analysts" because their parents are famous.

Americans worship the infamous as well as the famous. They love the good and the bad. It is why they care how many times a celebrity has been in rehab. They want to know how many times they have sex and cheat on their partners. They have salacious appetites for how many times they have driven drunk, been in fights, were divorced, or how often they were arrested for theft or shoplifting. Americans have an endless curiosity about the famous and infamous. If Hitler had been an American they would want to know what kind of breakfast cereal he ate, his favorite restaurant, and his favorite teacher.

American Celebrities also feel entitled to comment and give their advice on issues where they clearly have no expertise, which is why movie actor Steven Segal and basketball player Dennis Rodman feel they are entitled to be the ambassadors to Russia and North Korea respectively. It is why they feel entitled to give advice to the President and the US State Department on these two delicate relationships. It is why in 2012 Republican Presidential nominee Mitt Romney approved a prime time speech at the GOP convention featuring an old and angry and seemingly confused Clint Eastwood yelling at an empty chair. That this buffoonery is not just tolerated by the American public but often encouraged is very troubling.

In America, actors, musicians, and athletes seem to have a monopoly on charities and non profits. Actors like Oprah Winfrey give advice and the whole nation gives her the kind of rapt attention of a Socrates or Plato, which of course many Americans have never heard of.

Most Americans think of their society as some kind of egalitarian meritocracy, but their beliefs are mocked by their participation in a very rigid class system, a system that rewards the upper class "important people" and the rich and famous with valet parking, special and reserved seating everywhere, exclusive areas in restaurants and night clubs, box seats, priority entrance ahead of the public, celebrity events, priority entrance to colleges and universities based upon their parent's status rather than their merit (George W. Bush attending Yale is one example), and red carpets like they are royalty, which in America celebrities are. It even mocks the majority's self-proclaimed Christianity as this worship of false gods and idols called celebrities is frequently more ardent than their worship of their god. America's cult of celebrity reflects just how culturally shallow many Americans can be.

CHAPTER 24. AMERICAN ECONOMICS AND THE RELIGION OF CAPITALISM

> Under capitalism, man exploits man; under communism it is just the opposite.

> —American economist John Kenneth Galbraith

> We can have democracy in this country, or we can have great wealth concentrated in the hands of a few, but we can't have both.

> —Justice Louis Brandeis

Economics is simple. And contrary to popular belief economics are not about math or even money. Math and money are the measuring sticks, not the art. Economics is simpler than these measurements. It is how a society chooses to divide the wealth among its people. Economics is about wealth creation, but this is secondary to who will benefit by the wealth. Wealth created with little or no benefit to the majority of a society has no value. Wealth in the hands of the few is anti-economics.

In the aftermath of the 2008 economic collapse, Congress asked Alan Greenspan, the former Chairman of the Federal Reserve Bank, to explain his failed belief that capitalist markets could regulate themselves in a free market. They asked if he still believed that capitalism required no regulation. Greenspan admitted: "Yes, I found a flaw. I don't know how significant or permanent it is, but I've been very distressed by that fact...The reason I was shocked [is] because I had been going for forty years or more with very considerable evidence that it was working exceptionally well."

The question that begs to be asked: is there really a free market, and does it work? It appears that both capitalism as practiced by the United States and communism as it was practiced by the Soviet Union and China are dead or dying concepts. Soviet Communism collapsed in disaster in the late 1980s. American capitalism came to a near fatal collapse in 2008 and its on-going survival appears less than certain as it continues to concentrate wealth into fewer and fewer hands. It seems that these economic systems are going the way of feudalism and mercantilism.

In their purest forms capitalism is the complete private ownership of all property while Soviet communism was the complete ownership of all property by the state. In practice most economies were somewhere in between. China and Vietnam, both communist nations, have some private ownership and a growing economy. China's new economy with some private ownership is what even some Americans would call a free market. On the opposite side, even the pro-capitalist United States has many public and state owned properties; the national park system and the national forests are but two good examples. Even hard core capitalists and conservative Republicans believe in some forms of state ownership. Wally Hickel the conservative Republican Governor of Alaska and Nixon's Secretary of the Interior said that things like the waters, forests, and the air were what he called "the commons" and should always be in public ownership. Hickel also fought for oil and gas resources in Alaska to be protected and used as public resources.

US capitalism and Soviet and Maoist communism were created for nineteenth century industrial societies. They are systems whose relevance appears to be limited as they were applied to large industrial nation states of the nineteenth and twentieth centuries, where large numbers of both societies would be employed in industry. Both systems are now losing most of their relevance in the global economy as corporations are international and not national, and where they are becoming so productive that the concept of work for wages and universal employment, which supposedly define both economic systems, is ending. This threatens most current systems which are based upon a wage for work, which is fast becoming obsolete, at least in terms of employing large masses of people. These trends were first noted by economist Jeremy Rifkin in 1996 in his book, *The End of Work: The Decline of the Global Labor Force and the Dawn of the Post-Market Era.*

Corporations are still producing ever increasing amounts of goods and services, but they are becoming so productive that they need fewer and fewer workers to accomplish this. They are also international and no longer controlled by or contribute to their nation-states in their taxes, or more importantly their wages. The industrial society was defined by its occupations and employment. In these industrial societies individual economic worth has been defined by a job and its value as a needed skill. A medical doctor, for example, because of having skills and training that are relatively scarce, is paid more than a manual laborer with no special skills and training. Such manual laborers are also more numerous than doctors. In the United States and much of the Western world, jobs define a person's skill value. Compensation is based upon skills and the value of the work. As labor unions became a force, wages were augmented with benefits which included the limited work week (forty hours in the US) along with vacation time, sick pay, holiday pay, medical and dental benefits, and retirement pay. But all these wages and benefits were still based upon employment. A restaurant dishwasher, a low skill worker, would not have the same wages and benefits that skilled professional worker or an industrial laborer represented by a union. This compensation system works if everyone that wants to work, and is fit enough to work, can readily find a job with wages and benefits befitting their training and talents, and only works if employment in the society is universal and readily available.

Capitalism never completely worked as there were economic ups and downs with periods of high unemployment. There were also powerful corporations and employers who habitually tried to short change this system and their workers regardless of their skills or the value of their work output. Capitalism was supposed to be a meritocracy. It never really was, as the saying went "it isn't what you know, but who you know," but there is still a false belief that it is a meritocracy. And there is an almost religious devotion in American society that continually proclaims it is a meritocracy and that social upward mobility is an actuality, which it isn't. The *New York Times* recently debunked these myths in a series of articles called *Class Matters*.

The capitalist system does not seem to have an answer to these periodic economic downturns with mass unemployment. Nor are there solutions to the negative effects of class and race. Capitalism cannot truly justify that it is a meritocracy where wealth is given to the hardest working. The system cannot justify why so many professions were closed societies to all but their members, their friends and families. It cannot explain why higher education was frequently limited by class, race, ethnicity and of course by incomes. Capitalism and the free market provide no limits on the rich and powerful who control money and politics. But capitalists do limit the wages and benefits paid by them to their workers regardless of skills or the amount or value of the work given to them. Capitalism and its false claim of free markets never was what Americans thought or still claim it to be. Like communism, capitalism and free markets are a utopian concept that was never fully realized. In fact it can be more easily argued that the "free market" and capitalism are complete opposites.

Even Adam Smith, the father of American capitalism, stated that a free market cannot exist when it relies on the decisions of the wealthy and powerful. He said the rich and powerful would always manipulate the markets for their personal gain at the expense of others and the free market. His solution was "The Invisible Hand," the idea that some unknown natural force, or that god would always intervene on behalf of the market. However economics, including the "free market," are cultural inventions of man and they are not products regulated by either nature or a deity, and since America relied on this false assumption of an "invisible hidden hand," and that economics was somehow regulated by nature and god, unregulated American capitalism has slowly strangled the myth of the "free market." The Great Depression and 2008 economic collapse, along with declining American household incomes and unemployment are the proof of this.

Perhaps the final proof comes from none other than Alan Greenspan, the Ayn Rand disciple most dedicated to "free market capitalism." The former guru, the American anti-regulatory master of the free enterprise banking system and the proponent of laissez faire, was forced to admit to Congress in the wake of the 2008 economic crash that his belief in the free market's ability to check the greed of capitalism was wrong.

The twenty-first century is different. Work as we know it is ending. It has been almost twenty years since Jeremy Rifkin published his book, *The End of Work*, which began a serious discussion about the decline of the American and global workforce. Productivity is steadily decimating the jobs of the industrial society, not just in America, but globally. In the 1880s it took over 80% of the American population to produce enough food and fiber for the United States. But by 1950 it took less than 1% to produce all the food and fiber necessary for the US, which by 1950 also included a very large surplus to export to the rest of the world. Increased productivity in agriculture caused this revolution, producing more goods with much less labor. Machinery, chemicals, etc., took away ninety-nine percent of the jobs in what was once the world's main source of work. Is it any wonder that rural areas suffered massive population losses and went into a terminal economic depression? Is it any wonder that the small unit family farm has lost out and been run over by the large corporate farms and the powerful agricultural corporations of Monsanto, ADM and Cargill?

The other economic sectors have suffered job losses in the same manor, as they too have become "more productive." In the 1920s a majority of Americans were employed in manufacturing, transportation and utilities. The largest employer in the US during the industrial age was the railroads. But by the 1980s these giants of industry were employing less than half the number they employed at their peak in the 1920s. This too was due to the use of increasingly productive technology and processes. The amount of goods manufactured in the factories and moved by the railroads and trucking systems has multiplied many times, while the number of jobs in these industries has tumbled and they continue to decline.

In the 1950s retail goods and services became the dominant employment sector in the US as the large and small shopping malls replaced main street. I call this the "Malling of America." Service and retail jobs began replacing some, but not all, of the jobs that were formerly found in the manufacturing, transportation and utility sectors, but unfortunately these jobs are not valued as highly. Service and retail jobs lack the pay and the benefits of the manufacturing sector. That is why the American concept of the "living wage" began to dramatically decline. It is not a coincidence that most of these service and retail jobs were not represented by unions and therefore could not demand living wages and benefits. It was not that this sector could not afford to pay living wages, but rather their capitalist owners chose to maximize profits at the expense of wages—that is the essence of capitalism: to make money for capitalists (investors).

It also meant that since the wealth went to the investors, not the workers, more wealth would continually concentrate at the top. Billionaire retailers like Sam Walton and his family, and their Wal-Mart stores, have become the new model. Retail laborers in this sector have become "part time associates" with low wages and no or very few benefits. It has become so bad that some workers, as in the case of Wal-Mart, have been forced to work extra unpaid hours, "off the clock," just to keep their jobs, some are paid less because they are women and both of these are shown to be true by recent court cases against the company. These workers have no union representation and no say in their livelihood, and generally they receive little or no benefits. But even these jobs are disappearing as online orders replace people and stores. And automated checkouts and automated shelf stocking and storage systems are replacing workers. It is the same in the banking sector where ATMs and on-line banking have replaced tellers and other bank personnel.

The capitalists now have total control of their corporations and the US and the world economies. You can either take a job on the employer's terms or you don't take any job. They say it is a "free market decision" to work for them or not, although realistically you are lucky to get any job whatsoever, and so most workers have no choice at all. It is becoming wage slavery.

Arguments periodically arise from the defenders of the status quo that these service sector workers somehow deserve their fate because they lack the skill or education to compete for the "new economy jobs" in the information age. Supposedly, the available jobs are now in the computer sciences or in "green technology." But such training or education is not available to everyone, as you would expect it to be in the American meritocracy. Without some type of assistance such as the GI Bill or veteran's benefits, this education and training is not available even to the many who have performed military service. Because of its rising cost education has become available to far fewer people. There are student loans, but Congress periodically ponders if these should be continued and subsidized. And even if these loans continue, with the cost of today's education, a person going to college by this method would find themselves with a Bachelors degree and generally over $40,000 in debt with interest—even if he or she attends a State college. It is unaffordable. Scholarships cover very few people and many of these also presume that the student will need to borrow significant amounts of money. And graduating from college hardly ensures that debt-ridden young adults will find a job in their chosen field — or any job at all.

It is with some irony that Governor Mitt Romney, the 2012 Republican candidate for president and a champion of American big money capitalism, when confronted with a question about the unaffordable cost of education, advised that students should borrow from their parents. It was an amazingly callous statement, but even more amazing was the fact that he actually thought that the average American parent would have such funds to lend. Even presidential candidates with Romney's supposed vast business acumen fail to understand the mechanics of what is happening to the American economy.

Further, there aren't as many "new economy" or information jobs in the new economy as we are led to believe. And those who think a job in the computer industry is the solution might stop to think that the industry—which is all about productivity—has become very good and efficient at their own productivity. In other words, this industry is very good at cutting labor requirements in its own field as well as others. Jobs in this industry are losing themselves to the god of productivity as computers and machines are designing, maintaining, repairing and fixing computers and programs. They are doing away with jobs that used to be done by a person. The information and computer science industry are on the cutting edge of productivity, including their own. It is one of the major reasons why there are fewer jobs in this new industry than in the other sectors at their inception.

Computers, automation and robotics are rapidly replacing people in the workplace. Grocery and other retail stores used to employ many stock workers who have now been replaced by automated inventory systems, increasingly automated and robotic, so many fewer workers are needed. Automated checkout lines are eliminating the need for cashiers. And while some stores continue to retain cashiers, it is only because their customers haven't as yet fully accepted this coming reality, just as it was inconceivable to do banking without talking to a person until recent times. Today in banking, ATM machines and other automated systems have changed all that.

We have blamed China and a host of other countries for these job losses. And while many jobs are lost to low-wage overseas workers, as capitalists — owner-investors — seek to further increase their profits by reducing labor costs and minimize national oversight and regulation, the real issue is that the number of total jobs is rapidly declining.

As all industries continue to increase their productivity, causing ever greater job losses, and as fewer employed workers are collectively represented by unions, wages are going down rapidly and fewer benefits are offered. It also means that without national regulation of the markets, international corporations will continue to find lower wage workers somewhere else in the global marketplace and places free from any regulations or oversight. It is an employer's market, not a free market, and that means that even fewer dollars will be shared with ever fewer people, and that society will receive fewer benefits. It also means that safety and environmental issues will be unaddressed as the corporations free themselves of national regulation in the global marketplace.

Those with the money, the capitalists, have prevailed. They no longer need the large numbers of managers, employees, serfs or servants they once needed. Employment is becoming a very poor means of dividing the wealth of a society. If economics is defined by how a society equitably divides its wealth among the people, then what we now have is anti-economics. Although the myth persists that these wealthy businessmen and corporations are the "job creators," they have ceased to be the job providers they were in the past. Instead they continue to increase their wealth as they grow more businesses that employ fewer workers, at lower wages and without the benefits provided in the past. They will also increasingly ignore larger societal costs like safety and the environment.

The international corporations have become the depositories of most of American wealth. Although corporate ownership is supposedly open to all, at least when it comes to "public" corporations, in reality very few people actually own a significant number of shares in these economic behemoths. And the parts that are frequently touted as belonging to small shareholders are actually managed by large institutional investors (pension funds and other funds). These investments are almost always directed by wealthy professional managers who have their own agendas and economic interests, which may not coincide with the best interests of their trusting investors — as was evidenced in the 2008 economic crisis. In the aftermath of the crisis there were many lawsuits and legal actions against these investment managers. Wells Fargo Bank, for one example, was accused of mismanaging their investors' funds for their own benefit. The small individual shareholders in these large institutional funds have no power and no say in corporate affairs. In fact many of these small investors have no idea what corporations they are actually invested in at any given time, as mutual funds and pension funds shift in and out of various investments.

Small shareholders and their power is a myth. The wealthy, including these institutional money managers, use pensions and small shareholders funds to satisfy their personal and corporate ambitions.

Economics is defined as the science deals with the production, distribution, and consumption of goods and services for the material welfare of humankind. If capitalism is now restricting the amount of goods and services available to mankind, it must be said that capitalism has become a form of anti-economics. It is an antiquated system that no longer works.

Money and wealth is finite, not infinite, and for every wealthy capitalist there must be many who are poor to give them this wealth. A billionaire can only be made at the expense of many people who must be poor. This is not a socialist statement, it is just simple math.

The world we face in the twenty-first century is a world with fewer jobs. And since we are still using our industrial-job-based value system, it means fewer and fewer people will have the opportunity to earn a living wage. Poverty will continue to grow rapidly. The possibility of a large middle class is not a reality under the current economic systems either capitalist or quasi-communist. We must find a new economic system.

Despite the palaver of the Conservative Right, economics is neither natural law nor divine intervention. But rather it is a man-made cultural institution that states how a society will divide its wealth to benefit the entire society. During the industrial age the job value system worked enough to distribute a good portion of wealth to a large number of people. This system is now broken beyond repair and in need of replacement. Wealth has now and is increasingly concentrating in fewer hands. And with this mass concentration of wealth, the purchasing power and the political power is also concentrating into many fewer hands. The wealthy can now buy anything including the politicians who make the laws and the judges who rule on these laws assuring their continued wealth, and to buy the necessary security to make them invulnerable to any wishes, interference or protest by the majority. The consequences of this concentration of power may prevent Americans from making necessary changes to this system. What the wealthy fear most is a fair redistribution of the wealth, and it becomes less likely and more difficult to achieve this fair division as the money and power concentrates into fewer hands. Since wealth is finite, and if most of the wealth is in the hands of the few, it means many will live in poverty to support this rapid concentration of wealth and that the vast majority will be increasingly powerless to change it. The Koch brothers and their buying of national, state and even local elections are an example of this growing power and the inability of the majority to contain this power.

There is a fallacy in America that as a "free society" we can make changes—either peacefully or even forcefully, if deemed necessary. But the power that is currently massing would prevent change either by ballot or protest. If the corporations control the political process, and with it the police and military, the people will be controlled with or without their beloved guns. In America, the wealthy keep much of their wealth in offshore banks, in the Cayman Islands and other international accounts—if there is a forced "bail-out" as was recently imposed in Cyprus, those holding the most money simply won't be participating. However everybody with a normal bank account in his hometown bank will be forced to participate.

There is a window of opportunity to make needed changes to the economic system. Most likely it is a window that appears to be slightly open, but one that could quickly close.

As the corporations have become international and more powerful than nations or even groups of nation states, the nation states are also losing their relevance. Global and regional issues are becoming more dominating than national issues. Corporations are growing even more powerful than the so called super powers, or are at least independent of their powers. The financial crises that we have had at the beginning of the twenty-first century are a likely sign that our Old World mercantilist beliefs about economies and the capitalistic and communist systems are no longer viable or relevant.

US capitalism and Soviet communism were born to suit the industrial society and they achieved their zenith in the twentieth century when both systems competed with each other for dominance. Led by the United States, Western Europe and post-World War II Japan, capitalism assumed the dominant role. However communism or more precisely her totalitarian sisters, Soviet and Maoist communism, competed with and dominated the eastern hemisphere led by the USSR. These two giant economic engines, capitalism and communism, and their super power nation states so dominated the planet that the rest of the globe was relegated to a third class status called the "Third World." These third class nations were forced to choose which system they would adopt and or which super power they would serve. It was a form of colonialism as the super powers forced their narrow economic views upon and demanded loyalty from the smaller nation states.

US capitalism, which most Americans think is magically synonymous with both "democracy" and prosperity, has become a belief system with a distinct religious fervor. Its followers tend to believe that their system is the one and only true economic system for everyone on the planet. The cold war and all the hot little wars that followed were fought like something akin to religious crusades.

The US and its allies celebrated the fall of the USSR and saw the decline of Soviet communism as proof certain that capitalism was the one true economic religion. But soon capitalist nations also started showing signs of inadequacies in their systems. Western Europe, Japan and the United States have come to near financial collapse more than once in the last 30 years as their systems have begun to fail and their wealth began to be concentrated ever more in the hands of the few at the expense of the many. Their corporations, including their banks, became powerful international entities that could no longer be properly regulated by nation states, even by the powerful United States. Corporations now freely move about the globe to avoid taxes, to unjustly take advantage of cheap labor, and to find places where they can avoid safety and environmental regulation and costs.

Soviet and Maoist communism have been replaced or dramatically modified. It is becoming more and more apparent that American capitalism, too, may be inadequate in its current form, as it is failing to meet the challenges of the new century and a post-industrial society.

Southern Culture, Politics & Economics

> The incommensurability between the modern economic system and the people who staff it explains why modern workers have so often been depicted as 'cogs' in the larger 'machinery' of industrial civilization; for while the practical rationalization of enterprise does require workers to be consistent, predictable, precise, uniform, and even to a certain extent creative, it does not really require them to be persons, that is, to live examined lives, to grow, to develop character, to search for truth, to know themselves, etc.
>
> —Craig M. Gay, *Way of the Modern World*

> The test of our progress is not whether we add more to the abundance of those who have much it is whether we provide enough for those who have little.
>
> —*Franklin Roosevelt*

Southern culture has had both a regional and national impact on American culture. Depending on your perspective these impacts have sometimes been very positive and sometimes very negative. Religious Fundamentalism is one of the significant impacts on American culture and politics, and has been particularly notable in the late twentieth and early twenty-first century. Southern religious historian Sam Hill summarized it in an essay in 1998, *Fundamentalism in Recent Southern Culture* as follows: "Beginning in the mid-1970s, Fundamentalism attained an unprecedented prominence in the South. It disrupted two major denominations, the Presbyterian and the Southern Baptist, altering the place of each in the society. It also brought into being and prominence various new congregations, fellowships, media networks, and educational institutions that we will refer to here as a kind of 'third force' among southern Protestants. Further, Fundamentalism's ascent took place concurrently with the rise of the Republican Party as the White population's political home of choice."

Fundamentalism has been one of the principal driving forces of Southern culture as documented by historians like William Robert Glass. Economics based upon slave and cheap labor is another key element in Southern culture. After the abolition of slavery the South created a system of sharecroppers and convict labor that effectively extended slavery. These workers were not that much better off than the former slaves and also had little choice or freedoms.

The convict system was particularly abusive in the South where a person, both Blacks and Whites would be charged with some minor crime, some real many others not, and given lengthy prison and jail sentences. They were then sold by the Sheriffs or the prison systems to mines, factories and other Southern businesses as slave labor.

The sharecropper system was another form of slavery in that these farmers would become increasingly indebted to the large landowners and company stores and were forced to continue working to pay off their growing debts, which was not possible with their poor wages.

Southern economics is based upon the Southern plantation culture of Thomas Jefferson. Defense of this plantation economic culture was the primary reason Jefferson championed the "States Rights" argument against Washington and Adams and the federal government and why the right-wing and conservatives continue to use this argument to this day. These Republican Fundamentalists have described this plantation culture as "Free Market Capitalism." And as a consequence it has kept the South much more poor and uneducated than the three other large regions and it is currently infecting American economics with the spread of Southern plantation economics nationally. In the twenty-first century corporations like Wal-Mart and Tyson Chicken have made this Southern cheap labor economics system a national epidemic.

These plantation economics have taken over the conservative agenda in America and the Republican Party, and many other non-Southern corporations have adopted the Southern plantation economics to compete in, or to dominate their markets. It is how Monsanto, Archer Daniel Midlands, and Cargill have taken over the entire agricultural industry. It is how Wal-Mart and Target are taking over the retail industry, and how the energy business is once again concentrating into fewer hands like those of the Koch brothers. It is how the fast food industry through the National Restaurant Association controls minimum wage and makes sure their workers are kept poor and powerless.

These corporations argue that these wages are necessary to keep consumer prices low and say this is why Americans should support these low wages, but it is a lie, low wages maximize profits. Eric Schlosser in his book, *Fast Food Nation,* stated that for every dollar increase in a fast food worker's hourly wage will result in an increase of just eleven cents in the cost of a fast food hamburger. Schlosser also points out how the fast food corporations have duped and lobbied the Congress into actually paying their labor costs by a so called training fee that these restaurants receive for employing "poor people" and training them. It should be pointed out that they are poor because they work at fast food restaurants. Schlosser also found that a Department of Labor study of this subsidy showed that these restaurants actually provided little or no training and that the federal government is paying for their labor cost for nothing in return. This, they argue is free market capitalism, and is another example of why capitalism isn't working.

Milton Friedman and the Chicago School

> I am in favor of cutting taxes under any circumstances and for any excuse and for any reason.
>
> —Milton Friedman

> The theories of Milton Friedman gave him the Nobel Prize; they gave Chile General Pinochet.
>
> —Eduardo Galeano, Latin American journalist and writer

> Fascism should more appropriately be called Corporatism because it is a merger of state and corporate power.
>
> —Benito Mussolini

Capitalism took a decided right turn when the "free market" economists of the "Chicago School" also known as the "Chicago Boys" came to prominence starting in the 1950s. Today their policies are revered by conservatives. Even so-called moderate politicians like Bill and Hillary Clinton abide by their principles, which was why they dismantled the New Deal AFDC the program for the nation's poor children. Milton Friedman and his policies were the foundation of Reaganomics and George H. W. Bush's "Ownership Society." They are the policies that controlled Clinton and inspired George

W. Bush's nation building and his quest to "privatize" Social Security. They are the policies that hamstring Barack Obama.

The Chicago school sought to dismantle the New Deal and to refute Thorstein Veblen and Keynesian economics. They are proponents of a laissez-faire "free market" and seek the abolishment of all market regulations, taxation and government supports. They are against unions, minimum wage, Social Security, Medicare, environmental regulations and any type of government social program. They wish to dismantle the US Post Office, public school systems, and National Parks. They believe all these to be government interference in their magical free market. Naomi Klein in her book *Shock Doctrine, The Rise of Disaster Capitalism* gave an excellent account of the Chicago School and their failings.

A listing of some of those associated with the Chicago School and their beliefs are as follows:

Robert Fogel was one of the "Chicago Boys." Fogel preposterously argued that pre-civil war slaves in the South had a higher standard of living than the White workers in Northern States. He believed this apparently justified Southern economics and his arguments that the government should stay out of these affairs. He also argued that the building of the railroads in the 19th century with the assistance of government was a gross mistake and that they didn't contribute to meaningful economic growth. A theory denounced by many as the railroads were actually the largest employer in America during its industrial era and gave rise to massive economic development.

Another well respected "Chicago Boy," Ronald Coase was a strict libertarian and believed that laws and regulations are not as necessary "as lawyers and government believe." He believed that the government should do nothing, pass few laws and no regulations and let the wealthy and corporations find the best solutions on their own.

George Stigler was the developer of "Capture Theory" which claims that in an efficient market that the government and industry regulators will soon become captured by the industry they are regulating and are therefore redundant and unneeded.

Richard Posner advocated that law and justice should be about efficiency, because in a world of scarce resources waste should be regarded as immoral. Therefore resources and goods should be allocated to those who would use them the most efficiently, meaning the corporations.

But the most influential and the man who caused the most damage was Milton Friedman. Friedman was a capitalist zealot. His almost religious belief in a capitalist free and unregulated market was so strong that he was willing to see mass poverty and unemployment, war, murder, and torture used to meet his goals. Although he didn't participate in these activities directly he did inspire, advise, condone and encourage those who under took these evils on his behalf. The tortuous regime of Augusto Pinochet in Chile was his first client and his inspiration. He inspired the coup that overthrew the democratic government of Chile, he advised the government and Pinochet personally, and some of his "Chicago Boys" actually held positions in the government. The previously mentioned book by Naomi Klein illustrates this quite well. Friedman and the Chicago School were also involved with the military coups that destroyed the democratic governments of Argentina and Brazil. They were also involved in Uruguay. They became the financial and economic advisors to these repressive regimes and strongly encouraged further repression to achieve their economic goals when the local populations objected. They advised harsh military crackdowns on any groups or individuals that disagreed with their vision. They saw this as their living laboratory to demonstrate the wisdom of their economic theories.

They failed miserably. In Chile, where Friedman and his acolytes spent the most time, the economy was in shambles. Unemployment went from about 3% under the former democracy to about 30% under the military dictator Pinochet. Under the guidance of the "Chicago Boys" the country went into hyperinflation during their watch. They destroyed all financial regulations and the unregulated corporations and speculators then raided the Chilean economy causing a national debt of about $14 billion. Chile, which was a prosperous country with a poverty rate of about 9%, much less than the poverty rate in the United States, became poverty stricken under the Chicago Boys guidance and about half of the Chilean people, 45%, sank into poverty during these free market experiments. Food became scarce and unaffordable to many. Pensions and medical assistance from the government stopped. The economic catastrophe only stopped when Pinochet realized he was headed for economic ruin and he stopped implementing Friedman and his "Chicago Boys" theories. Uruguay, Brazil and Argentina all had similar results under Friedman and the Chicago School's direction. It was economic disaster. As one of Friedman's Latin American critics said of him, "Thousands of people were imprisoned so that his markets could be free."

Despite these bloody coups and gross economic failures the growing neoconservative movement embraced the philosophy of Friedman and the Chicago School. They became the foundation of conservative and Republican politics. The Chicago School's policies were implemented with zeal by Presidents Reagan, Bush Sr., Clinton, and Bush Jr. and particularly by Treasury Secretary Allan Greenspan. And the result was a widening gap between the rich and poor as the wealth has concentrated in the top one percent. It also brought about the massive failure of the unregulated markets in 2008 which nearly destroyed the economy of the United States and much of Europe. Even Greenspan a staunch advocate of Milt Freiedman had to admit to Congress that his desire to achieve unregulated free markets had been wrong. Unfortunately conservatives and Republicans still push the Friedman and Chicago School agenda.

Chapter 25. Anti-Communism—The Ultimate in American Xenophobia

> Communism has decided against god, against Christ, against the Bible and against all religion.
>
> —Reverend Billy Graham

> For us in Russia, communism is a dead dog, while, for many people in the West, it is still a living lion.
>
> —Aleksandr Solzhenitsyn

> This (Russia) is without question our No. 1 geopolitical foe. They fight for every cause for the world's worst actors. The idea that he (Obama) has more flexibility in mind for Russia is very, very troubling indeed.
>
> —Mitt Romney 2012

> The communist Chinese are funding Obama's political operation. The communist Chinese are funding his slush funds. Union buddies, community activist buddies, massively expand the federal bureaucracy. This is not an empty accusation. This is demonstrably true.
>
> —Rush Limbaugh 2010

The anti-hero of the American play is always communism and socialism, as evidenced by the quotes of the 2012 Republican presidential nominee Mitt Romney and conservative talk show host Rush Limbaugh. Communism, as Aleksandr Solzhenitsyn said, "is a dead dog." However it still remains the straw man for the conservatives and many other Americans. It is a whipping boy to blame all the troubles upon, a scary apparition hiding under the bed ready to get

Americans when they least expect it. It is pure xenophobia.

Communism and socialism are irrational American cultural taboos. Most Americans cannot reasonably define either communism or socialism, nor can they adequately define capitalism to which they profess their allegiance. Since the beginning of the twentieth century the greatest insult to an American politician is to say that he or she is a communist or a socialist. It has power beyond the words. It implies that they are un-American, anti-Christian, and are devious spies set to undermine and destroy America and her people.

Confusion over the recent coup in Kiev and the separatist movements by Russian-speaking regions in Ukraine have raised these fears again, even though communism is no longer an issue. Most Americans fail to understand is that the Crimea is vital to the long term well-being of Russia. It is home to the Russian Navy and is historically connected to Russia. The Soviets administratively joined it to the Ukraine as an afterthought in the 1950s when the Ukraine was part of the USSR. It was never intended that Russia would give up any claim on the Crimea.

America's first battle with Soviet communism occurred in 1918 when an American military force of eight thousand men invaded Russia, who ironically was an ally at the time in World War I. It was an odd thing to do to an ally and was also not very successful as America attempted to intervene in the Russian revolution against the communists. This invasion was called an intervention and said to be for Russia's own good. However the Russians didn't see it that way and have since remained suspicious of the United States, including in this post-communist period.

Since Karl Marx had declared in his writings that religion was the opiate of the people, it was reasoned by conservative and religious Americans that communism was a mortal enemy of Christians. Anti-communism became a religious cause, and because of this, capitalism was further strengthened and tied to the American Christian religious belief system.

Anti-communism has caused periodic bouts of insane American xenophobia. They produced two periods of modern witch trials as Americans searched to uncover communist witches, spies and traitors in their midst. During World War I the American Attorney General Thomas W. Gregory suppressed the free speech of socialists and communists under the Sedition and Espionage Acts. Disregarding his sworn oath to uphold the Constitution Gregory said, "Free expression is dangerous to American institutions." He then prosecuted 1500 people who were socialists and union advocates for their "dangerous" free speech.

At the end of President Wilson's presidential term, when he was too ill to govern, a new Attorney General came to power. A. Mitchell Palmer was a ruthless and ambitious man who wanted to become president, he served as Attorney General from 1919 to 1921. And in American tradition he thought that a witch hunt would guarantee him the headlines to launch his presidential ambitions. He began to proclaim that America was under siege by "god-less communists" whom he labeled "the Red Menace."

A very ill Wilson tried to intervene by telling Palmer, "do not let the country see red," but Wilson was by that time so ill that Palmer felt free to ignore his warning. Palmer was assisted by a young anti-communist employee of the Justice Department with ambitions of his own, J. Edgar Hoover, who would later go on to be the infamous Director of the FBI and would also later encourage and support Senator Joe McCarthy in his anti-communist witch hunt in the 1950s.

In the winter of 1920, Palmer began ordering raids to arrest supposed communists who were in reality mostly low-level labor leaders seeking to protect workers' rights. In one night he ordered raids by federal agents in thirty-three cities to arrest "communists" that he claimed were actively trying to overthrow the government of the United States. Palmer had over four thousand people arrested; most of them labor leaders and new immigrants. He detained them up to a week in jail, many without food. The courts found almost all of those arrested innocent of any charges and ordered their release. Despite his poor conviction rate Palmer continued, and since he couldn't get convictions in court, he began to arrest new immigrants and deport them as undesirable citizens, claiming they were communists. J. Edgar Hoover at the US Justice Department was his primary accomplice in this activity.

His abuses were so vile that two US Senators, Warren G. Harding (who would later become president) and Charles Evans Hughes, began to denounce Palmer and his communist witch hunt. Palmer called the senators traitors and communist dupes.

After the arrest of about two thousand people whom Palmer and Hoover planned to deport, Labor Secretary William Wilson asked his deputy Louis Post to intervene. Post freed the two thousand people, enraging Palmer and Hoover, and they appeared before Congress and asked that Post be fired for "his support of communism" and "his tender solicitude for social revolution."

Post was then ordered to appear before the Congress, which was considering his forced termination, but he gave such a rousing speech about American liberties and rights (which was printed in the newspapers) that the Congress let him go with just a warning. Although Post was not fired, Palmer and Hoover now felt they had congressional support for their anti-communist campaign and they went for the big finish. In April of 1920, Palmer began claiming that there would be, on May 1, a violent communist uprising in the United States. He warned America to prepare, claiming he was the only man who could prevent this uprising. The US Army and National Guard units were put on alert. New York City took Palmer's warning so seriously and they were so fearful of a revolution that on May 1, they put the entire police department on a twenty-four hour shift.

When May 1 passed without so much as a rock being thrown, Palmer became a national joke, despite claiming that his warning had prevented the revolution. The Army, guardsmen and police who had to perform extra duty were angry and America's first communist witch hunt ended. Palmer's career was destroyed, but Hoover slunk away into the shadows of the Justice Department, claiming that he was just performing as Palmer had ordered. He survived the incident.

America is slow to learn lessons and this xenophobia returned in the 1950s. Senator Joe McCarthy, a German-Irish Catholic from Wisconsin, was first elected to the Senate in post World War II America as a returning veteran, and by falsely claiming he was a tail gunner on a B-17 bomber, one of the most heroic and hazardous duties in the war. He campaigned under the name "Tail Gunner Joe." He was a charlatan and had actually served very safely as a briefing officer during the war. McCarthy had also forged a commendation letter from Admiral Chester Nimitz to make himself out to be a hero, and had falsely claimed a combat wound for a Purple Heart, which was later revealed as an accident on a ship while drinking with sailors and celebrating his first crossing of the equator. The accident had occurred far from combat. He also shamelessly campaigned on the premise that the holocaust was a lie, to appeal to the large group of German Catholic voters in Wisconsin.

As a senator he had a poor voting record due to absences that may have been due to his addiction to morphine and his alcoholism. He was in danger of losing re-election, when his priest and J. Edgar Hoover suggested that a campaign against communists would be welcome and very popular.

In 2006, columnist Arnold Beichman in *The Politics of Personal Self-Destruction* documented just how dishonest McCarthy was. McCarthy took on the idea of anti-communism with great enthusiasm despite the fact that he had been very pleased to accept and was elected to his first term in the Senate with large support and money from the communist-controlled United Electrical, Radio and Machine Workers' Union, which preferred McCarthy to his opponent, the openly anti-communist and progressive Robert M. La Follette.

In 1950, McCarthy became the most visible public face of the Cold War. His false accusations of communists in government fueled fears of widespread communist subversion and imminent takeover. He was noted for making claims in Congress and on television that there were large numbers of Communists and Soviet spies and sympathizers inside the United States. He said they had infiltrated the State Department, the federal agencies, the military, Hollywood, the media, and elsewhere. In his wake hundreds were accused and lost their jobs or saw their careers destroyed. The people he forced to testify before the House Committee on Un-American Activities Committee began to "cooperate" by saying they suspected certain friends and colleagues so they themselves would appear as loyal Americans and not lose their jobs.

McCarthy accused President Truman's State Department of harboring "205 known Communists" which was a claim he never proved or tried to prove. Truman's Secretary of Defense George Marshall was the target of some of McCarthy's most irrational hatred. A five star general, George Marshall had been the Army Chief of Staff during World War II and also served as Truman's Secretary of State. In addition to being one of America's most respected generals, Marshall was a highly respected statesman, and the Marshall Plan was named for him. When the immediate post-war program to destroy Germany's industry left millions without work or food, and the Soviet alternative started to gain appeal, the Marshall Plan was a much ballyhoo'd program credited with funding reconstruction which saved Europe. Marshall was awarded the Nobel Peace Prize in 1953. McCarthy made a lengthy speech about Marshall and also published a book titled *America's Retreat From Victory: The Story of George Catlett Marshall.* In both the speech and his book McCarthy charged that Marshall was directly responsible for the loss of China to Communism. In his speech McCarthy also implied that Marshall was guilty of treason and accused him of being part of "a conspiracy so immense and an infamy so black as to dwarf any previous venture in the history of man."

Unfortunately it was one of America's darkest hours and men like President Eisenhower, who had served under Marshall, and who could have ended McCarthy's witch-hunt, remained quiet for fear of retaliation.

Even the Kennedy family was guilty of supporting McCarthy. McCarthy became a close friend of Joseph Kennedy Sr., who was also a fervent anti-Communist Catholic. McCarthy was a frequent guest at the Kennedy compound in Hyannis Port. He dated two of Kennedy's daughters, Patricia and Eunice, and was the godfather to Robert Kennedy's first child, Kathleen. Robert Kennedy was also chosen by McCarthy as a counsel for his investigatory committee.

McCarthy became such an intolerant angry bully and a belligerent that by 1954 his Senate colleagues had enough and began to speak openly about disciplining him. On December 2, 1954, the Senate voted to "condemn" McCarthy by a vote of 67 to 22. The Democrats that were present unanimously voted for condemnation, but the Republicans were split evenly. The only senator not on record was John F. Kennedy, who was hospitalized for back surgery. Kennedy never indicated how he would have voted. The McCarthy era was over.

One of the side effects of America's silencing of the left and driving communists and socialists from America was that the conversation about capitalism became extremely one-sided. There are few critics to question capitalist dogma or to point out its weaknesses or to make needed changes. Capitalism has become an unchallenged idea, a cultural universal, and so dogmatic that along with Christianity it has become America's dominant religion. Without debate and criticism, needed improvements and adjustments are not made. Yet without changing, America will likely fall from power as it refuses to adapt to the post-industrial world of the twenty-first century.

There is still time to make a change, but there is little indication that American culture will allow this change. America is an ethnocentric country whose dogmatic belief in capitalism and American exceptionalism may have locked us into an outdated position.

CHAPTER 26. CONCLUSIONS FROM AMERICAN CULTURE

> What has destroyed every previous civilization has been the tendency to the unequal distribution of wealth and power.
>
> — economist Henry George

> America will never be destroyed from the outside. If we falter and lose our freedoms, it will be because we destroyed ourselves.
>
> —Abraham Lincoln

> There is not a liberal America and a conservative America — there is the United States of America. There is not a black America and a white America and Latino America and Asian America — there's the United States of America.
>
> — Barack Obama

As America is now well into the twenty-first century, it is very easy to be pessimistic about the nation's future. Many Whites lament that their majority is ending and that the culture will change and leave them behind. Christians worry they will no longer dominate, and they fear that society will lose its moral compass if secularism takes hold. Republicans and conservatives are beginning to recognize the declining demographics of their base of support. African-Americans are frustrated and worried that Republicans and conservatives — recognizing their voting preferences for liberalism and Democratic politics — will enact more voter restrictions designed to exclude them, as is evidenced by their attempts in the 2012 presidential election and in the 2014 congressional elections. Latino voters are angry that immigration issues are thinly disguised bias and that many Americans treat all American Latinos as outsiders. Women are frustrated because after all their gains, their rights are still questioned, they still lack equal pay for equal work, and their reproductive rights are still continually under siege. The GLBT community is angry and frustrated because their civil rights are slow in coming despite the fact that a majority of Americans now feel they should have them. Liberals and Democrats are frustrated that conservatives and Republicans still control Congress and are obstructionists to any progress. American voters are disturbed because the Courts have said that corporations and the wealthy can legally buy elections and elected officials. They are concerned that congressional districts are artificially gerrymandered to assure the few can enforce their will on the many. Americans are distraught about the declining state of the health care system, with the country evenly divided on possible solutions.

Wealth keeps concentrating into fewer and fewer hands; the American middle class is disappearing and the working class is becoming more poverty stricken. Older Americans worry they will die in poverty and their grandchildren's futures will be limited. Higher education, once supposedly universal in America, is becoming unaffordable for the vast majority, and without a good education system America will become a second class nation. Libertarians, the religious right, and economic conservatives fight over the declining remnants of the Republican Party, further dividing them. President Obama, the Democrats and liberals can't seem to rally a majority to make changes and break through the Republican roadblocks.

The loss of jobs continues, in part as productivity rises and routine jobs are automated. American corporations continue to send jobs overseas. They move their corporate headquarters out of the country to avoid regulation and taxes. Capitalism, a nineteenth-century economic system for an industrial society, is no longer relevant or workable, but it may be difficult to change under the current American culture.

There is much reason to be pessimistic about America's culture and politics, which now appear hopelessly splintered. Each faction seems to be pulling in a different direction. America appears to be in a spiral of decline.

But there are glimmers of hope. The culture is changing. The newest American generation, the "Nexters" (also called the "Y generation), and "the Millennials," are different. They seem to have no racial, ethnic, religious, or sexual bias and have little time for those who are biased. They don't look at race or ethnicity, or religion or sex or sexual preference, as their elders do. They care less that America will be secular and multi-ethnic and multi-racial. They are open to change. They are less married to the past than their elders. They are less xenophobic and less nationalistic than previous generations. As a generation they believe in and are appalled by climate change and the deterioration of the natural environment. They are comfortable with new technology and rapid change and embrace both. According to Stephanie Armour in a *USA Today Money* article, "Generation Y: They have Arrived at Work with a New Attitude," the Nexters prefer flexible hours and expect competitive salaries based on market trends. They like working as part of a team, and would not stay at a place where they sensed they were being micro-managed. They think for themselves and freely access the internet in search of diverse ideas rather than accept quick answers. On the downside the Nexters are not known as being either loyal to employers or willing to put in the time or hard work that their Baby Boom elders or Generation X do.

These generational changes along with the rapidly changing religious, ethnic, racial and political demographics will make America more open to change and innovation. America will likely move from politics that have been far right of center for many years, to a more moderate or left of center political stance.

There is no assurance that America will change rapidly enough to make the needed changes of the twenty-first century, but it is becoming apparent that some changes will be made. And while there is no indication that the country will suffer a complete collapse, there is also no assurance that America will remain the dominant world power, either. Indeed, history suggests that ongoing American supremacy is unlikely; such empires and world powers have always peaked and diminished.

There will likely be many bumps in the road, and the cultural changes that are coming in American may or may not help preserve American power. Despite this, and barring a swing of the political pendulum even further to the right wing, these cultural changes will very likely provide a good future for American generations to come.

American culture has been both magnificent and disastrous. It has been both inclusive and intolerant. Now it stands at a crossroads and we must decide which direction to turn. Will we enter a renaissance or a dark age?

BIBLIOGRAPHY

A Religious History of the American People, Sidney E. Ahlstrom, 2004; Yale University Press

African American English: A Linguistic Introduction, Lisa J. Green, 2002; Cambridge University Press

Albion's Seed: Four British Folkways in America, David Hackett Fischer, 1989; Oxford University Press

American Indian Holocaust and Survival: A Population History Since 1492, Thomas Russell, 1990; The University of Oklahoma Press

American Indian Languages: The Historical Linguistics of Native America, Lyle Campbell, 2000; Oxford University Press

American Sphinx: The Character of Thomas Jefferson, Joseph J. Ellis, 1997; Knopf

Atlas of the North American Indian, Carl Waldman, 1985; Facts On File Publications

Benjamin Franklin: An American Life, Walter Isaacson, 2004; Simon & Schuster

Bolton and the Spanish Borderlands, Herbert Eugene Bolton, Edited by John Francis Bannon, 1974; University of Oklahoma Press

Cesar Chavez: an Autobiography of La Causa, Jaques E. Levy, 2007; University of Minnesota Press

Community and Class in American Education, 1865-1918, Patricia Albjerg Graham, 1974; John Wiley & Sons

Community and Class in Education 1865 to 1918, Patricia A. Graham, 1974; John Wiley & Sons

Education in the United States, Robert L. Church, 1976; Free Press

Encyclopedia of American Indian History, Bruce E. Johansen and Barry Pritzker, 2008; CIO-Clio

Evolution of Modern Popular Music: A history of Blues, Jazz, Country, R&B, Rock and Rap, Mark Vinet, 2004; Wadem Publishing

Exemplar of Liberty: Native America and the Evolution of Democracy, by Donald A. Grinde Jr. and Bruce E. Johansen, 1990; American Indian Studies Center

Fast Food Nation: The Dark Side of the All-American Meal, Eric Schlosser, 2001; Houghton Mifflin

Flashback, a Brief History of Film, Louis Gianetti and Scott Eyman, 2009; Pearson

Great Fortune, The Epic of Rockefeller Center, Daniel Okrent, 2004; Penguin Books

Guns, Germs and Steel, the Fates of Human Societies, Jared Diamond, 1999; W.W. Norton & Co.

Gus Hall, Mark Isaakovitch Lapitskii, 1985; Progress Publishers

Hi There, Boys and Girls! America's Local Children's TV Programs, Tim Hollis, 2001; University of Mississippi Press

How to Talk Minnesotan: A Visitor's Guide, Howard Mohr, 1987; Penguin Books

Illiterate America, Jonathan Kozal, 1986; Plume

Immigration in the United States, William Dvorak, 2009; H.W. Wilson & Co.

Kill the Indian, Save the Man; The Genocidal Impact of American Indian Residential Schools, Ward Churchill, 2004; City Lights

Life Upon These Shores: Looking at African American History, 1513-2008, Henry Louis Gates Jr., Published 2011; Knopf

Luce and His Empire, W. A. Swanberg, 1972; Scribner

Magical Urbanism: Latinos Reinvent the US City, Mike Davis, 2000; Verso

Malcolm X: A Life of Reinvention, Manning Marable, 2011; Penguin Books

Mark Twain: A Biography, Connie Ann Kirk, 2004; Greenwood Press

Martin Luther King, Jr., Malcolm X, and the Civil Rights Struggle of the 1950s and 1960s: A Brief History with Documents, David Howard-Pitney, 2004; Bedford/St. Martin's

Muhammad Ali: His Life and Times, Thomas Hauser, 1992; Simon & Schuster

Official and Confidential: The Secret Life of J. Edgar Hoover, Anthony Summers, 1993; Putnam

Oxford School Dictionary of Word Origins, John Ayto, 2002; Oxford University Press

Red over Black: Black Slavery Among the Cherokee Indians, R. Halliburton, 1997; Greenwood Press

Roots: The Saga of an American Family, Alex Haley, 2007; Vanguard Press

---

Spain in America / España en América, Edward Gaylord Bourne, 2013; Lulu Enterprises

Strangers from a Different Shore: A History of Asian Americans, Ronald Takai, 1998; Little, Brown & Co.

Sweet Air: Modernism, Regionalism, and American Popular Song, Edward P. Comentale, 2013; University of Illinois Press

The Age of Revolution: 1789-1848, Eric Hobsbawm, 1996; Vintage Press

The Columbia History of American Television, Gary Edgerton, 2009; Columbia University Press

The Emigrants, Vilhelm Moberg, 1999; Buccaneer Books

The End of Work: The Decline of the Global Labor Force and the Dawn of the Post-Market Era, Jeremy Rifkin, 1996; Tarcher

The Gourmet Atlas, Susie Ward, Claire Clifton, Jenny Stacy, 1997; John Wiley & Sons

The History of Cuba, Clifford L. Staten, 2005; McMillan

The History of The Blues: The Roots, The Music, The People, Francis Davis, 2003; Da Capo Press

The Life and Times of Joe McCarthy: A Biography, Thomas C. Reeves, 1997; Madison Books

The Making of the Slave Class, Jerry Carrier, 2010; Algora Publishing

The Mark of the New World Order, Terry L. Cook, 2009; Bible Belt Publishing

The Oxford History of the American People, Volume 1 & 2, Samuel Eliot Morison, 1994; Meridian

The Politics of Heroin in Southeast Asia, Alfred W. McCoy, 1972; Harper & Row

The Shock Doctrine: The Rise of Disaster Capitalism, Naomi Klein, 2007; Metropolitan Books

Two Spirit People by Sue-Ellen Jacobs, Wesley Thomas, and Sabine Lang, 1997; University of Illinois Press

Webster's New Universal Unabridged Dictionary, Published 1996; Random House Value Publishing

Whiteout: The CIA, Drugs and the Press, Alexander Cockburn and Jeffery St. Clair 1999; Verso

Periodicals and Media Sources

Northeast Indian Quarterly, 1988. "It's Time to Take Away the Veil, Indian Roots of Democracy", Donald Grinde Jr.

JALA International, "Telework and Telecommuting Frequently Asked Questions"

Atlantic Monthly, June 2000, "Harvard and the Making of a Unabomber," Alston Chase

USA Today, Money, November 6, 2005, "Generation Y: They have Arrived at Work with a New Attitude," Stephanie Armour

The Boston Review, June 1, 2006, "The Power and the Glory, the Myth of American Exceptionalism," Howard Zinn

Washington Post, November 24, 2006, "Putting the Bite On Pseudo Sushi and Other Insults," Anthony Faiola

Lincoln Journal Star, January 11, 2011, "40 Years after Wounded Knee, Trial Judge Reflects," Kevin Abourezk

Colonial Quills, Literacy in Colonial America, June 15, 2011, colonialquills.blogspot.com

Eater DC, November 10, 2011, "10 Chinese Dishes That Real Chinese People Don't Eat," Eater Staff, *DC.Eater.COM*

The Chicago Tribune, August 6, 2012, "American Exceptionalism, Our Tedious Boast," Eric Zorn

The New York Times, January 16, 2013, "Schooling Ourselves in an Unequal America," Rebecca Strauss

Sonoran News, June 26, 2013, "We Must Overhaul the Role of the TSA," Glenn Mollette

Film

Daniel K. Inouye: An American Story, Producer/Director Heather H. Giugni, Released 2009 Juniroa Productions, Inc.

Government and Nonprofit Research Entities and Publications

1992 and 2003 National Assessment of Adult Literacy (NAAL)

2012 Pew Hispanic Center Report

2013 Pew Forum on Religion and Public Life

Air War College, Air War University, Maxwell Paper No. 10 1997, Military Culture a Paradigm Shift, Karen O. Dunivin

American Religious Identification Survey (ARIS) 2008

Department of Homeland Security Authorized Budget for Fiscal Year 2012

Immigration Report 2007, US Congressional Budget Office

Politico.com, 2008 & 2012 Elections

The Hoover Institution, Stanford University, *Policy Review* No. 135, February 1, 2006, "The Politics of Personal Self-Destruction," Arnold Beichman

The National Defense Authorization Act for 2013

The Southern Poverty Law Center website, Teaching Tolerance

United States v. Banks and Means (Wounded Knee) Center for Constitutional Rights, ccrjustice.org

United States v. Banks, 383 F. Supplement 389 (D. S.D. 1974)

US Census Bureau Statistical Abstract of the United States: 2007 & 2012, US Department of Commerce.

US Department of Veteran Affairs, the Office of the Actuary

US National Research Council's study: *The New Americans: Economic, Demographic, and Fiscal Effects of Immigration*, James Smith the Rand Corporation

Acknowledgements

I would like to thank and acknowledge the work of my wife, Mike, and Ron, along with other colleagues who reviewed and commented during the writing of this book. I would also like to thank Andrea Sengstacken, my editor at Algora Publishing, for her hard work.

INDEX

A

Abernathy, Ralph, 33
Abourezk, James, Senator, 16
Abrams, Creighton, 135
Adams, James Truslow, 113
Adams, John, President, 64-66
Adams, Samuel, 62, 65
African Americans, 14, 28, 36-42, 45-47, 52, 64, 72, 79, 101, 102, 105, 109, 118, 150, 164, 224
African American Vernacular English (AAVE), 105
AIDS, 143
Albee, Edward, 172
Algonquin, 170
Ali, Muhammad, 44, 112
Allen, Paula Gunn, 10
Allen, Woody, 135, 197
American Exceptionalism, 3, 5-7, 169, 170, 233
American Indian Movement (AIM), 16-18
American Sign Language, 3, 11
Anderson, Ken, 210
Angelou, Maya, 168
Animals, The, 137, 175
Appalachia, 61, 62, 123
Arab Americans, 50, 54
Armstrong. Louis, 40
Art, 2, 14, 35, 39-41, 55, 75, 89, 91, 124, 125, 133, 134, 136, 137, 151, 152, 154, 157, 160, 171, 173, 175, 213, 215
Ashcroft, John, 88, 111, 120
Ashkenazi, 95, 96

AT&T, 146
Attucks, Crispus, 36
Audubon, John James, 171
Autry, Gene, 152
Aztecs, 22

B

Baby Boomers, 131, 135, 136, 152
Bachmann, Michele, Congresswoman, 72, 88, 120
Backus, Jim, 161
Bahamas, 22, 24, 36
Bain, Donald, 139
Baldwin, James, 35, 41
Bartram, William, 171
Basie, Count, 40
Bay of Pigs Invasion, 30, 76
Beach Boys, The, 137
Beatles, The, 137
Beichman, Arnold, 232
Berlin, Irving, 82
Berry, Chuck, 136
Big Bopper, The, 136
Big Brother and the Holding Company, 137
Blacks. See African Americans
Blaine Amendments, 166
Blair, James, 168
Blakey, Art, 173, 175
Bogart, Humphrey, 160
Booth, Ballington, 119
Boston Latin School, 60, 62, 164